Chocolate

AND THE ART
OF LOW-FAT DESSERTS

Chocolate

AND THE ART
OF LOW-FAT DESSERTS

....

Alice Medrich

Photographs by Michael Lamotte

Photo Styling by Sara Slavin

Design by Jacqueline Jones Design

WARNER BOOKS

A Time Warner Company

Also by Alice Medrich, *Cocolat: Extraordinary Chocolate Desserts*

Copyright © 1994 by Alice Medrich

Warner Books, Inc.
1271 Avenue of the Americas,
New York, NY 10020
Ⓦ A Time Warner Company

Printed in Italy by Amilcare Pizzi S.p.A.
First Printing: October 1994
10 9 8 7 6 5 4 3 2 1

Library of Congress Cataloging-in-Publication Data
Medrich, Alice.
    Chocolate and the art of low-fat desserts / Alice Medrich.
        p. cm.
    Includes bibliographical references and index.
    ISBN 0-446-51666-X
    1. Low-fat diet—Recipes.   2. Desserts   3. Cookery (Chocolate)
I. Title.
RM237.7.M435 1994   94-3042
641.5'638—dc20   CIP

Photography by Michael Lamotte
Photo Styling by Sara Slavin
Food Styling by Alice Medrich
Design by Jacqueline Jones Design
Design assistance by Kristen Jester

For Elliott and Lucy—my sweet ones.

Acknowledgments

....

My husband, Elliott Medrich, saw the "light" before anyone. I thank him for knowing that I, of all people, could create light desserts and write about them. His clear vision and unwavering belief contributed immeasurably to this book.

I thank my editor, Liv Blumer, for including friendship and enthusiasm in the professional package, and the team at Warner Books for making it happen once again. Thanks also to Susan Derecskey, copy editor extraordinaire.

Thanks to my agent Jane Dystel for her care and support throughout.

Designer Jackie Jones of Jacqueline Jones Design, photographer Michael Lamotte, and stylist Sara Slavin created a book beautiful beyond my dreams. Thanks to Kristen Jester for design assistance, and to Bill Checkvala for photo assistance and perfect espresso.

My thanks to Paul Bauer, Sue Fisher King, and Fillamento, all of San Francisco, for generously lending props.

Publicist Cynthia Traina, among other things, pushed me to teach my first low-fat dessert class. I thank her and Joan Hall and the staff and students of Summit Hospital's Cancer Education and Prevention Center.

Thanks to Harold McGee, Jenifer Peale, Zelda Gordon, Flo Braker, Carole Walter, Barbara Kafka, Maida Heatter, and Marion Cunningham for their own good work, technical advice, and the willingness to chat.

Thanks to Maria Morales, the "other mom" at our house, for keeping my kitchen always ready for action.

This book was constantly propelled by small sparks—little ideas or artifacts, idle comments, or chance remarks that became some of the most important and exciting recipes and findings. Small sparks were provided by friends, family, and colleagues, sometimes even without their knowledge. Thus my warm thanks to Beryl Radin, Merle Fajans, Lubov Armstrong-Mazur, Joan Nackerud, Christine Blaine, Martha Finkelstein, Bea and Herman Abrams, Libby Medrich, and Lucy Medrich. They provided encouragement and inspiration, recipes and ideas, reality checks, testing, and even the mundane reminder that home cooks sometimes use glass pans.

Berkeley, California, 1993

Table of Contents

....

The Journey

....

Over the past sixteen years my name has become synonymous with dessert: rich, elegant, chocolate dessert. Since I created Cocolat, the dessert and chocolate company, my friends and customers have come to expect chocolate nirvana—desserts to swoon over, fabulous endings to marvelous meals. We never counted the calories or fat; we said, "This is so rich and delicious that just a small serving is sufficient." But in recent years I have been asked more and more often about making my desserts less rich and less caloric. Believing, as I did, and do, that a little bit of something very good is more satisfying than a large portion of something mediocre, I used to answer automatically, "Take a smaller portion, or choose a lighter main course."

In the spring of 1989 I was asked to teach a dessert class for the Celebrated Chefs program of the Summit Hospital Cancer Education and Prevention Center in Oakland, California. The mandate was to prepare great desserts with less than thirty percent of the calories from fat. I accepted the challenge out of curiosity. I scanned some of the "light" cookbooks both here and in France. Quite sensibly, they were filled with lovely fruit desserts. Some recipes used strange food substitutes or what I call fake ingredients—something I oppose vehemently. Chocolate desserts were rare and anemic at best.

Now I know, if anyone does, that for a significant portion of the dessert-eating public, it isn't dessert if it isn't chocolate. These wonderful people were my clients at Cocolat and my personal friends as well. One friend said outright, "Thank you so much for offering to bring dessert. You won't bring fruit will you?"

For the first time I thought seriously about lighter desserts, but on my own very particular terms. Could I create desserts within the required guidelines that would please the palates of serious dessert lovers? Could I devise decadent, indulgent desserts with less fat and fewer calories without compromising quality or using fake ingredients? Most important of all, could I do it with chocolate?

○○○○○○○○○○○○○○○○○○○○○○○○

It was difficult, but my students seemed very pleased with my first three low-fat desserts. Once I learned that it was possible, I became hooked on the challenge. I taught the class again the following year with three new desserts. This time I explained my philosophy and my mission—to lower fat and calories and still maintain an extremely high pleasure and satisfaction quotient using only real ingredients. This meant that recipes would not necessarily be the very lowest in calories and fat, but that they would meet the Surgeon General's guidelines and still appeal to those of us who adore desserts, especially very chocolatey ones. The idea met with so many murmurs and nods of approval, it remained only for me to prove myself.

The three new desserts were even more successful than the first batch. The tremendous response to this class took me aback. I saw the same excitement that I see after one of my classes where no holds are barred when it comes to butter, eggs, chocolate, and cream. One of the participants told me that she had served one of my "new" desserts at a party next to a dessert with a very high fat and calorie content. Both desserts received raves. Guests were invited to guess which dessert was the light one. They guessed wrong! By now I was obsessed.

Today I know that the health-conscious changes we have made in our diets—even subtly—over the last decade have also changed our palates. Even those of us who love food have begun to taste things differently, to have less tolerance for fat and rich foods, and to derive more pleasure from good-tasting, well-made lighter food. I know too that if we are to eat desserts regularly, we must do two things: We must eat smaller portions of our enduring "big splurge" favorites and we must learn to choose and make more delicious desserts with reduced fat. I also believe that the best new desserts will be created by passionate pastry chefs rather than nutritionists or scientists.

Lowering our overall diet to thirty percent of calories from fat is the target set by the Surgeon General and accepted by the American Heart Association and many cancer education organizations. The *average* calories from fat consumed in a reasonable period of time—a whole day or even a week—is more significant than the fat calories in an individual dish or meal. The sensible approach is to vary our overall diets, eating more foods that are naturally fat free or inherently low in fat, so that we can also enjoy some high-fat splurges from time to time.

Even though it is not essential that each dessert we eat meet such rigorous standards, most of the recipes in this book contain less than thirty percent of calories from fat and from four to eight grams of fat per serving. Exceptions are still much leaner than similar old-fashioned recipes. I believe that a repertoire of truly indulgent desserts that meets these rigorous standards will make us more comfortable about eating dessert as often as we like. And, as our tolerance for fat declines, these desserts will become even more in tune with our tastes and desires.

I have tried to keep calories per serving under three hundred, with many many wonderful desserts averaging between two hundred and two hundred and fifty calories. Several are shockingly lean. Each recipe includes a chart showing calories per serving; grams of fat, protein, and carbohydrates; milligrams of cholesterol; and percentage of calories from fat. Each recipe also includes working and cooking times and tips for doing ahead, storing, and freezing. My own favorite cookbooks are thick with tips, notes, advice, and variations, and so I have liberally given the reader a "piece of my mind" throughout. In addition, I have outlined my overall approach in the chapter The Theory and Practice of Creating Rich Desserts with Less Fat (page 166). I urge you to read it, especially the parts about measuring and mixing (page 172) and time and temperature (page 173). In baking, these details are crucial, more than ever when you're making low-fat desserts.

This collection is personal and eclectic, reflecting my own interests and preferences as well as notes and advice from readers of my first book. I did not include recipes or categories that I was unable to make delicious.

The word *gourmet* is pretentious and often applied to food which is not. Yet in the best sense these desserts are gourmet. You may already enjoy being the host or hostess with the mostest—a reputation for show-stopping to-die-for desserts. My goal is to add winning new desserts to your repertoire without a sense that these are a special category or "not bad for low fat" but sensational desserts by any measure.

I did not want simply to create leaner versions of the original *Cocolat* recipes, but I could not resist tinkering with some of my signature desserts (Chocolate Decadence, Chocolate Marble Cheesecake, and Bittersweet Chocolate Marquise). I was delighted to find that I could recast these old favorites—and create dozens more—with the intense flavor, rich texture, and elegance always associated with my desserts. This is hardly diet food. These are the new desserts of the future for people who cook and eat with pleasure and discrimination. The bonus comes with the pleasure of knowing something that your guests do not and seeing the surprised faces when you tell. Let dessert remain one of life's great simple pleasures. Once again, sweet dreams and bon appetit!

The Low-Fat Diary

....

When I began developing recipes for this book, I had very little knowledge of how to go about creating luscious desserts with fewer calories and less fat. I learn best by doing. I like to start with a clean slate and few preconceived notions, so I was less worried about what I didn't know than I was challenged and excited by the new ideas to come and the steep learning curve of a new project. This is not to say that there weren't moments when I asked myself, "Why did I ever say I would do this?"

I have been rewarded with an extraordinary learning experience. Nothing was ever quite as expected. Solutions that should have come easily did not, and many difficult problems almost solved themselves. I have never done so much experimentation; and I have never thrown out or donated so many failures. Nonetheless I have loved almost every minute of it.

Early on I began a diary to record my progress and my discoveries—and my mood. As I reviewed my notes, some things became clear. I was never aiming to make desserts that emphasized their own lightness. Coming from a profession where most everything I created was very rich, I used to chuckle when a customer referred to one or another of our desserts as light or less rich. More often than not, the dessert in question was not light at all, only perceived as such because of color, texture, or flavor. We called this delusion "perceived lightness"—and thanked our stars for it.

When desserts are truly light, however, perception of lightness is not really the point. Perception of richness is. When I was preparing for my second light dessert class, I found myself short of time and despairing about what to present. I thought a lovely poached pear with vanilla frozen yogurt and a nice light sauce would fill the bill. My husband said, "If you're going with the pear, you can just phone it in. What they want from you is rich chocolate desserts—the stuff that dreams are made of."

○○○○○○○○○○○○○○○○○○○○○○○○○

Conversations with friends and acquaintances along the way strengthened my resolve to emphasize richness instead of lightness. When I mentioned that I was doing a dessert book with less fat and fewer calories, some people nodded wisely and said, "Oh well, I guess you'll be doing a lot of fruit desserts and such."

Others, knowing my relationship with chocolate, said, "I guess you'll have to use a lot of cocoa since you won't be able to use that rich bittersweet chocolate you love so much." One well-known pastry chef put it most diplomatically. "There are some lovely things you can do with cocoa," he said. Almost everyone asked, "What are you using to replace the fat?" One of my favorite food-magazine editors said, "Oh, but I hope you will still do some of your glamorous and decadent desserts for our magazine?"

I was intrigued by the assumptions. Desserts with less fat and calories are mostly fruit, can't have real chocolate, have to use fat replacements, and are neither glamorous nor decadent! Not exactly high expectations. This was all I needed to hear. I decided that I would not emphasize fruit desserts, that I would absolutely never abandon my favorite chocolate, and that my desserts would be both elegant and decadent.

I never think in terms of fat replacement. I have approached my desserts with the idea that not all of the fat in traditional recipes is necessary. Some desserts can be lightened without further adjustment. Others require modifications to compensate for the loss of qualities traditionally provided by fat. Still others require a total leap of faith. I think in terms of rearranging recipes, juggling ingredients, and using fat strategically rather than replacing it.

My diary entries are peppered with two alternating phrases: "This is harder than I thought" and "Gee, this is fun." Otherwise the entries record a journey of discovery. Sometime in early 1992, I noted the following: In the old days, after days of testing traditional dessert recipes, I would wake up with a terrible "richness hangover," not to mention the weight gain. These lighter desserts are entirely different. One morning, after far too many tastes, I felt fine and had no hangover. I have not gained any weight during this project.

Later, in frustration, I wrote: One of the hardest things about using less fat has to do with getting a dessert to "perform"—mousses to stand up, frostings to hold peaks, pastries to resist sogginess, fillings to retain moisture without bleeding or draining. Pastry chefs have it the hardest of all—after all, no one asks a chicken breast to stand up on its own or cares if the sauce just lies there next to it!

I also found that my years of experience with classic desserts did not always help: The elements in lean desserts must be composed with great finesse or the flavors all stick out separately like elbows and knees. Trying to pair sauces, frostings, toppings, and glazes with chocolate desserts, I can't predict what will work. Some toppings make the cake taste strange, others taste irrelevant, or cover up the taste of the cake. I have to taste every imaginable combination and take nothing for granted. Pastry chefs will need to reeducate themselves!

There are several entries in my diary like this one: I gain courage each time I bring a light dessert to someone's house for dinner. I always come home beaming from the response. I like it best when the guests don't know in advance that the dessert is not a conventional one.

Finally, and perhaps best of all: I'm beginning to hear things like, "This is delicious; it certainly tastes like one of your desserts, but somehow it's easier to eat." How the times are changing.

Tea Loaves and Pound Cakes

....

These so-called plain cakes are delicious and appealing beyond their modest billing (unless you were taught, as I was, that "plain is best"). You'll treasure them for being so easy to make, store, and serve. You'll make them often, invent your own variations, and give them as gifts.

Chocolate Pound Cake

Cocolat customers used to stop me in the street to rave about our exquisitely simple but excellent Chocolate Pound Cake.

This version is inspired by the popular original, but with only half the fat per serving. The recipe may be divided in half for a smaller cake;

indeed, half a recipe is included in Double Chocolate Layer Cake (page 46).

WORK TIME: 30 MINUTES
BAKE TIME: 45–55 MINUTES

INGREDIENTS

2-1/4 CUPS SIFTED ALL-PURPOSE
  FLOUR (9 OUNCES)

3/4 CUP PLUS 1 TABLESPOON
  UNSWEETENED DUTCH PROCESS
  COCOA

3/8 TEASPOON BAKING SODA

3/8 TEASPOON BAKING POWDER

1/2 TEASPOON SALT

2 EGGS

4 EGG WHITES

2 TABLESPOONS INSTANT ESPRESSO
  OR COFFEE POWDER

2 TEASPOONS VANILLA EXTRACT

3/4 CUP LOW-FAT (1%) BUTTERMILK

12 TABLESPOONS UNSALTED BUTTER

2-2/3 CUPS SUGAR

EQUIPMENT

12-CUP TUBE OR BUNDT PAN OR TWO
  5-CUP LOAF PANS

NUTRITION INFORMATION

CALORIES PER SERVING: 196

FAT: 7 G

% CALORIES FROM FAT: 31%

PROTEIN: 3.1 G

CARBOHYDRATES: 32.4 G

CHOLESTEROL: 33.4 MG

Serves 20 to 24. Best if baked 1 day before serving.

1. Have all ingredients at room temperature (68°-70°F.). Position the rack in lower third of the oven and preheat to 350°F. Spray pans with vegetable oil spray.

2. Combine and sift together the flour, cocoa, baking soda, baking powder, and salt. Set aside. Whisk the whole eggs with the egg whites in a small bowl. Set aside. Dissolve the espresso powder in 3 tablespoons warm water and combine with the vanilla and buttermilk in a small bowl.

3. Cut the butter into chunks and place in an electric mixer bowl. Using a stand mixer, beat to soften, about 1 minute. Add sugar gradually, beating constantly for about 3 minutes at medium speed. Gradually dribble eggs into sugar mixture, beating at medium-high speed for 2 to 3 minutes. On medium-low speed, beat in a third of the flour mixture, scraping the bowl as necessary. On medium speed, gradually dribble in half of the buttermilk mixture, scraping the bowl as necessary. On low speed, beat in half of the remaining flour followed by the rest of the buttermilk, always scraping the bowl as necessary. Beat in remaining flour mixture until well combined. Batter may look slightly curdled; this is okay.

4. Scrape batter into the pan or pans and smooth the top as necessary. Bake loaves for 45 to 50 minutes, or until cake starts to shrink from the sides of the pan and a toothpick inserted into the center comes out barely clean. Cake in a tube or bundt pan will bake in 50 to 55 minutes. Do not overbake.

5. Cool cake, in the pan, on a rack for 10 minutes. Invert and remove pan. Turn right side up if baked in loaves. Cool completely on the rack before storing. *Cake remains moist and delicious for 4 to 5 days, well wrapped. Cake may be frozen for up to 2 months.*

....

Kahlúa Fudge Ring

Cookbook author Carole Walter's hot Kahlúa and honey soak and my Rich Chocolate Glaze turn Chocolate Pound Cake into a superb party cake.

Serves 20 to 24. Best if baked 1 day before serving.

1. Make the cake. As soon as it comes out of the oven combine the Kahlúa, ½ cup water, and honey in a small saucepan and simmer for 2 to 3 minutes. Unmold the cake on a rack set on a plate. Pierce cake all over with a skewer. Spoon the hot syrup slowly over the cake, allowing it to absorb entirely. Cool cake on the rack. *Cake can be prepared to this point and stored in an airtight container for several days or frozen for up to 2 months.*

2. Spoon the glaze over the cake, leaving some bare spots showing.

VARIATIONS
....

• For a less rich glaze, substitute Chocolate Buttermilk Glaze (page 147).

• Omit the glaze.

WORK TIME: 1 HOUR
BAKE TIME: 45–55 MINUTES

INGREDIENTS

1 CHOCOLATE POUND CAKE (PAGE 18)
1 CUP KAHLÚA
1/4 CUP HONEY
1 CUP RICH CHOCOLATE GLAZE
　(PAGE 148), MADE AND COOLED

NUTRITION INFORMATION

CALORIES PER SERVING: 277
FAT: 8 G
% CALORIES FROM FAT: 26%
PROTEIN: 3.8 G
CARBOHYDRATES: 47 G
CHOLESTEROL: 34 MG

Chocolate Marble Cake

Deep dark chocolate swirled into a snowy white yogurt batter. This cake is so beautiful when it comes out of the pan that I can never decide whether it looks best upside down or right side up.

WORK TIME: 30 MINUTES
BAKE TIME: 45–50 MINUTES

INGREDIENTS

2 CUPS CAKE FLOUR (8 OUNCES)

1 TEASPOON BAKING POWDER

1/2 TEASPOON BAKING SODA

1/2 TEASPOON SALT

1 TEASPOON INSTANT ESPRESSO OR
   COFFEE POWDER

1/3 CUP UNSWEETENED DUTCH
   PROCESS COCOA

1-1/3 CUPS SUGAR

1 WHOLE EGG

1 EGG WHITE

6 TABLESPOONS UNSALTED BUTTER

1 CUP NONFAT YOGURT

2 TEASPOONS VANILLA EXTRACT

Serves 12.

1. Have all ingredients at room temperature (68°–70° F.). Position the rack in lower third of the oven and preheat to 350° F. Spray the pan with vegetable oil spray.

2. Use a wire whisk to combine the flour with the baking powder, baking soda, and salt. Sift together. Set aside. In a small bowl, combine the espresso powder, cocoa, and ⅓ cup of the sugar with ¼ cup water. Whisk until smooth. Set aside. In another small bowl, whisk whole egg with egg white. Set aside.

3. Cut the butter into pieces and place in an electric mixer bowl. Beat for about 1 minute to soften. Gradually add remaining 1 cup of sugar and beat at high speed for about 3 minutes. Dribble eggs in slowly, about 1 tablespoon at a time, beating constantly for about 2 minutes. On low speed, beat in a third of the flour mixture. On medium-high speed, beat in half of the yogurt. On low speed, beat in half of the remaining flour. On high speed, beat in the rest of the yogurt and the vanilla. On low speed, beat in the remaining flour.

4. Measure out 1½ cups of yogurt batter and mix into the cocoa mixture; set aside.

5. Use a large spoon to fill the bottom of the pan with about three quarters of the white batter placed in dollops. Cover the white batter with dollops of chocolate batter. Top the chocolate batter with small dollops of white batter spaced so that the chocolate batter shows through. Use a table knife to marble the batters together with a circular or zigzag motion; be careful not to blend them too much. Bake for 45 to 50 minutes, or until the cake begins to pull away from the sides of the pan and a toothpick inserted into the center of the cake in several places comes out clean.

6. Cool for 10 to 15 minutes on a rack. Unmold the cake. Cool completely before serving or storing. Serve cake upside down or right side up. *Cake may be stored, well wrapped, at room temperature for 3 to 4 days or frozen for up to 2 months.*

EQUIPMENT

8- TO 10-CUP TUBE PAN

NUTRITION INFORMATION

CALORIES PER SERVING: 230

FAT: 6.9 G

% CALORIES FROM FAT: 26%

PROTEIN: 4 G

CARBOHYDRATES: 39.7 G

CHOLESTEROL: 33.5 MG

....

Buttermilk Pound Cake

Pound cake of course is a misnomer, not only because we wouldn't dare use a pound of butter and a pound of eggs, but because the traditional slightly dry texture of the classic pound cake has fallen out of favor and been replaced by moister incarnations. A good buttermilk cake with lots of vanilla is my favorite. This version is leaner than usual and remarkably good. If you are a pound cake lover, try this plain beauty, then go ahead and have your way with her.

Serves 10 to 12. Best if baked 1 day before serving.

1. Have all ingredients at room temperature (68°–70° F.). Position the rack in lower third of the oven and preheat to 325° F. Spray pan with vegetable oil spray.

2. Whisk to combine the flour, baking powder, baking soda, and salt. Sift together. Set aside. In a small bowl, whisk together the whole egg with the egg whites. Set aside. Combine the vanilla and buttermilk. Set aside.

3. Cut the butter into chunks and place in an electric mixer bowl. Beat to soften, about 1 minute. Add sugar gradually, beating constantly for about 3 minutes. Gradually dribble beaten eggs into sugar mixture, beating at medium-high speed for 2 to 3 minutes. On low speed, beat in a third of the flour mixture, scraping the

WORK TIME: 30 MINUTES
BAKE TIME: 35–70 MINUTES

INGREDIENTS

1-1/2 CUPS SIFTED ALL-PURPOSE
FLOUR (6 OUNCES)

1/4 TEASPOON BAKING POWDER

1/4 TEASPOON BAKING SODA

3/8 TEASPOON SALT

1 EGG

2 EGG WHITES

1-1/4 TEASPOONS VANILLA EXTRACT

1/2 CUP LOW-FAT (1%) BUTTERMILK

5 TABLESPOONS UNSALTED BUTTER

1 CUP SUGAR

EQUIPMENT

5-CUP LOAF PAN OR 5- TO 6-CUP
BUNDT OR TUBE PAN

NUTRITION INFORMATION

CALORIES PER SERVING: 171

FAT: 5.44 G

% CALORIES FROM FAT: 28%

PROTEIN: 2.96 G

CARBOHYDRATES: 28 G

CHOLESTEROL: 30.9 MG

bowl as necessary. On medium-high speed, gradually dribble in half of the buttermilk mixture, scraping the bowl as necessary. On low speed, beat in half of the remaining flour. On medium-high speed, beat in the rest of the buttermilk, always scraping the bowl as necessary. On low speed, beat in the remaining flour mixture until well combined. Batter may look slightly curdled; this is okay.

4. Scrape batter into the pan and bake until the cake starts to pull from the sides of the pan, the top is golden brown, and a toothpick inserted into the center of the cake comes out clean. In a tube pan, the cake will bake in 35 to 40 minutes; in a loaf pan, 65 to 70 minutes.

5. Cool for 10 to 15 minutes on a rack. If using a tube pan, run a knife around the tube if necessary to release cake. Invert the pan and unmold on a rack to cool completely. When cool, wrap well in plastic wrap. Cake is slightly moister the second day. *Cake may be stored, well wrapped, at room temperature for 3 to 4 days or frozen for up to 2 months.*

6. To serve: Slice about ⅜ inch or thinner and serve 2 to 3 slices per serving.

VARIATIONS

....

Egg Nog Pound Cake: Prepare the cake, adding ¼ teaspoon ground nutmeg with the sugar. While the cake is baking, prepare a liquor soak: Simmer 3 tablespoons brandy and 3 tablespoons dark rum with 2 tablespoons sugar for 2 minutes. Set aside to cool. Also prepare a glaze: Combine ¼ cup powdered sugar with 1 tablespoon each brandy and rum. Unmold cake on a rack set over a plate. Plunge a skewer into the cake all over. Spoon the soaking liquid slowly over the cake. Remove the plate from beneath the rack and collect the excess liquid. Replace plate under rack and spoon the liquid over the cake again. Repeat as often as necessary until all syrup has soaked into the cake. Brush the glaze over the top and sides and center core of cake; use all of the glaze. Cool cake completely before storing or serving.

Rum Raisin Pound Cake: Plump ⅔ cup of golden raisins in enough rum to cover for 15 minutes or more. Drain raisins, saving rum for liquor soak. Fold drained raisins into completed batter at the end of Step 3. Prepare a liquor soak as for Egg Nog Pound Cake, using 2 tablespoons sugar and 6 tablespoons rum; omit the brandy. Likewise, prepare a glaze with ¼ cup powdered sugar and 2 tablespoons rum.

You could also use chopped dried apricots and brandy, prunes in Armagnac, grappa with raisins or dried pears—you take over from here. To add dried fruit without liquor, plump chopped fruit pieces in a strainer or steamer basket suspended over simmering water. Cover and steam for 1 to 2 minutes to soften. Spread pieces on paper towels and blot dry.

Cranberry Pecan Cake

Too easy! Too pretty! Lots of tangy cranberries in a light yogurt cake with a nuance of orange and a handful of nuts make this an obvious choice for the holidays both for gift giving and serving.

Serves 10 to 12.

1. Have all ingredients at room temperature (68°-70°F.). Position the rack in lower third of the oven and preheat to 350°F. Spray the pan with vegetable oil spray.

2. Whisk together the flour, baking powder, baking soda, and salt. Sift together. Set aside. In another small bowl, whisk the whole egg with the egg white. Set aside.

3. Cut the butter into pieces and place in an electric mixer bowl. Add the orange zest and beat for about 1 minute to soften. Gradually add the sugar and continue to beat on high speed for about 3 minutes. Dribble eggs in slowly, about 1

WORK TIME: 30 MINUTES
BAKE TIME: 40–45 MINUTES

INGREDIENTS

2 CUPS CAKE FLOUR (8 OUNCES)
1 TEASPOON BAKING POWDER
1/2 TEASPOON BAKING SODA
1/2 TEASPOON SALT
1 WHOLE EGG
1 EGG WHITE
5 TABLESPOONS UNSALTED BUTTER
GRATED ZEST OF 1 LARGE ORANGE

1 CUP SUGAR

1 CUP NONFAT YOGURT

2 TEASPOONS VANILLA EXTRACT

2 CUPS CRANBERRIES

1/2 CUP CHOPPED PECANS OR WALNUTS
 (2 OUNCES)

3 TABLESPOONS ORANGE LIQUEUR,
 SUCH AS GRAND MARNIER,
 CURAÇAO, OR TRIPLE SEC

6 TABLESPOONS POWDERED SUGAR

EQUIPMENT

8-CUP TUBE PAN

NUTRITION INFORMATION

CALORIES PER SERVING: 256

FAT: 8.5 G

% CALORIES FROM FAT: 30%

PROTEIN: 4.3 G

CARBOHYDRATES: 40.6 G

CHOLESTEROL: 30.9 MG

tablespoon at a time, beating constantly for about 2 minutes. On low speed, beat in a third of the flour mixture. On medium-high speed, beat in half of the yogurt. On low speed, beat in half of the remaining flour. On high speed, beat in the rest of the yogurt and the vanilla. On low speed, beat in the rest of the flour. Use a rubber spatula to fold in the cranberries and nuts.

4. Scrape into prepared pan. Bake for 40 to 45 minutes, or until a toothpick inserted into the center of the cake in several places comes out dry. Cool for 10 to 15 minutes on a rack. Meanwhile, whisk liqueur and powdered sugar together to form a glaze. Unmold the cake. Brush the glaze over the top and sides of the cake until all the glaze is used. Cool cake completely before serving or storing. *Cake may be stored, well wrapped, at room temperature for 3 to 4 days or frozen for up to 2 months.*

VARIATION

....

In high summer, instead of cranberries fold in fresh berries and serve for breakfast or brunch.

....

Apricot Yam Loaf

Roy Andries de Groot's sensational Candied Yams with Apricots and Sweet Vermouth provided the inspiration for this fragrant loaf. It makes a perfect hostess gift and a lovely addition to anyone's holiday repertoire. Try it with one cup canned pumpkin or pureed hubbard squash instead of yams.

WORK TIME: 30 MINUTES
COOK TIME: 20 MINUTES
BAKE TIME: 50–55 MINUTES

Serves 16 to 18.

1. Have all ingredients at room temperature (68°–70°F.). Position the rack in the lower third of the oven and preheat to 350°F. Spray pans with vegetable oil spray or line with paper: Tear off a 12 x 10-inch piece of wax or parchment paper and press into pan, pleating corners neatly to fit.

INGREDIENTS

2/3 CUP FINELY DICED DRIED APRICOTS
    (4 OUNCES)

1/2 CUP SWEET VERMOUTH

2 CUPS SIFTED ALL-PURPOSE FLOUR
    (8 OUNCES)

3/4 TEASPOON SALT

1/4 TEASPOON BAKING POWDER

1 TEASPOON BAKING SODA

1 CUP SUGAR

1/2 CUP LIGHT OR DARK BROWN SUGAR

1 LARGE LEMON

6 TABLESPOONS UNSALTED BUTTER

1 EGG

1 EGG WHITE

1 CUP YAM PUREE (SEE NOTE)

2/3 CUP CHOPPED WALNUTS
    (3 OUNCES)

EQUIPMENT

TWO 5-CUP LOAF PANS OR ONE 8-CUP
    TUBE OR BUNDT PAN

NUTRITION INFORMATION

CALORIES PER SERVING: 219

FAT: 7.2 G

% CALORIES FROM FAT: 29%

PROTEIN: 3 G

CARBOHYDRATES: 35.7 G

CHOLESTEROL: 22.1 MG

2. Place apricot pieces with sweet vermouth in a small cup. Cover and let stand for at least 15 minutes. Pour through a sieve set over a small bowl, pressing apricots lightly to extract all the juice.

3. Whisk together and sift the flour, salt, baking powder, and baking soda. Set aside. Combine sugar and brown sugar in a small bowl. Use your fingers to pinch and separate brown sugar lumps. (Or process sugars in a food processor to eliminate lumps.) Set aside.

4. Grate lemon zest directly into the large bowl of an electric mixer. Add butter and beat until creamy. Add sugars and beat on high speed until mixture starts to come together in a mass. Add whole egg and egg white, beating until smooth. On low speed, add half of the flour mixture, stopping to scrape the bowl as necessary and beating only until barely combined. On medium-high speed, beat in the liquid drained from the apricots. Add the remaining flour mixture and beat on low speed just until incorporated. Scrape bowl as necessary. Beat in the yam puree on medium speed. By hand, stir in the walnuts and the drained apricots.

5. Divide into prepared pans. Smooth the tops. Bake for 50 to 55 minutes, or until a skewer inserted in the center tests dry. Cool for 10 minutes on a rack. Unmold loaves and turn right side up to cool completely on a rack. When completely cool, wrap well in plastic wrap or foil. *Loaves may be kept, well wrapped, at room temperature for several days or frozen for up to 2 months.* They are delicious with a slightly crispy crust on the day they are baked. They are even more delicious —and easier to slice—a day later when the flavors have married, although, alas, the crust is soft.

Note

To make yam puree: Peel a yam weighing at least 10 ounces with a vegetable peeler and cut into large pieces. Simmer gently in water to cover for 15 to 20 minutes, or until fork-tender. Drain. Puree in a food processor or push through a ricer. Cool before using.

Spicy New Orleans Gingerbread

Simplicity itself, this moist and very gingery cake is so lean that you might consider a dollop of
low-fat sour cream or Enlightened Crème Fraîche (page 160) and maybe some sliced bananas to accompany it.
Low-fat vanilla yogurt also makes a nice partner.

WORK TIME: 20 MINUTES
BAKE TIME: 25–35 MINUTES

INGREDIENTS

1 CUP ALL-PURPOSE FLOUR (5 OUNCES)
1/2 TEASPOON GROUND CLOVES
3/4 TEASPOON GROUND CINNAMON
1/2 TEASPOON POWDERED MUSTARD
1/8 TEASPOON SALT
3/4 TEASPOON BAKING SODA
1/2 TEASPOON INSTANT ESPRESSO
    OR COFFEE POWDER
1/2 CUP LIGHT BROWN SUGAR
6 TABLESPOONS DARK OR LIGHT
    UNSULPHURED MOLASSES
1 EGG
1 EGG WHITE
2-1/2 TABLESPOONS MELTED BUTTER
2-1/2 TABLESPOONS FINELY MINCED OR
    GRATED FRESH GINGER
2 TABLESPOONS BABY-FOOD PRUNES
    OR STRAINED APPLESAUCE
1/4 CUP BOILING WATER

EQUIPMENT

5- TO 6-CUP TUBE OR BUNDT PAN OR
    8-INCH ROUND CAKE PAN

NUTRITION INFORMATION

CALORIES PER SERVING: 198
FAT: 4.46 G
% CALORIES FROM FAT: 20%
PROTEIN: 3.2 G
CARBOHYDRATES: 36.8 G
CHOLESTEROL: 36.2 MG

Serves 7 to 8.

1. Position the rack in lower third of the oven and preheat to 325°F. Spray pan with vegetable oil spray.

2. In a bowl, whisk together the flour, cloves, cinnamon, mustard, and salt. Set aside. In a small cup, mix together baking soda and espresso powder. Set aside.

3. Place the brown sugar in a medium bowl. Add the molasses, whole egg, egg white, butter, ginger, and prunes. Whisk together until combined. Stir in the flour mixture. Dissolve baking soda and espresso powder in boiling water. Stir into batter just until combined.

4. Scrape batter into pan. Bake until a toothpick inserted into the center of the cake comes out dry, about 25 to 30 minutes for a round pan, 30 to 35 minutes for a ring mold. Cool cake on a rack for about 10 minutes. Unmold. *Cake may be stored, well wrapped, at room temperature for 3 to 4 days or frozen for up to 2 months.*

Note

If you want to double the recipe, divide the batter between 2 pans rather than using 1 large one. The additional time that is required to bake in a large pan (even a tube pan) toughens the cake—frighteningly. This discovery was a revelation. It seems to hold true in general for recipes where fat has been all or partially replaced with a fruit puree.

California Fruit and Nut Cake

I lowered the fat just a little in this recipe, which was given to me by my friend Christine Blaine, retail director at Cocolat for many years. Christine knew I would like this nontraditional fruitcake, which is filled with dried fruits and nuts and not a single candied fruit. This is rich! rich! rich! Slice it very thin—it's almost a confection.

WORK TIME: 30 MINUTES
BAKE TIME: 1 HOUR 10 MINUTES
TO 1 HOUR 40 MINUTES

Makes 24 to 36 thin slices.

1. Position rack in lower third of the oven and preheat to 300°F. Line the pan with parchment paper or spray with vegetable oil spray.

2. In a large mixing bowl, whisk the flour, baking soda, baking powder, and salt to combine. Add the brown sugar, apricots, dates, and walnuts and mix with your fingers. Set aside.

3. In a small bowl, beat the eggs and egg white with the vanilla until light. Pour the egg mixture over the dry ingredients and mix well with a wooden spoon or your hands until all the fruit and nut pieces are coated.

4. Scrape into the pan. Bake until the top is deep golden brown and batter clinging to the fruit seems set, 1 hour 10 to 20 minutes for 2 small loaves, 1 hour 30 to 40 minutes for 1 large loaf. If loaves become too dark very early, cover them with a tent of aluminum foil. Cool on a rack. When completely cool, remove from pan and wrap airtight in foil or plastic wrap. *Cake may be stored, well wrapped, at room temperature for several weeks, or in the refrigerator for at least 3 months. Cake can be frozen for at least 6 months.*

5. To serve: Slice ⅜ inch thick with a heavy sharp knife.

INGREDIENTS

3/4 CUP ALL-PURPOSE FLOUR (3-3/4 OUNCES)
1/4 TEASPOON BAKING SODA
1/4 TEASPOON BAKING POWDER
1/2 TEASPOON SALT
3/4 CUP LIGHT OR DARK BROWN SUGAR
1-1/4 PACKED CUPS DRIED APRICOT HALVES (7-1/2 OUNCES)
2-1/4 CUPS QUARTERED DRIED DATES (13-1/2 OUNCES)
2 CUPS WALNUT HALVES (6-1/2 OUNCES)
2 EGGS
1 EGG WHITE
1 TEASPOON VANILLA EXTRACT

EQUIPMENT

8-CUP LOAF PAN OR TWO 4-CUP LOAF PANS

NUTRITION INFORMATION

CALORIES PER SLICE (SMALL/LARGE LOAF): 112/168
FAT: 3.8 G/5.7 G
% CALORIES FROM FAT: 29%
PROTEIN: 2 G/2.9 G
CARBOHYDRATES: 19 G/28.8 G
CHOLESTEROL: 11.8 MG/17.7 MG

New Dessert Classics

....

Of all desserts, I come back
most often to those with a
certain easy elegance. I like them
simple but very rich in effect—
and often very chocolatey! New
classics thus include my
beloved chocolate tortes and
The New Chocolate Decadence,
astonishingly creamy cheese
cakes, rich chocolate
soufflés, a marvelous flan,
and much, much more.

The New Chocolate Decadence

In the late seventies and the eighties, the ultimate chocolate dessert was called Chocolate Decadence. Made with only one tablespoon of flour and a full pound of dark chocolate, it was so rich it needed whipped cream and raspberry sauce to lighten it! If you loved it then and yearn for it now, salvation is at hand. With half the calories and a quarter of the fat per serving (even less if you count the whipped cream that went with the original), this may be the richest light dessert in the world. Be sure to use a superb brand of chocolate and the best cocoa you know.

WORK TIME: 30 MINUTES
BAKE TIME: 30 MINUTES
CHILL TIME: 24 HOURS

INGREDIENTS

5 OUNCES BITTERSWEET OR SEMI-
    SWEET CHOCOLATE, CHOPPED FINE
1 WHOLE EGG
1 EGG, SEPARATED
1 TEASPOON VANILLA EXTRACT
1 EGG WHITE
1/8 TEASPOON CREAM OF TARTAR
1/2 CUP PLUS 1/2 TABLESPOON
    UNSWEETENED DUTCH PROCESS
    COCOA
2 TABLESPOONS ALL-PURPOSE FLOUR
2/3 CUP PLUS 1/4 CUP SUGAR
3/4 CUP LOW-FAT (1%) MILK
1-1/4 CUPS OR MORE RASPBERRY
    SAUCE (PAGE 161)
ENLIGHTENED WHIPPED CREAM
    (PAGE 161) (OPTIONAL)

EQUIPMENT

8-INCH ROUND CAKE PAN WITH A SOLID
    BOTTOM, 1-1/2 TO 2 INCHES DEEP
OVENPROOF BAKING DISH OR SKILLET,
    AT LEAST 2 INCHES DEEP AND 2
    INCHES WIDER THAN THE CAKE PAN

Serves 12. Make 1 day before serving.

1. Position the rack in the lower third of the oven and preheat to 350°F. Spray the sides of the cake pan with vegetable oil spray and line the bottom with parchment paper. Put a kettle of water on to boil for Step 4.

2. Place the chocolate in a large mixing bowl. Combine 1 whole egg and 1 egg yolk in a small bowl with the vanilla. Place the 2 egg whites in a medium bowl with the cream of tartar. Set all 3 bowls aside.

3. Combine the cocoa, flour, and ⅔ cup sugar in a 1- to 1½-quart heavy-bottomed saucepan. Whisk in enough of the milk (about half) to form a smooth paste. Mix in the remaining milk. Cook over medium heat, stirring constantly with a wooden spoon or heatproof paddle to prevent burning (especially around the bottom edges), until mixture begins to simmer. Simmer very gently, stirring constantly, for 1½ minutes. Pour the hot mixture immediately over the chopped chocolate. Stir until the chocolate is completely melted and smooth. Whisk in egg and vanilla mixture. Set aside.

4. Beat the egg whites and cream of tartar at medium speed until soft peaks form. Gradually sprinkle in the remaining ¼ cup sugar, beating at high speed until stiff but not dry. Fold a quarter of the egg whites into the chocolate mixture to lighten it. Fold in remaining egg whites. Scrape mixture into the cake pan and smooth the top. Set cake pan in baking pan and place on oven rack. Pour enough boiling water into the baking pan to come about a third to halfway up the sides of the cake pan. Bake for exactly 30 minutes. The surface of the torte will spring back when very gently pressed but it will still be quite gooey inside. Remove cake pan and water pan from oven. Remove the cake pan from the water and cool completely on

NUTRITION INFORMATION

CALORIES PER SERVING: 184

FAT: 6 G

% CALORIES FROM FAT: 26%

PROTEIN: 3.7 G

CARBOHYDRATES: 33.5 G

CHOLESTEROL: 35.9 MG

a rack. Wrap in plastic and refrigerate overnight before serving. *Dessert may be refrigerated for up to 2 days or frozen for up to 2 months.*

5. To serve: Unmold by sliding a thin knife or metal spatula around the sides of the pan to release the torte. Place a piece of wax paper on top of torte. Invert a plate on top of the wax paper and invert torte onto plate. Remove pan and peel away paper liner. Turn torte right side up again and remove wax paper. Cut into wedges with a sharp thin knife. Dip the knife in hot water and wipe it dry between each slice. Or cut with dental floss like a moist cheesecake. Serve each slice with about 2 tablespoons of Raspberry Sauce and a dollop of Enlightened Whipped Cream, if desired.

Fallen Chocolate Soufflé Torte

*I wanted a light but real chocolate torte—something rich, moist, and chocolate, like my favorite Queen of
Sheba Torte with ground almonds, chocolate, and brandy. This is it: deep chocolate flavor, moist and dense, yet somehow light.
My closest Cocolat staff and toughest audience tasted it first. I was in heaven when they loved it.
Enthusiasm from the rest of the staff was the icing on the cake since they didn't know they were tasting a light dessert.*

Serves 10.

1. Position the rack in the lower third of the oven and preheat to 375°F. Place a round of parchment paper in the bottom of the pan and spray the sides with vegetable oil spray.

2. In a food processor or blender, grind the almonds with the flour until very fine. Set aside.

3. Combine the chopped chocolate, cocoa, and ¾ cup of the sugar in a large mixing bowl. Pour in the boiling water and whisk until mixture is smooth and chocolate is completely melted. Whisk in the egg yolks and brandy. Set aside.

4. Combine the egg whites and cream of tartar in a medium mixing bowl. Beat on medium speed until soft peaks form. Gradually sprinkle in the remaining sugar and beat on high speed until stiff but not dry. Whisk the flour and almonds into the chocolate. Fold about a quarter of the egg whites into the chocolate mixture to lighten it. Fold in the remaining egg whites. Scrape the batter into the pan and level the top if necessary.

5. Bake for 30 to 35 minutes, or until a toothpick or wooden skewer inserted into the center comes out with a few moist crumbs clinging to it. Cool in the pan on a wire rack. Torte will sink like a soufflé.

6. Taking care not to break the edges of the torte, slide a knife between the torte and the pan and run it around the pan to release the cake completely. Invert cake onto a plate and remove pan and paper liner. Turn right side up on a card-

WORK TIME: 20 MINUTES
BAKE TIME: 30–35 MINUTES

INGREDIENTS

1/4 CUP BLANCHED ALMONDS
 (1 OUNCE)
3 TABLESPOONS ALL-PURPOSE FLOUR
3 OUNCES BITTERSWEET OR SEMI-
 SWEET CHOCOLATE, CHOPPED FINE
1/2 CUP UNSWEETENED DUTCH
 PROCESS COCOA
1 CUP SUGAR
1/2 CUP BOILING WATER
2 EGG YOLKS
1 TABLESPOON BRANDY
4 EGG WHITES, AT ROOM TEMPERATURE
SCANT 1/4 TEASPOON CREAM OF
 TARTAR
2 TO 3 TEASPOONS POWDERED SUGAR
ENLIGHTENED WHIPPED CREAM
 (PAGE 161) (OPTIONAL)

EQUIPMENT

8-INCH SPRINGFORM PAN, 2-1/2 TO
 3 INCHES DEEP
8-INCH CARDBOARD CAKE CIRCLE
 (OPTIONAL)

NUTRITION INFORMATION

CALORIES PER SERVING: 179

FAT: 6.4 G

% CALORIES FROM FAT: 29%

PROTEIN: 4.2 G

CARBOHYDRATES: 30.2 G

CHOLESTEROL: 42.4 MG

board circle or platter. *Torte may be stored, covered, at room temperature for 1 day or frozen for up to 2 months.*

7. **To serve:** Sieve powdered sugar over the top. Serve with Enlightened Whipped Cream, if desired.

Note

I like the sunken-soufflé look of this torte served right side up with a dusting of sugar, but there are other options. If you plan to dust powdered sugar through a decorative stencil and/or would prefer a flat, even surface, level and invert the torte as follows: Slide a knife around the sides of the pan to release the torte. With torte still in the pan, use your fingers to press the raised edges down gently all around, so that the edges of torte are even with the center. Release the sides of the springform and invert the torte onto a cake circle or another pan bottom or a plate. Peel away the paper liner and leave the torte upside down.

VARIATION
....

Fallen Chocolate Soufflé Torte with Raspberries: Level and invert the torte as described in Note. Make a glaze by simmering ¼ cup red currant jelly or seedless raspberry jam for 1 or 2 minutes. Brush evenly over the top and sides of torte (reserve any leftover glaze for another use). Arrange 1 pint of raspberries in concentric circles on top of the torte until it is completely covered. Dust with powdered sugar just before serving, if desired.

Chocolate Walnut Torte

This flavor combination always pleases. The fat budget is largely spent on walnuts and lots of bittersweet chocolate,
so I banned all butter and reduced the egg yolks to a bare minimum.

Serves 10.

1. Position the rack in lower third of the oven and preheat to 350°F. Place a round of parchment paper in the bottom of the pan and spray the sides with vegetable oil spray.

2. In a food processor or blender, grind the walnuts with the flour until very fine. Set aside.

3. Combine the chopped chocolate, cocoa, and ¾ cup of the sugar in a large mixing bowl. Pour in boiling water and whisk until the mixture is smooth and chocolate is completely melted. Stir in the egg yolk, rum, and vanilla. Set aside.

4. Combine the egg whites and cream of tartar in a medium bowl. Beat at medium speed until soft peaks form. Gradually sprinkle in the remaining sugar and continue to beat at high speed until stiff but not dry. Whisk the walnuts into the chocolate. Fold a quarter of the egg whites into the chocolate batter to lighten it. Fold in the remaining egg whites. Scrape the batter into the pan and smooth the top. Bake until a skewer or toothpick inserted into the center of the torte comes out with a few moist crumbs clinging to it, about 25 to 30 minutes. Cool torte in the pan on a rack. It will sink dramatically in the center as it cools, leaving a raised crust around the edge. *Torte may be stored, covered, at room temperature for 1 or 2 days or frozen, well wrapped in foil or plastic, for up to 2 months.*

5. **To serve:** Slide a thin knife around the sides of the pan to release the torte. Remove sides and bottom of springform or invert cake pan to unmold. Remove

---

WORK TIME: 30 MINUTES
BAKE TIME: 25—30 MINUTES

INGREDIENTS

1/3 CUP COARSELY CHOPPED WALNUTS
   (1-1/3 OUNCES)

3 TABLESPOONS ALL-PURPOSE FLOUR

2-1/2 OUNCES BITTERSWEET OR SEMI-
   SWEET CHOCOLATE, CHOPPED FINE

1/3 CUP UNSWEETENED DUTCH
   PROCESS COCOA

1 CUP SUGAR

1/3 CUP BOILING WATER

1 EGG YOLK

1 TABLESPOON RUM

1/2 TEASPOON VANILLA EXTRACT

4 EGG WHITES

SCANT 1/4 TEASPOON CREAM OF
   TARTAR

ABOUT 2 TEASPOONS POWDERED
   SUGAR, FOR DUSTING

1 TO 1-1/2 CUPS MAIDA'S CREAM
   (PAGE 160) OR ENLIGHTENED
   CRÈME FRAÎCHE (PAGE 160) OR
   ENLIGHTENED WHIPPED CREAM
   (PAGE 161) OR 1 PINT VANILLA
   FROZEN YOGURT (OPTIONAL)

EQUIPMENT

8-INCH SPRINGFORM OR ROUND CAKE
   PAN, 2-1/2 TO 3 INCHES DEEP

8-INCH CARDBOARD CAKE CIRCLE
   (OPTIONAL)

NUTRITION INFORMATION

CALORIES PER SERVING: 169

FAT: 5.9 G

% CALORIES FROM FAT: 29%

PROTEIN: 3.5 G

CARBOHYDRATES: 28.6 G

CHOLESTEROL: 21.2 MG

paper liner from bottom and turn torte right side up on a cake circle or platter. Sieve a little powdered sugar on top and serve plain or with a dollop of Maida's Cream, Enlightened Cream, or a scoop of frozen yogurt, if desired.

VARIATION

. . . .

Chocolate Walnut Torte with Rich Chocolate Glaze: Level and invert the torte, as described in the Note on page 34. Make the Rich Chocolate Glaze (page 148). You will need about 1 cup to glaze the torte. Refrigerate or freeze the rest for another use. Spread top and sides of torte with a very thin coating (less than ¼ cup) of cooled Rich Chocolate Glaze. Let dry for 15 minutes or longer. Pour the remaining ¾ cup of glaze in the center of the torte and use a metal icing spatula to smooth it over the top and sides of the cake, letting the excess run off the sides. Let set at room temperature until dry. Transfer to a serving platter. Store and serve at room temperature.

Chocolate Chestnut Torte

Here my favorite chestnut puree is just a vehicle, providing a rich moist texture with only a hint of flavor in an otherwise very bittersweet chocolate torte.

Serves 10. Best served at room temperature.

1. Position the rack in lower third of the oven and preheat to 350°F. Place a round of parchment paper on the bottom of the pan and spray sides with vegetable oil spray.

2. Combine the chopped chocolate, cocoa, and half of the sugar in a large mixing bowl. Pour in boiling water and whisk until mixture is smooth and chocolate is completely melted. Stir in the chestnut spread, egg yolks, rum, and vanilla. Set aside.

3. Combine the egg whites with the cream of tartar. Beat at medium speed until soft peaks form. Gradually sprinkle in the remaining sugar and continue to beat at high speed until stiff but not dry. Whisk the flour into the chocolate mixture. Fold in a quarter of the egg whites to lighten it. Fold in the remaining egg whites. Scrape the batter into the pan and smooth the top. Bake until a skewer or toothpick inserted into the center of the torte comes out with a few moist crumbs clinging to it, about 30 to 35 minutes. Cool torte in the pan on a rack. It will sink in the center as it cools. *Torte may be prepared to this point and stored, covered, at room temperature or refrigerated for 1 or 2 days or frozen, well wrapped, for up to 2 months.*

4. To serve: Slide a thin knife or spatula around the sides of the pan to release the torte. Remove the sides and bottom of springform or invert cake pan to unmold. Remove the paper liner from the bottom and turn torte right side up. Sieve

---

WORK TIME: 30 MINUTES
BAKE TIME: 30—35 MINUTES

INGREDIENTS

4 OUNCES BITTERSWEET OR SEMISWEET
  CHOCOLATE, CHOPPED FINE
1/2 CUP PLUS 1/2 TABLESPOON
  UNSWEETENED DUTCH PROCESS
  COCOA
3/4 CUP SUGAR
1/2 CUP BOILING WATER
1/2 CUP CHESTNUT SPREAD
  (SWEETENED CHESTNUT PUREE)
2 EGG YOLKS
1 TABLESPOON RUM
1 TEASPOON VANILLA EXTRACT
4 EGG WHITES
SCANT 1/4 TEASPOON CREAM OF
  TARTAR
1/4 CUP ALL-PURPOSE FLOUR
1 TO 2 TEASPOONS POWDERED SUGAR,
  FOR DUSTING
MAIDA'S CREAM (PAGE 160) OR ANY
  ONE OF THE ENLIGHTENED CREAMS
  (PAGES 160—161) OR 1 PINT VANILLA
  FROZEN YOGURT (OPTIONAL)

EQUIPMENT

8-INCH SPRINGFORM OR ROUND CAKE
  PAN, 2-1/2 TO 3 INCHES DEEP
8-INCH CARDBOARD CAKE CIRCLE
  (OPTIONAL)

NUTRITION INFORMATION

CALORIES PER SERVING: 188

FAT: 6.2 G

% CALORIES FROM FAT: 27%

PROTEIN: 4.2 G

CARBOHYDRATES: 33.3 G

CHOLESTEROL: 42.4 MG

a little powdered sugar over the torte. Serve with a dollop of Maida's Cream, a dollop of Enlightened Cream, or a scoop of frozen yogurt, if desired.

VARIATION

....

Chocolate Chestnut Torte with Cream Cheese Fudge Glaze: Level and invert the torte, as described in the Note on page 34. Spread the top and sides with a very thin coating (about ¼ cup) of cooled Cream Cheese Fudge Glaze (page 146). Let dry at room temperature for 15 minutes or longer to set the glaze. Rewarm the remaining glaze to a thick pouring consistency. Pour it through a fine strainer to remove air bubbles. Pour strained glaze into the center of the torte and use a metal icing spatula to smooth it over the top and sides. There will be just enough glaze. Let set at room temperature until dry. Transfer to a serving platter. Store and serve at room temperature.

> *Throughout the development and testing of recipes for this book, I found it surprisingly tricky to pair lower-fat desserts with appropriate sauces, toppings, and frostings. The obvious was almost never correct. Alas, there was no such thing as one good all-purpose chocolate glaze or frosting. This particular torte, for example, was tasted with all three of the frosting/glazes presented in this book—only the Cream Cheese Fudge Glaze really worked. We also tasted the torte with sweetened low-fat sour cream (fine but higher in fat than I wanted), a combination of sweetened yogurt and low-fat sour cream (much too tangy), medium quality vanilla low-fat yogurt (fair), really good quality vanilla low-fat frozen yogurt (good!), and sweetened pureed low-fat cottage cheese (good as long as it was sweet enough). From my experience, particularly with this torte, I learned to keep on trying.*

Sweet Chestnut Torte

For sweetened chestnut cream lovers especially. I was hooked twenty-five years ago, when inexpensive restaurants in Paris served great goblets of the stuff (right from the can) with huge dollops of crème fraîche. Some restaurants still do it and, believe me, it's still good.

Serves 10. Best served at room temperature.

1. Position the rack in lower third of the oven and preheat to 350°F. Place a round of parchment paper in the bottom of the pan and spray the sides with vegetable oil spray.

2. Combine the chestnut spread, egg yolks, brandy, and vanilla in a medium mixing bowl. Whisk in the flour. Set aside.

3. In a medium mixing bowl, combine the egg whites with the cream of tartar. Beat at medium speed until soft peaks form. Gradually sprinkle in the sugar and continue to beat at high speed until stiff but not dry. Fold a quarter of the egg whites into the chestnut mixture to lighten it. Fold in the remaining egg whites. Scrape batter into the pan and smooth the top. Bake until a skewer inserted in the center of the torte comes out nearly clean (a few moist crumbs may still cling to it), about 25 to 30 minutes. Cool torte in the pan on a rack. *Torte may be stored, covered, at room temperature or refrigerated for 1 or 2 days or frozen for up to 2 months.*

4. **To serve:** Slide a thin knife or spatula around the sides of the pan to release the torte, as necessary. Remove the sides and bottom of springform or invert cake pan to unmold. Remove paper liner from bottom and turn torte right side up. Sieve a little powdered sugar over the top. Serve with a dollop of sour cream, Enlightened Cream, Maida's Cream, or a scoop of frozen yogurt, if desired.

WORK TIME: 20 MINUTES
BAKE TIME: 25–30 MINUTES

INGREDIENTS

1 CUP CHESTNUT SPREAD
   (SWEETENED CHESTNUT PUREE)
2 EGG YOLKS
2 TABLESPOONS BRANDY
1 TEASPOON VANILLA
1/4 CUP ALL-PURPOSE FLOUR
4 EGG WHITES
1/8 TEASPOON CREAM OF TARTAR
1/4 CUP SUGAR
ABOUT 2 TEASPOONS POWDERED
   SUGAR, FOR DUSTING
1 TO 1-1/2 CUPS LIGHT SOUR CREAM
   SWEETENED WITH 4 TO 6 TEASPOONS
   SUGAR, OR TO TASTE, AND 1/4
   TEASPOON VANILLA EXTRACT OR
   ONE OF THE ENLIGHTENED CREAMS
   (PAGES 160–161) OR MAIDA'S
   CREAM (PAGE 160) OR 1 PINT
   VANILLA FROZEN YOGURT (OPTIONAL)

EQUIPMENT

8-INCH SPRINGFORM OR ROUND CAKE
   PAN, 2-1/2 TO 3 INCHES DEEP

NUTRITION INFORMATION

CALORIES PER SERVING: 113
FAT: 1.5 G
% CALORIES FROM FAT: 12%
PROTEIN: 2.76 G
CARBOHYDRATES: 22.2 G
CHOLESTEROL 42.4 MG

Chocolate Marble Cheesecake, page 44

The New Cheesecake

A superb plain cheesecake is a thing of beauty unto itself. It is also an irresistible invitation to marble beautiful colors and flavors together. Two combinations follow this recipe—one for chocolate and vanilla, almost primal choices, and the other for vanilla and Lemon Curd. Finally, since my cheesecake is baked in a pan of water like a custard, I thought why not divide the batter into individual custard cups? For that matter, why not line the cups with caramel? A star is born!

Serves 10. Make 1 day ahead.

1. Position the rack in lower third of the oven and preheat to 350°F. Place a round of parchment paper on the bottom of the pan and spray the sides with vegetable oil spray. Put a kettle of water on to boil for Step 4.

2. Process the cottage cheese in a food processor for 2½ to 3 minutes, or until silky smooth, scraping the sides and bottom of the bowl once or twice as necessary. Set aside.

3. In a small microwavesafe bowl, soften the cream cheese in microwave on High for about 30 seconds. Or warm gently in the top of a double boiler. Stir until smooth. Scrape into the processor. Add the eggs, sugar, vanilla, lemon juice, and salt. Pulse until incorporated and perfectly smooth. Do not overprocess. Pour into pan.

4. Slide oven rack part way out. Place the cheesecake pan in a baking dish or skillet and set on oven rack. Carefully pour boiling water around the pan to a depth of about 1 inch. Slide oven rack in gently to avoid sloshing water. Bake until cheesecake has puffed and risen slightly and is just beginning to shrink from the edges of the pan, about 40 to 45 minutes. Remove cheesecake from water bath and cool on a rack. When cool, cover and chill for at least 12 hours or up to 2 days before serving. *Cheesecake may be refrigerated for up to 2 days.*

5. **To unmold and serve:** Cover pan with tightly stretched plastic wrap. Place a flat dish on top of plastic. Invert and rap pan gently until cheesecake is released from pan. Remove pan and peel parchment liner from bottom of cheesecake. Place

---

WORK TIME: 25 MINUTES
BAKE TIME: 40–45 MINUTES
CHILL TIME: AT LEAST 12 HOURS

INGREDIENTS

2 CUPS LOW-FAT (2%) SMALL-CURD
  COTTAGE CHEESE
8 OUNCES LIGHT CREAM CHEESE
3 EGGS
1 CUP SUGAR
1 TABLESPOON VANILLA EXTRACT
1-1/2 TEASPOONS STRAINED LEMON
  JUICE
1/4 TEASPOON SALT
3 TO 4 TABLESPOONS GRAHAM
  CRACKER OR ZWIEBACK CRUMBS

EQUIPMENT

8-INCH ROUND PAN WITH A SOLID
  BOTTOM, AT LEAST 2 INCHES DEEP
OVENPROOF BAKING DISH OR SKILLET,
  AT LEAST 2 INCHES DEEP AND 2
  INCHES WIDER THAN THE CAKE PAN
8-INCH CARDBOARD CAKE CIRCLE
  (OPTIONAL)

NUTRITION INFORMATION

CALORIES PER SERVING: 204

FAT: 7.4 G

% CALORIES FROM FAT: 32%

PROTEIN: 10.7 G

CARBOHYDRATES: 24 G

CHOLESTEROL: 83.4 MG

cake circle or serving plate on the cake and carefully invert so that cake is right side up. Remove plastic wrap. Press crumbs around sides of cake. Cut with a sharp thin knife. Dip the knife in hot water and wipe it dry between each cut.

Note

The suave texture of this cheesecake relies on ultra-smooth cottage cheese. This requires a food processor and at least 2½ to 3 minutes of processing, no cheating.

When I began to work on a lighter cheesecake,
I tested a number of published recipes.
Usually all or most of the cream cheese was traded for
cottage cheese and flour was added to thicken
and absorb the extra moisture in the cottage cheese.
The results were lighter in fat and calories but
quite leaden in taste and texture. Where was the
creaminess? How could something so light
be so heavy? I tried cornstarch instead of flour.
My tasters grimaced and said "ugh" (they are
not gentle) "is there starch in this?" I abandoned
starch and flour and wrung the cottage
cheese out in dishtowels. This helped a little, but
I hated the messy dishtowels. I abandoned the
dishtowels, added one more egg to bind up
excess moisture, and baked the cheesecake in
a hot water bath. The result was incredible!
A creamy rich cheesecake without
weird flavors, without overcooked edges,
and without cracks.

Baby Caramel Cheesecakes: Set out eight or nine 4- to 5-ounce soufflé or custard cups and an ovenproof pan or pans large enough to hold the cups. Preheat the oven as in Step 1. Using 1 cup of sugar and ½ cup of water, make caramel on the stove or in the microwave and line the soufflé cups as directed on page 158. Make the batter as in Steps 2 and 3. Divide the batter among the cups and put them in the baking pan with hot water. Bake until cheesecakes are puffed but still jiggle, about 25 to 30 minutes. Remove from the water bath and cool on a rack. Chill for at least 12 hours. Unmold to serve. If desired, set cups in simmering water bath for 2 to 3 minutes to melt caramel stuck to the bottom. Pour extra caramel over cheesecakes. This serves 8 to 9.

Chocolate Marble Cheesecake: Preheat the oven and prepare pan as in Step 1 of The New Cheesecake (page 41). Make the batter as in Steps 2 and 3. Whisk 3 tablespoons unsweetened Dutch process cocoa, ¼ teaspoon instant espresso or coffee powder, and 1 tablespoon sugar with 3 tablespoons of water in a small bowl until smooth. Stir 1 cup of cheesecake batter into this chocolate mixture. Set aside. Pour about three fourths of the remaining cheesecake batter into the pan. Pour all the chocolate batter in the center of the pan on top of the plain batter, leaving a thick ring of plain batter showing all around the edges. Pour the reserved plain batter in the center of the chocolate batter, leaving a ring of chocolate batter showing. Using a table knife or teaspoon, make circular strokes to marble the batters until nicely but not completely mingled. Bake, cool, and chill as in Step 4. Unmold and serve as in Step 5, coating the sides with crushed Plain Chocolate Cookies (page 121) instead of graham cracker or zwieback crumbs, if desired. This serves 10 to 12.

Lemon Marble Cheesecake: Prepare ⅔ cup Lemon Curd (page 141) and set aside to cool to room temperature. Meanwhile, preheat the oven and prepare the pan as in Step 1 of The New Cheesecake (page 41). Make the cheesecake batter as in Steps 2 and 3. Scrape the cheesecake batter into the pan. Distribute slightly rounded tablespoons of Lemon Curd evenly over the cheesecake batter. Using a table knife or teaspoon, make circular strokes to marble the batters until the colors are nicely but not completely mingled. Bake, cool, and chill as in Step 4. Unmold and serve as in Step 5. This serves 10 to 12.

Chocolate Roulade

This simple chocolate roulade was the first dessert that I created for the Celebrated Chefs series put on by Summit Hospital Cancer Education and Prevention Center. Its success surprised me and convinced me to think more seriously about light desserts.

Serves 12.

1. In a food processor fitted with a steel blade, process the cottage cheese, Kahlúa, sugar, vanilla, 2 tablespoons of cocoa, the espresso powder, and Amaretto for 2 to 3 minutes, or until very smooth and no longer curdy. Set aside.

2. Sieve about 1 tablespoon of cocoa over a sheet of foil. Run a small knife around the edges of the soufflé pastry to release it from the pan. Invert it onto the foil. Peel parchment liner from pastry.

3. Spread the cottage cheese mixture evenly over the pastry. Use foil to help roll up the pastry lengthwise. Roulade will crack as you roll. Wrap roulade tightly in foil. Refrigerate for at least 3 hours. *Roulade may be refrigerated up to 1 day.*

4. **To serve:** Unwrap the roulade and trim ends, if necessary, to neaten. Dust with cocoa, if desired. Transfer to a serving platter. Serve slices with Raspberry Sauce and, if desired, raspberries.

WORK TIME: 30 MINUTES
BAKE TIME: 15–17 MINUTES
CHILL TIME: AT LEAST 3 HOURS

INGREDIENTS

2 CUPS (4% FAT) COTTAGE CHEESE

2 TABLESPOONS KAHLÚA

1/4 CUP SUGAR

1 TEASPOON VANILLA EXTRACT

3 TO 4 TABLESPOONS UNSWEETENED
    DUTCH PROCESS COCOA

1/2 TEASPOON INSTANT ESPRESSO
    OR COFFEE POWDER

2 TO 3 TEASPOONS AMARETTO

1 SHEET CHOCOLATE SOUFFLÉ PASTRY
    (PAGE 148), BAKED AND COOLED

1-1/2 TO 2 CUPS RASPBERRY SAUCE
    (PAGE 161)

1 PINT FRESH RASPBERRIES
    (OPTIONAL)

NUTRITION INFORMATION

CALORIES PER SERVING: 207

FAT: 6.9 G

% CALORIES FROM FAT: 29%

PROTEIN: 7.6 G

CARBOHYDRATES: 30.3 G

CHOLESTEROL: 5.58 MG

Double Chocolate Layer Cake

At Cocolat we needed a simple chocolate layer cake that was less sophisticated than our chocolate tortes

with nuts and liqueurs. The solution was to use our Chocolate Pound Cake for the layers and frost it with chocolate. It was an

instant success. I took the hint and transformed my low-fat Chocolate Pound Cake likewise. Voilà!

A great birthday cake. The two chocolate frostings are equally delicious; the Rich Chocolate is somewhat richer.

WORK TIME: 1 HOUR 30 MINUTES
BAKE TIME: 45–50 MINUTES

INGREDIENTS

1 CUP PLUS 2 TABLESPOONS SIFTED
    ALL-PURPOSE FLOUR (4-1/2
    OUNCES)
1/3 CUP PLUS 1 TABLESPOON
    UNSWEETENED DUTCH PROCESS
    COCOA
SCANT 1/4 TEASPOON BAKING SODA
SCANT 1/4 TEASPOON BAKING POWDER
1/4 TEASPOON SALT
1 EGG
2 EGG WHITES
1 TABLESPOON INSTANT ESPRESSO
    OR COFFEE POWDER
1-1/2 TABLESPOONS HOT WATER
1 TEASPOON VANILLA EXTRACT
1/4 CUP PLUS 2 TABLESPOONS LOW-FAT
    (1%) BUTTERMILK
6 TABLESPOONS UNSALTED BUTTER
1-1/3 CUPS SUGAR
ABOUT 2 CUPS CHOCOLATE
    BUTTERMILK FROSTING (PAGE 147)
    OR RICH CHOCOLATE FROSTING
    (PAGE 148)
FINE CHOCOLATE SHAVINGS (PAGE
    162), FOR DECORATION (OPTIONAL)

Serves 10 to 12. Best served at room temperature.

1. Have all ingredients at room temperature (68°-70°F.). Position the rack in lower third of the oven and preheat to 350°F. Line the bottom of the pan with a round of parchment paper and spray the sides with vegetable oil spray.

2. Combine and sift together the flour, cocoa, baking soda, baking powder, and salt. Set aside. Whisk the whole egg with the egg whites in a small bowl. Set aside. Dissolve the espresso powder in the water and combine with the vanilla and buttermilk in a small bowl. Set aside.

3. Cut the butter into chunks and place in an electric mixer bowl. Beat to soften, about 1 minute. Add the sugar gradually, beating constantly for about 3 minutes. Dribble in the eggs gradually, beating at high speed for 2 to 3 minutes. On low speed, beat in a third of the flour mixture, scraping the bowl as necessary. On medium speed, gradually dribble in half of the buttermilk mixture, scraping the bowl as necessary. On low speed, beat in half of the remaining flour, followed by the rest of the buttermilk, always scraping the bowl as necessary. On low speed, beat in the remaining flour mixture until well combined. Batter may look slightly curdled.

4. Scrape batter into the pan and smooth the top. Bake for 40 to 45 minutes, or until cake starts to shrink from the sides of the pan and a toothpick inserted into the center comes out barely clean. Do not overbake. Cool cake in the pan on a rack for 5 to 10 minutes. Invert onto a plate and remove pan and paper liner. Turn right side up and cool completely before filling or storing. *Cake can be prepared to this point and stored, wrapped airtight, for up to 1 day or frozen for up to 2 months.*

5. Assemble the cake. Place cake right side up on a cardboard cake circle or serving platter. Using a long serrated knife, cut the cake horizontally into 3 thin layers. Remove the top 2 layers and spread ⅓ cup of frosting over the bottom layer. Place the second layer on top and spread with another ⅓ cup of frosting. Place the final cake layer on top and check to see that the cake layers are centered on top of one another. Spread a thin layer (¼ to ⅓ cup) of frosting over the top and sides of cake. Allow cake to set, at room temperature, for 20 minutes or more. Spread the remaining frosting over the top and sides of the cake. Decorate top or sides of cake with Fine Chocolate Shavings, if desired. *Cake may be stored at room temperature for 1 day.*

EQUIPMENT

8-INCH ROUND CAKE PAN,
  2 INCHES DEEP
8-INCH CARDBOARD CAKE CIRCLE
  (OPTIONAL)

NUTRITION INFORMATION

CALORIES PER SERVING: 242
FAT: 7.8 G
% CALORIES FROM FAT: 27%
PROTEIN: 4.2 G
CARBOHYDRATES: 42.9 G
CHOLESTEROL: 33.9 MG

Mini Misùs

Tiramisù, Italian for "pick me up," has certainly captured the imagination of the nation.
Mine are single servings—light but spirited.

Serves 9 or 10.

1. Position rack in the middle of the oven and preheat to 350˚F.

2. Place the Ladyfinger Layers on a baking sheet and toast for 5 minutes. Remove from oven and cool on a rack.

3. **Make the filling.** Place the cottage cheese in a food processor and process for at least 2½ to 3 minutes, or until perfectly smooth. Add the cream cheese, brandy, vanilla, and ⅓ cup of the sugar. Pulse just until combined. Do not over-process. Filling may be completed to this point, covered, and refrigerated for up to 1 day.

4. **Make the safe meringue.** In a large skillet, bring 1 inch of water to a boil. In a 4- to 6-cup stainless steel bowl, combine the cream of tartar and 1 teaspoon of water. Whisk in the egg white and remaining 2 tablespoons of sugar. Place thermometer near stove in a mug of very hot tap water. Set bowl in skillet. Stir mixture briskly and constantly with a rubber spatula, scraping the sides and bottom often to avoid scrambling the whites. After 45 seconds, remove bowl from skillet. Quickly insert thermometer, tilting bowl to cover stem by at least 2 inches. If less than 160˚F., rinse thermometer in skillet water and return it to mug. Replace bowl in skillet. Stir as before until temperature reaches 160˚F. when bowl is removed. Beat on high speed until cool and stiff. (For more details on safe meringue, see pages 138–140.)

5. Fold a quarter of the meringue into the filling, then fold in the remaining meringue.

6. **Assemble the dessert.** Brush the top of each layer with coffee. Place a generous 2 tablespoons of filling in the center of half of the layers. Sprinkle the filling with half of the chocolate. Set a second layer on top of each mound of filling and press down slightly to spread filling almost to the edge of the bottom layer. Divide the remaining filling among the pastries, centering a dollop on top of each. Use the back of a spoon to smooth and spread the filling gently. Refrigerate in a covered container for at least 2 hours. *Dessert may be refrigerated for up to 1 day.*

7. **To serve:** Top each dessert with remaining chocolate.

WORK AND BAKE TIME: 60 MINUTES
CHILL TIME: AT LEAST 2 HOURS

INGREDIENTS

EIGHTEEN TO TWENTY 3-INCH
  LADYFINGER LAYERS A (PAGE 149),
  BAKED AND COOLED
1-1/2 CUPS LOW-FAT (2%)
  SMALL-CURD COTTAGE CHEESE
6 OUNCES LIGHT CREAM CHEESE
2 TABLESPOONS BRANDY
1/2 TEASPOON VANILLA EXTRACT
1/3 CUP PLUS 2 TABLESPOONS SUGAR
1/16 TEASPOON CREAM OF TARTAR
1 EGG WHITE
1/2 CUP VERY STRONG BLACK COFFEE
  OR ESPRESSO
2 OUNCES BITTERSWEET OR SEMI-
  SWEET CHOCOLATE, CHOPPED FINE
  OR MADE INTO CHOCOLATE
  SHAVINGS, THIN CHOCOLATE
  SHARDS, OR CHOCOLATE SPLINTERS
  (PAGE 162–163)

EQUIPMENT

INSTANT-READ THERMOMETER

NUTRITION INFORMATION

CALORIES PER SERVING: 230
FAT: 7 G
% CALORIES FROM FAT: 30%
PROTEIN: 9.7 G
CARBOHYDRATES: 30.8 G
CHOLESTEROL: 78.4 MG

Panna Cotta

This dressy combination of vanilla pudding, chocolate sauce, raspberries, and a caramelized sugar tuile was inspired by the original creation of Tra Vigne Chef Michael Chiarello in Napa, California. Michael's heavenly recipe is not, uh, quite so light as mine. But he generously shared his recipe for Sugar Tuiles, which I have only slightly revised.

WORK TIME: 45 MINUTES
BAKE TIME: 12 MINUTES
CHILL TIME: AT LEAST 1 HOUR

INGREDIENTS

VANILLA PUDDING (RECIPE FOLLOWS)

1-1/2 OUNCES BITTERSWEET OR SEMI-SWEET CHOCOLATE, CUT INTO SMALL PIECES

1/2 OUNCE MILK CHOCOLATE, CUT INTO SMALL PIECES

1-1/2 TABLESPOONS LOW-FAT (1%) MILK

4 TO 5 SUGAR TUILES (PAGE 156–157), FLAT OR CURVED

1 CUP RASPBERRIES

EQUIPMENT

4 OR 5 INDIVIDUAL DESSERT DISHES, PREFERABLY WIDE AND SHALLOW, OR ROUND OR OVAL RAMEKINS OR CUSTARD CUPS

NUTRITION INFORMATION

CALORIES PER SERVING: 232

FAT: 7.9 G

% CALORIES FROM FAT: 29%

PROTEIN: 7.3 G

CARBOHYDRATES: 35.3 G

CHOLESTEROL: 91.8 MG

1. Make the pudding through Step 3.

2. **Make the chocolate sauce.** Combine all the chocolate and milk in a small bowl. Set bowl in a pan of barely simmering water and stir until melted and smooth. Or microwave on Medium (50% power) for about 30 seconds. Stir until melted and smooth. Set aside. *Sauce may be refrigerated for up to 2 days.*

3. **To serve:** Just before serving, rewarm the sauce if necessary. Drizzle 1 tablespoon of chocolate sauce over each pudding. Top with a Sugar Tuile. Scatter a few raspberries over or around the tuile. Serve at once.

Vanilla Pudding, Plain or Fancy

Unadorned, this old-fashioned style pudding may remind you of your childhood (only better). Caramelize the top and/or add summer berries and invite your friends. Or use the pudding to make Panna Cotta (page 50).

Serves 4 to 5.

1. Combine the sugar with the cornstarch and a pinch of salt in a small bowl. Add enough of the milk to make a smooth paste. Set aside. Scald the remaining milk with the nutmeg in a heavy nonreactive 2-quart saucepan.

2. While the milk is heating, whisk the eggs and vanilla in a medium bowl. Set aside.

3. Gradually whisk a third of the hot milk into the sugar mixture. Return to saucepan. Cook, stirring constantly, until milk begins to bubble around the edges. Simmer very gently, stirring constantly, for about 2 minutes. Remove from the heat and ladle about 1 cup of hot liquid into the beaten eggs, whisking briskly to prevent eggs from scrambling. Scrape egg mixture back into saucepan. Cook over medium heat for about 2 minutes, stirring constantly, without allowing pudding to simmer or boil. Pour it immediately into a serving dish or divide among ramekins. Chill for 1 or 2 hours before serving, longer if you plan to caramelize the top. *Pudding may be refrigerated for up to 1 day.*

4. Caramelize the tops on individual puddings, if desired. Shortly before serving, sprinkle the top of each pudding evenly with ½ tablespoon sugar. Caramelize with a torch (page 159). Chill in the freezer for at least 10 minutes before serving. Repeat for each ramekin. Or caramelize under the broiler. Preheat the broiler and position the rack 3 to 4 inches from the heat source. Sprinkle sugar on desserts and place in a baking pan. Fill the baking pan with lots of ice cubes and water nearly to the top of the pudding cups. Slide under the broiler and watch the surface of puddings carefully until caramelized, 3 minutes or longer. It's best to test with 1 pudding first. Or, if desired, top each pudding with a Caramel Round or Sugar Tuile. Serve immediately.

VARIATION

....

Chocolate Pudding: Prepare as for Vanilla Pudding, increasing the sugar to 6 tablespoons and adding ⅓ cup unsweetened Dutch process cocoa in Step 1. Omit the nutmeg.

WORK TIME: 15 MINUTES
CHILL TIME: AT LEAST 1 HOUR

INGREDIENTS

1/3 CUP SUGAR
2 TABLESPOONS CORNSTARCH
PINCH OF SALT
2 CUPS LOW-FAT (1%) MILK
PINCH OF NUTMEG
2 EGGS
1-1/2 TEASPOONS VANILLA EXTRACT
2-1/2 TABLESPOONS SUGAR OR 4 TO 5
    CARAMEL ROUNDS (PAGE 158) OR
    SUGAR TUILES (PAGE 156)
    (OPTIONAL)

EQUIPMENT

FOUR OR FIVE 4- TO 5-OUNCE
    RAMEKINS OR CUSTARD CUPS OR
    A 3- TO 4-CUP SERVING BOWL
PROPANE TORCH (OPTIONAL)

NUTRITION INFORMATION

CALORIES PER SERVING: 134
FAT: 3 G
% CALORIES FROM FAT: 20%
PROTEIN: 6 G
CARBOHYDRATES: 21 G
CHOLESTEROL: 88.7 MG

Chocolate Soufflés

I like my soufflés dark and very rich in chocolate flavor, never light and ethereal!
These meet my standards—and no one will suspect how light they really are. The bonus is that you can make them
hours or even a day ahead and simply pop them into the oven twenty minutes before serving.

WORK TIME: 20 MINUTES
BAKE TIME: 15–20 MINUTES

INGREDIENTS

5 TEASPOONS SUGAR, FOR CUPS
    (OPTIONAL)
1 CUP POWDERED SUGAR
1/2 CUP UNSWEETENED DUTCH
    PROCESS COCOA
2 TABLESPOONS FLOUR
1/2 CUP LOW-FAT (1%) MILK
4 EGG WHITES, AT ROOM TEMPERATURE
1/8 TEASPOON CREAM OF TARTAR
3 TABLESPOONS PLUS 1 TEASPOON
    GRANULATED SUGAR
2 EGG YOLKS
1/2 TEASPOON VANILLA EXTRACT
2 TO 3 TABLESPOONS POWDERED
    SUGAR, FOR DUSTING

EQUIPMENT

EIGHT 4- TO 5-OUNCE SOUFFLÉ CUPS
BAKING SHEET

Serves 8.

1. Position the rack in lower third of the oven and preheat to 350°F. Spray soufflé cups with vegetable oil spray. If you are sugaring the cups, pour a little granulated sugar in 1 soufflé cup and tilt it to coat the bottom and sides. Tap out excess sugar into the next cup and continue until all the cups are sugared.

2. Sift the powdered sugar, cocoa, and flour into the top of a double boiler. Add the milk and ½ cup water and whisk until smooth. Cook over gently simmering water, whisking continuously, for about 10 minutes, or until thickened. Remove from heat. Set aside.

3. Beat the egg whites with the cream of tartar on medium speed until soft peaks form. Gradually sprinkle in sugar, beating at high speed until stiff but not dry.

4. Whisk the egg yolks and vanilla into the chocolate mixture. Fold about a quarter of the egg whites into the chocolate mixture to lighten it. Fold in the remaining whites. Divide mixture evenly among the cups. It can come to about ¼ inch below the rims. *Soufflés may be cooled, covered, and refrigerated for up to 1 day.*

5. Place the cups on a baking sheet and bake for 15 to 17 minutes (19 to 20 minutes if soufflés were prepared in advance and refrigerated), or until soufflés have puffed well above the cups and a bamboo skewer or toothpick inserted from the side deep into the center comes out with moist crumbs clinging to it. Do not overbake.

6. To serve: Sieve a little powdered sugar over each soufflé and serve immediately.

NUTRITION INFORMATION

CALORIES PER SERVING: 127

FAT: 2.6 G

% CALORIES FROM FAT: 17%

PROTEIN: 4.3 G

CARBOHYDRATES: 24.6 G

CHOLESTEROL: 53.6 MG

Notes

• These are excellent just as they are. If you're a lily gilder or just can't serve anything like this without some kind of accompaniment, try a small scoop of really good, slightly softened vanilla frozen yogurt, Enlightened Whipped Cream, or Enlightened Crème Fraîche (pages 160–161).

• For another kind of splurge, tuck a ¼-ounce piece of bittersweet or semisweet chocolate deep into each soufflé before baking or fold ⅓ cup of chocolate chips into the batter with the egg whites.

Pumpkin Nests

Pumpkin pie crust is frequently a soggy abomination. At Thanksgiving my Mom simply makes what she calls pumpkin pudding (the filling without the crust) and then devotes her energy to the best apple pies in the world. Everyone happily eats both with fewer groans and no regrets. I scoop my pumpkin pudding into flaky phyllo nests and top them with spun sugar and/or shards of caramel. The phyllo stays crisp since it is not baked with the pumpkin.

WORK TIME: 40 MINUTES
BAKE TIME: 70–75 MINUTES

INGREDIENTS

2 EGGS, LIGHTLY BEATEN
1-3/4 CUPS SOLID PACK PUMPKIN
    (15-OUNCE CAN)
3/4 CUP SUGAR
1/2 TEASPOON GROUND GINGER
1 TEASPOON GROUND CINNAMON
1/4 TEASPOON GROUND CLOVES
1/4 TEASPOON GROUND NUTMEG
1/2 TEASPOON SALT
2 TABLESPOONS BRANDY OR RUM
1-1/2 CUPS EVAPORATED MILK
    (12-OUNCE CAN)
8 PHYLLO NESTS (PAGE 156), BAKED
    AND COOLED
CARAMEL SHARDS AND/OR SPUN SUGAR
    (PAGES 158–159) OR ENLIGHTENED
    WHIPPED CREAM (PAGE 161) OR
    ENLIGHTENED SOUR CREAM (PAGE
    161) (OPTIONAL)

EQUIPMENT

8-INCH ROUND GLASS BAKING DISH,
    2 INCHES DEEP

NUTRITION INFORMATION

CALORIES PER SERVING: 228
FAT: 7.2 G
% CALORIES FROM FAT: 28%
PROTEIN: 6 G
CARBOHYDRATES: 35.7 G
CHOLESTEROL: 72.4 MG

Serves 8.

1. Position the rack in lower third of the oven. Preheat to 325°F.

2. **Make the pumpkin pudding.** In a medium bowl, mix eggs, pumpkin, sugar, spices, and salt. Stir in brandy and evaporated milk. Pour into baking dish and bake until a knife plunged into the center of the pudding comes out nearly clean, about 55 minutes. Cool. *Pumpkin pudding may be refrigerated, covered, for up to 2 days.*

3. **Assemble the nests.** Just before serving, scoop pudding into nests. Garnish with Caramel Shards and/or Spun Sugar, if desired. Or garnish with a dollop of the cream. Serve immediately.

Raspberry Genoise

When you have finally had your fill of fresh raspberries and are willing to bake some, this ultra-simple dessert
is light and tangy enough for breakfast or brunch and delightful after a casual supper. Measure all ingredients in advance and you'll be able
to put the cake together in less than fifteen minutes and serve it shortly after it has cooled.

Serves 10. Best served soon after cake has cooled.

1. Preheat the oven to 350°F. If the cake pan is only 2 inches deep, make a foil collar. Tear off a sheet of aluminum foil about 30 inches long and fold it lengthwise in half and then in half again to make a long band 3 inches wide. Wrap the foil around the outside of the pan and fold the edges together tightly to form a collar about 1 inch taller than the pan. Spray the bottom and sides of the pan and the collar lightly with vegetable oil spray.

2. Use a large fork to mix the berries lightly with ⅓ cup of sugar (or a little more if the berries are very tart). Spread evenly over the bottom of the pan. Set aside.

3. Mix the Genoise A according to the directions on page 152. Turn the batter immediately into the pan on top of the berries.

4. Bake until the cake shrinks slightly from the edges and the top springs back when pressed, 30 to 35 minutes. Cool the cake in the pan on a rack for 10 to 15 minutes. Slide a small knife or metal spatula around the edges of the cake to release it. Invert onto a plate. Lift off the pan. Allow cake to cool. Serve shortly after cake has cooled.

Note

Do not use a pan with a removable bottom; the berry juices will leak. Do not use a glass pan; the Genoise would take longer to bake and so the berries would overcook.

WORK TIME: 30 MINUTES
BAKE TIME: 30–35 MINUTES

INGREDIENTS

3-1/2 CUPS FRESH RASPBERRIES
1/3 CUP SUGAR, OR MORE TO TASTE
GENOISE A, MADE WITH ALL-PURPOSE
   FLOUR (PAGE 152), INGREDIENTS
   ONLY

EQUIPMENT

9-INCH ROUND NONREACTIVE OR NON-
   STICK METAL CAKE PAN WITH A
   SOLID BOTTOM, AT LEAST 2 TO 3
   INCHES DEEP

NUTRITION INFORMATION

CALORIES PER SERVING: 185
FAT: 4.7 G
% CALORIES FROM FAT: 22%
PROTEIN: 4 G
CARBOHYDRATES: 32.7 G
CHOLESTEROL: 71.3 MG

The sweetness of berries varies greatly. I would rather err on the side of adding too
little sugar and then pass a big shaker of sugar at the table—for those who must—as
they used to do in Paris bistros when unglazed strawberry tarts were served.

Flans with Brandied Prunes

This recipe was adapted from a nonfat recipe by cookbook author Steve Raichlen. It's as satisfying as a flan should be.
I do believe that steeping vanilla beans, cinnamon stick, and citrus peel in milk instead of using extracts and flavorings convinces our palates
that we are eating something very rich indeed. The macerated prunes add richness and sophistication.

WORK TIME: 40 MINUTES
BAKE TIME: 35–40 MINUTES
CHILL TIME: AT LEAST 6 HOURS

INGREDIENTS

6 MOIST PITTED PRUNES

3 TO 4 TABLESPOONS BRANDY,
  ARMAGNAC, OR RUM

1 LEMON

3 CUPS LOW-FAT (1%) MILK

1/2 VANILLA BEAN, SPLIT LENGTHWISE

2-INCH PIECE CINNAMON STICK

1 CUP SUGAR

2 WHOLE EGGS

2 EGG WHITES

EQUIPMENT

SIX 4- OR 5-OUNCE SOUFFLÉ OR
  CUSTARD CUPS

BAKING DISH LARGE ENOUGH TO HOLD
  THE CUPS

NUTRITION INFORMATION

CALORIES PER SERVING: 242

FAT: 2.9 G

% CALORIES FROM FAT: 11%

PROTEIN: 7.7 G

CARBOHYDRATES: 46.7 G

CHOLESTEROL: 75.5 MG

Serves 6.

1. Soak prunes in liquor to cover for 30 minutes, or until needed. Cut strips of zest from a quarter of the lemon.

2. Combine the milk, vanilla bean, cinnamon stick, and lemon zest in a medium saucepan. Bring to a simmer, lower the heat, and keep just below the simmer for about 15 minutes.

3. Preheat the oven to 350°F.

4. Using ½ cup of the sugar and ¼ cup of water, make a caramel as described on page 158, using either the microwave or stovetop method.

5. Quickly pour an equal amount of caramel into each soufflé cup. Tilt to spread caramel all over the bottom. Drain the prunes, reserving the liquid for another use. Place a prune in the center of the caramel in each cup. Put the kettle on to boil.

6. Beat eggs and egg whites with the remaining ½ cup of sugar until well combined. Strain the milk and gradually whisk it into the eggs. Strain again to eliminate foam and pour into cups up to ¼ inch from the rim. Set cups in a baking dish and pour boiling water halfway up the sides of the cups.

7. Bake until a knife inserted into the center of each flan comes out clean, about 35 to 40 minutes. Remove flans from pan and cool on a rack to room temperature. Refrigerate for at least 6 hours or overnight before serving. *Flans may be refrigerated for up to 1 day.*

8. To serve: Run a knife around the edge of each flan to loosen it. Tilt back and forth until flan begins to slide, then invert onto a dessert plate. Use a small rubber spatula to scrape any caramel sauce left in the cup onto the flan. Serve immediately or chill until needed.

Notes

• If prunes are not very moist and soft, cut them each into 5 or 6 pieces. They will be easier to eat than whole prunes but not quite as beautiful to look at.

• Try this dessert with other dried fruits like apricots with rum, dried pears with pear eau de vie, dried peaches with brandy or marsala, dried cherries with kirsch.

• If you want to reduce fat and cholesterol a little more, trade one of the yolks for an additional egg white.

Mexican Rice Pudding

Rick Bayless, owner of Chicago's Frontera Grill and Topolobampo, is one of my favorite American chefs. This fragrant custardy rice pudding is adapted from his wonderful recipe—lightened just a little but still subtly addictive.

WORK AND COOK TIME: 45 MINUTES

INGREDIENTS

PIECE LIME ZEST, 1-3/4 INCH

1-INCH PIECE CINNAMON STICK

SCANT 1/8 TEASPOON SALT

1/2 CUP MEDIUM-GRAIN OR SHORT-
   GRAIN WHITE RICE

1 EGG

1/4 TEASPOON VANILLA EXTRACT

2 CUPS LOW-FAT (1%) MILK

6 TABLESPOONS SUGAR

1/4 CUP RAISINS

1 TABLESPOON MELTED BUTTER, FOR
   GLAZING (OPTIONAL)

EQUIPMENT

DECORATIVE 1-1/2-QUART SERVING
   BOWL OR SIX 5- TO 6-OUNCE
   RAMEKINS OR CUSTARD CUPS

NUTRITION INFORMATION

CALORIES PER SERVING: 172

FAT: 1.8 G

% CALORIES FROM FAT: 9%

PROTEIN: 5.2 G

CARBOHYDRATES: 34.3 G

CHOLESTEROL: 38.7 MG

Serves 6.

1. Combine 1 cup water, the lime zest, cinnamon stick, and salt in a 1½- to 2-quart nonreactive heavy saucepan. Simmer, covered, for about 5 minutes. Stir in the rice. Bring back to a simmer. Stir rice once. Cover tightly; if lid is loose, weight it to slow the escaping steam. Reduce heat to very low and cook without uncovering or stirring for 20 to 25 minutes, or until all the liquid is absorbed and rice is tender.

2. While rice is cooking, whisk the egg with vanilla in a medium bowl. Set aside.

3. Add the milk and sugar to the rice. Cook over medium heat, stirring constantly, until milk thickens to the consistency of light cream, about 10 to 12 minutes. (If you double the recipe, simmer the pudding for 15 to 20 minutes.) Fish out and discard cinnamon and lime zest. Ladle about 1 cup of the rice mixture into the beaten egg, whisking briskly to prevent scrambling. Off heat, return the egg and rice mixture to the saucepan and whisk well to combine. Stir in raisins. Turn the mixture into a serving dish or ramekins. Cool to room temperature or chill before serving. *Pudding may be refrigerated for up to 2 days.*

4. If desired, glaze before serving: Brush top of rice with melted butter and run under a hot broiler just until browned.

Coconut Rice Pudding

Coconut has a subtle presence in this delicate rice pudding. I banished egg yolks to allow for the fat and calories in coconut and came up with this snowy white pudding.

WORK AND COOK TIME: 45 MINUTES

Serves 6.

1. Bring 1¼ cups of water and the salt to a boil in a heavy 1½- to 2-quart saucepan. Stir in the rice and coconut. Bring back to a simmer. Stir rice. Cover tightly; if lid is loose, weight it to slow the escaping steam. Cook on very low heat without uncovering or stirring for 20 to 25 minutes, or until all the liquid is absorbed and rice is tender.

2. While rice is cooking, whisk the egg whites and vanilla in a medium bowl. Set aside.

3. Add milk and ½ cup sugar to the rice. Cook over medium heat, stirring constantly, until milk thickens to the consistency of light cream, about 10 to 12 minutes. (If you double the recipe, allow 15 to 20 minutes.) Ladle about 1 cup of the rice mixture into the egg whites, whisking briskly to prevent scrambling. Off heat, return the mixture to the saucepan and whisk well to combine. Turn into a serving bowl or individual ramekins. Cool to room temperature or chill before serving. *Pudding may be refrigerated for up to 2 days.*

4. Serve the pudding plain or, if desired, sprinkle the tops with 3 to 4 tablespoons sugar and caramelize under the broiler or with a propane torch as described on page 159.

VARIATION

....

Use 1 cup grated fresh coconut instead of dried coconut. Cook the rice without coconut in 1 cup of water in Step 1. Add the fresh coconut with the milk in Step 3.

INGREDIENTS

SCANT 1/4 TEASPOON SALT

1/2 CUP MEDIUM-GRAIN OR SHORT-GRAIN WHITE RICE

1/2 CUP UNSWEETENED SHREDDED DRIED COCONUT

2 EGG WHITES

1/2 TEASPOON VANILLA EXTRACT

2-1/4 CUPS LOW-FAT (1%) MILK

1/2 CUP SUGAR

3 TO 4 TABLESPOONS SUGAR FOR CARAMELIZING (OPTIONAL)

EQUIPMENT

DECORATIVE 1-1/2-QUART SERVING BOWL OR SIX 5- TO 6-OUNCE RAMEKINS OR CUSTARD CUPS

PROPANE TORCH (OPTIONAL)

NUTRITION INFORMATION

CALORIES PER SERVING: 208

FAT: 5.2 G

CALORIES FROM FAT: 22%

PROTEIN: 5.9 G

CARBOHYDRATES: 35.2 G

CHOLESTEROL: 3.7 MG

Frozen Hot Chocolate

This simple frosty chocolate spoon drink is served, thick and slushy, in an iced goblet, as was the original ultra-rich version at New York's Serendipity. Or you could refreeze it and scoop it like sherbet. It's refreshing either way.

Serves 6 to 7.

1. In a small saucepan, combine the cocoa and sugar. Stir in just enough of the milk to form a smooth paste. Stir in all but 2 tablespoons of the remaining milk. Stir over low heat until the mixture is warm and sugar is dissolved.

2. Pour into a shallow pan or ice-cube trays, cover well, and freeze for at least 6 hours or overnight. *Mixture can be frozen for 1 week or more.*

3. Break frozen mixture into chunks with a fork or table knife. Place chunks in a food processor bowl fitted with the steel blade. Process with the remaining 2 tablespoons milk until no lumps remain and mixture is thick and light in color. Serve at once in frosted goblets as a spoon drink or scrape into a bowl, cover, and refreeze for at least 8 hours or overnight. Scoop and serve frozen.

Note

Increase or decrease the richness of this concoction to your taste by replacing some or all of the low-fat milk with whole or nonfat milk.

WORK TIME: 15 MINUTES
FREEZE TIME: 6 PLUS 8 HOURS

INGREDIENTS

1/2 CUP UNSWEETENED DUTCH
    PROCESS COCOA
3/4 CUP SUGAR
2-3/4 CUPS LOW-FAT (1%) MILK
    (SEE NOTE)

NUTRITION INFORMATION

CALORIES PER SERVING: 144
FAT: 2.3 G
% CALORIES FROM FAT: 13%
PROTEIN: 4.6 G
CARBOHYDRATES: 29.6 G
CHOLESTEROL: 3.85 MG

VARIATIONS

....

Frozen Chocolate Malt: Add 2 tablespoons malt powder to cocoa mixture in Step 1.

Frozen Mocha or Chocolate Espresso Bean: Add 4 teaspoons instant espresso or coffee powder to cocoa mixture in Step 1. Or add 4 teaspoons freshly ground espresso beans to the frozen mixture in Step 3.

Frozen Orange or Lemon Chocolate : Add ½ teaspoon freshly grated orange or lemon zest in Step 1.

Frozen Chocolate Mint: Add a scant ¼ teaspoon mint extract in Step 1.

Caramel Oranges with Rum

This is the simplest of desserts—and the perfect one after a spicy Mexican or Indian meal. Years ago at an elegant opening
night gala we placed an enormous crystal bowl of these oranges at the end of a table laden
with the most indulgent Cocolat chocolate desserts imaginable. At the end of a perfect evening we filled each guest's
empty champagne coupe with this refreshing grande finale.

WORK AND COOK TIME: 30 MINUTES

INGREDIENTS

8 EATING ORANGES, PREFERABLY
    SEEDLESS NAVELS
1/4 CUP DARK RUM
1 CUP SUGAR

EQUIPMENT

IMPROVISED SUGAR SPINNING TOOLS
    (PAGE 159)

NUTRITION INFORMATION

CALORIES PER SERVING: 176
FAT: .1 G
% CALORIES FROM FAT: 1%
PROTEIN: 1.4 G
CARBOHYDRATES: 41 G
CHOLESTEROL: 0 MG

Serves 6 to 8.

1. Use a zester to remove long thin slivers of zest from 2 oranges. Or use a vegetable peeler to peel wide pieces of zest from 1 orange, then cut the pieces into very fine slivers. Set aside.

2. Use a very sharp knife to remove all the skin and white membrane from the oranges. Cut oranges crosswise into ¼-inch slices or cut between membranes into segments (or do some of each). Remove seeds as necessary. Arrange slices or segments in a shallow serving dish. Splash rum over the oranges and sprinkle with the zest. Set aside.

3. Using the sugar and ½ cup cold water, make caramel as described on page 158, using the saucepan method.

4. Immediately set the pan in an ice bath for about 30 seconds to stop the cooking. Pour all but about 3 tablespoons of syrup over the oranges. Set aside the pan with remaining caramel. *Oranges may be prepared to this point and kept, covered, in the refrigerator for up to 2 days.*

5. **To serve:** Melt the remaining caramel in a saucepan over gentle heat until it is thick and sticky. Make Spun Sugar as described on page 159. Cover oranges with spun sugar and serve immediately.

Note

This dessert turns out quite different depending on how long it is chilled. A short chilling leaves some of the hardened caramel undissolved and brittle. Lengthy chilling allows the oranges to become infused with the rich rum and caramel syrup. The dessert is delicious either way. For the best of both, chill for the longer time and garnish with additional shards of hard caramel (page 159) just before spinning the sugar.

Banana Sherbet

This is delicious frozen or slushy. The method is easy and you can use it for other fruits or fruit combinations.
Try mango, cherimoya, or pineapple, or any favorite fruit smoothy combination.

WORK TIME: 15 MINUTES
FREEZE TIME: AT LEAST 6–14 HOURS

INGREDIENTS

1 CUP MASHED BANANA (ABOUT 2 VERY
   RIPE MEDIUM BANANAS)
1 CUP LOW-FAT YOGURT
1/4 CUP LIGHT BROWN SUGAR
4 TEASPOONS SUGAR
2 TEASPOONS VANILLA EXTRACT
4 TEASPOONS RUM

NUTRITION INFORMATION

CALORIES PER SERVING: 132
FAT: .9 G
% CALORIES FROM FAT: 6%
PROTEIN: 2.8 G
CARBOHYDRATES: 27.6 G
CHOLESTEROL: 2.8 MG

Serves 4 to 5.

1. Combine ingredients in bowl of food processor fitted with the steel blade. Process until smooth. Pour into a shallow pan or ice-cube tray. Freeze for at least 6 hours or overnight. *Mixture can be frozen for 1 week or more.*

2. Break up frozen mixture and place in food processor bowl. Process with 2 tablespoons cold water until smooth. Serve immediately as a spoon drink in a frosted goblet or compote, or scrape into a bowl, cover, and refreeze for at least 8 hours or overnight. Scoop frozen sherbet to serve.

Scorpio Sagittarian Fruit Compote

Since 1977, on the first Sunday in December six of us celebrate our late fall birthdays with an intimate brunch in Katherine Esmay's San Francisco Victorian flat. We sip champagne and share the year's adventures with each other until early evening. Katherine pampers us with elegant comfort food including this sensational compote originally from Mary Risley of Tante Marie Cooking School.

1. Make the syrup. Use a vegetable peeler to remove the zest of 2 oranges, both lemons, and the lime. Cut the zest into very fine shreds. Combine zest with the sugar and 1¼ cups of water in a medium saucepan. Stir over low heat until sugar dissolves. Boil, without stirring, for 5 to 6 minutes until syrupy. Chill at least 1 hour. *Syrup may be refrigerated for 1 week or longer.*

2. Peel, seed, and cut fruit into bite-size pieces. Do this in such a way as to collect the juice and include it in the compote. Pile the fruit into a bowl with the peaches, bananas, and any other fruit that turns brown on top. Squeeze the juice of 1 lemon and 1 lime over the fruit, particularly the peaches and bananas. Cover and chill until serving. *Compote may be prepared to this point 3 to 4 hours ahead.*

3. Just before serving, pour the syrup over the fruit and mix gently.

Note

Mary got this recipe from a friend in Toronto many years ago. The main thing is to improvise; certainly it is never followed to the letter. The first six ingredients are de rigueur in my book to establish the basic citrus nature of the compote and I insist on some bananas. Think of this as a winter compote—don't worry if there isn't much in the way of berries or peaches to be had—just add more of other things. I am sure no one has ever made this compote with all the ingredients that are listed in it. Katherine always adds sliced kiwis. Mary says never use cooked fruit or apples, but Katherine always includes apples anyway and we always love it. I think you get the idea.

WORK TIME: 30 MINUTES
CHILL TIME: 60 MINUTES

INGREDIENTS

4 ORANGES
2 LEMONS
1 LIME
2 CUPS SUGAR
2 GRAPEFRUITS
6 PEACHES
3 BANANAS
6 OUNCES MIXED GRAPES
1 SMALL CANTALOUPE
4 PLUMS
SOME RASPBERRIES AND/OR
   BLUEBERRIES
4 SLICES FRESH PINEAPPLE
1-1/2 CUPS STRAWBERRIES
PITTED CHERRIES

NUTRITION INFORMATION

CALORIES PER SERVING: 167
FAT: .5 G
% CALORIES FROM FAT: 3%
PROTEIN: 1.3 G
CARBOHYDRATES: 42.7 G
CHOLESTEROL: 0 MG

Dressy Desserts

....

*Special occasions sometimes
demand a little fuss. Recipes in
this chapter require a
bit more time, attention to detail,
or skill than some others.
None is really very difficult, and
all are beautiful. For those of
us who love to make dessert, the
process is part of the reward—
not to mention the oohs
and aahs from the gallery. Thus
you'll enjoy, as I do, making
roses out of baked apples for
tartlets, caramelizing phyllo
leaves for napoleons, arranging
a bouquet of fruit for
Primavera, or even making four
different recipes for one Triple
Mousse Celebration Cake.*

Chocolate Grand Marnier Cake

Chocolate mousse between layers of orange-scented Genoise—very elegant. My brother Albert (sharp of palate and annoyingly honest) declared this excellent without knowing for sure if it was one of my "new" desserts.

WORK TIME: 1 HOUR 30 MINUTES
BAKE TIME: 20–25 MINUTES
CHILL TIME: AT LEAST 4 HOURS

INGREDIENTS

ONE GENOISE B, MADE WITH CAKE
    FLOUR (PAGE 152), BAKED AND
    COOLED
1/4 CUP GRAND MARNIER
4 CUPS BITTERSWEET CHOCOLATE
    TRUFFLE MOUSSE (PAGE 142)
2 TO 3 TEASPOONS UNSWEETENED
    DUTCH PROCESS COCOA
1 TO 2 TEASPOONS POWDERED SUGAR,
    FOR DECORATION (OPTIONAL)
FINE BITTERSWEET OR SEMISWEET
    CHOCOLATE SHAVINGS (PAGE 162),
    FOR DECORATION (OPTIONAL)

EQUIPMENT

8-INCH SPRINGFORM PAN OR CHEESE-
    CAKE PAN WITH REMOVABLE BOTTOM
DOILY OR HANDMADE STENCIL, FOR
    DECORATION (OPTIONAL)

NUTRITION INFORMATION

CALORIES PER SERVING: 236
FAT: 8.2 G
% CALORIES FROM FAT: 30%
PROTEIN: 5.75 G
CARBOHYDRATES: 37.8 G
CHOLESTEROL: 85 MG

Serves 12.

1. With a long serrated knife, cut the Genoise horizontally into 3 layers. Place the top layer, upside down, in the bottom of springform pan. It will not fit tight; there will be a tiny bit of space between the pan and the layer. Brush layer liberally with Grand Marnier.

2. **Make the Bittersweet Chocolate Truffle Mousse.** As soon as the mousse is ready, pour about 1½ cups of it over the moistened Genoise layer. Tilt the pan to spread mousse and shake it back and forth and from side to side, jerking it gently, so that some of the mousse seeps into the space between the pan and the Genoise. Brush both sides of the middle layer lightly with Grand Marnier and place on top of mousse. Scrape all but 1 cup of remaining mousse on top. Tilt and shake pan as before. Brush both sides of third layer with Grand Marnier and place, bottom (brown side) facing up, on top of mousse. Top with remaining chocolate mousse. Tilt and shake pan as before. Cover pan and refrigerate for at least 4 hours, or until set. *Cake may be completed to this point and refrigerated for up to 1 day or it may be wrapped well in plastic wrap or foil or placed in an airtight container and frozen for up to 2 months.*

3. **To finish and serve:** Wrap a hot wet and wrung out towel around the pan to melt the mousse slightly. Remove the sides of the pan. Use a fine strainer to sieve cocoa evenly over top of cake. Center the doily or stencil over cocoa, sieve powdered sugar over it, and remove it carefully. If you have done a good job shaking the mousse in Step 2, the sides of the dessert will be covered with mousse, with no bare cake showing. No additional decoration is really necessary. I like to finish only the very bottom edge of the cake with a few very fine Chocolate Shavings. Use a metal spatula to pick up and apply shavings. If the sides of the dessert are not perfect, cover them completely with shavings, always using the spatula to lift and apply the delicate shavings. Refrigerate until ready to serve.

VARIATIONS

....

Substitute other mousses and liqueurs for the Bittersweet Chocolate Truffle Mousse and Grand Marnier to create a host of new desserts.

Rum and Lemon Mousse Cake: 4 cups Lemon Mousse (page 145) and rum.

Mocha Mousse Cake: 4 cups Mocha Mousse (page 143) and Kahlúa, brandy, or a nut liqueur.

Lemon Mousse Cake

A lemon mousse always seems light but it's usually rich with egg yolks and cream. This cake is a combination of light layers with rum and a lemon mousse that has about half the fat of my old standard. I don't think I'll ever look back!

Serves 10 to 12.

1. Turn the Ladyfinger Layers upside down and peel parchment from them. If layers have spread during baking, trim them about ½ inch smaller than the 9-inch pan all around.

2. Brush the tops of the layers liberally with most of the rum. Place 1 layer, moist side up, in the bottom of the pan. Moisten the bottom of the second layer with rum and set it aside.

3. **Make the Lemon Mousse.** Check that the layer is centered in the pan. Scrape almost half the mousse into the pan on top of the sponge layer. Spread the mousse to fill in between the pan and the layer all around. Center the second layer on top and press gently. Scrape the remaining mousse into the pan and spread to fill in the edges. Level the top of the mousse as perfectly as you can. I do this on a cake decorating turntable with a triangular cake comb with a serrated edge, turning the cake and holding the edge of the comb against the top of the mousse until it is as perfect as I can make it. You may improvise by folding a clean 3 x 5-inch index card lengthwise (to stiffen it). Hold the folded edge against the mousse as you rotate the cake. Use a rubber spatula or the tip of a knife wrapped with a moist paper towel to wipe clean the inside of the pan above the top of the mousse to prevent a ragged edge. Cover the pan with plastic wrap and refrigerate for at least 4 hours, or until set.

4. **Make the topping.** In a small cup, sprinkle the gelatin over cold water. Allow gelatin to soften for at least 1 minute without stirring. When softened, set cup in a pan of barely simmering water or microwave on High for 15 seconds to melt gelatin completely. Combine melted gelatin with orange juice, lemon juice, and sugar. Stir to dissolve sugar. Set aside until thickened to a slightly syrupy consistency, or until needed.

5. When mousse is set, check consistency of topping. If it has thickened beyond a syrupy consistency, set it in a pan of hot water or microwave for a few

WORK TIME: 1 HOUR 15 MINUTES
BAKE TIME: 8–10 MINUTES
CHILL TIME: AT LEAST 4 HOURS 30 MINUTES

INGREDIENTS

TWO 8-INCH LADYFINGER LAYERS B
  (PAGE 150), BAKED AND COOLED
3 TABLESPOONS DARK RUM
6 CUPS LEMON MOUSSE (PAGE 145)
1-1/4 TEASPOONS GELATIN
2 TABLESPOONS COLD WATER
1/2 CUP STRAINED ORANGE JUICE
2-1/2 TABLESPOONS STRAINED
  LEMON JUICE
1 TABLESPOON SUGAR

EQUIPMENT

9-INCH SPRINGFORM PAN

NUTRITION INFORMATION

CALORIES PER SERVING: 154
FAT: 4.2 G
% CALORIES FROM FAT: 25%
PROTEIN: 3.82 G
CARBOHYDRATES: 24.2 G
CHOLESTEROL: 79.6 MG

seconds on Low. Pour just enough on top of the mousse to form a thin glossy coating and tilt the pan in every direction to spread evenly. Chill for at least 30 minutes to set. *Dessert may be completed to this point and refrigerated for up to 1 day.*

6. To serve: Warm the sides of the pan for 20 to 30 seconds with a hot wet and wrung out towel. Release and remove pan sides carefully.

Note

Decorate top, if desired, or with a sprinkling of minced blanched pistachios (page 165), a few ultra-thin shards of white chocolate (pages 162), chocolate curls (page 163), slices of fresh lemon or candied lemon peel, or fresh berries.

VARIATIONS
....

This dessert may be made with 6 cups (1½ times the recipe) of Bittersweet Chocolate Truffle Mousse (page 142) or Mocha Mousse (page 143) or 6 cups of any other mousse.

Chocolate Haystack

It looks like a delectable haystack of chocolate twigs. The pencil-thin meringue shapes are called doigts de fée, *which is French for fairy fingers. They add crunch—and humor—to this layered chocolate mousse dessert.*

Serves 12 to 14.

1. Position the racks in upper and lower third of the oven and preheat to 200°F. Line 2 baking sheets with parchment paper. On one of the parchment liners, trace two 8-inch circles or 9 x 6-inch ovals with a heavy pen or pencil. Turn the parchment liners over; you should still be able to see the tracing through the paper.

2. In a food processor, combine ¼ cup of the sugar, the almonds, cocoa, and cornstarch. Process until mixture resembles a fine meal. Set aside.

3. Combine the egg whites, cream of tartar, vanilla, and almond extract in a medium mixing bowl. Beat at medium speed until soft peaks form. Gradually sprinkle in remaining ½ cup sugar, beating on high speed until very stiff but not dry.

4. Fold the nut mixture into the egg whites with a large rubber spatula. Scrape a little less than half of the meringue mixture into the pastry bag. Pipe long straight lengths of meringue from edge to edge across the length or width of the unmarked parchment paper. Leave about ⅜ inch between each rope. Use up all of the meringue in the bag. Divide remaining mixture equally between the 2 traced circles or ovals. Spread evenly within the lines.

5. Bake layers and long shapes for 1 hour. Turn oven off and allow layers to cool in the oven for at least 1 hour. Cool completely before using or storing. Wrap airtight until needed. *Nut meringue may be completed to this point and stored, airtight, for several weeks at room temperature.*

6. **Assemble the cake.** About 2 to 4 hours before serving, place 1 meringue layer on a serving plate. Cover the layer with a little less than half the mousse by gently spooning dollops of it over the layer. Try not to spread and smooth the mousse more than necessary. Place the second layer on top and press gently to level and compact the dessert slightly and push the mousse out to the edges of the

WORK TIME: 1 HOUR 30 MINUTES
CHILL TIME: AT LEAST 6 HOURS
BAKE AND COOL TIME: 2 HOURS

INGREDIENTS

3/4 CUP SUGAR, PREFERABLY FINE
   GRANULATED OR SUPERFINE

1/2 CUP PLUS 2 TABLESPOONS
   ALMONDS (3 OUNCES)

3 TABLESPOONS UNSWEETENED DUTCH
   PROCESS COCOA

4 TEASPOONS CORNSTARCH

1/2 CUP EGG WHITES, AT ROOM
   TEMPERATURE (3 TO 4)

1/4 TEASPOON CREAM OF TARTAR

1 TEASPOON VANILLA EXTRACT

1/8 TEASPOON ALMOND EXTRACT

4 CUPS BITTERSWEET CHOCOLATE
   TRUFFLE MOUSSE (PAGE 142) OR
   MOCHA MOUSSE (PAGE 143),
   CHILLED FOR AT LEAST 3 HOURS

1 TO 2 TEASPOONS COCOA, FOR
   DUSTING

1 TO 2 TEASPOONS POWDERED SUGAR,
   FOR DUSTING (OPTIONAL)

EQUIPMENT

2 HEAVY BAKING SHEETS

PASTRY BAG FITTED WITH A 5/16-INCH
   PLAIN TIP (ATECO #3)

layers. Cover the second meringue layer with the remaining mousse, as evenly as you can. Spread mousse over edges of meringue layer to cover. Break long meringue shapes into random lengths ½ to 2 inches long and arrange them everywhere over top and sides of dessert. *The torte may be refrigerated, covered, from 2 to 4 hours before serving.* (After about 4 hours the meringue layers soften and meld with the mousse—the torte is still delicious but without crunch.) The torte may also be served frozen. *Freeze overnight or for up to 2 months.*

7. To serve: Use a very fine strainer to sieve a little cocoa over the fairy fingers. Follow this with a light dusting of powdered sugar, if desired.

VARIATIONS

• Substitute walnuts, pecans, or toasted blanched hazelnuts (page 165) for almonds.

• Pipe heart-shape or square layers, or any shape to suit the occasion or to fit a favorite serving dish.

Mocha Hazelnut Mousse Torte

This is dressy. Serve this for a special dinner, and it will become an instant classic.

Serves 12 to 14.

1. Position the racks in the lower and upper third of the oven and preheat to 300°F. Line the baking sheets with parchment paper. Trace parchment with three 8-inch circles in heavy pencil or ink. Turn parchment upside down; you should be able to see the tracing through the paper.

2. Combine the sugar, hazelnuts, cocoa, espresso powder, and brandy in a food processor. Process until fine. With the motor running, slowly add just enough egg white (usually about 3 tablespoons) to form a thick sticky mixture the consistency of fudge frosting.

3. Divide the batter into 3 equal parts. With a metal icing spatula, spread very thin even layers within the traced circles. Neaten the edges with your finger if necessary. Bake for 15 to 20 minutes, or until the layers puff and crackle slightly and the tops look dry from edges to center. Rotate pans from top to bottom and front to back halfway through the baking time. Remove from the oven and cool completely before attempting to remove the parchment.

4. When completely cool, turn parchment upside down with layers still attached. Peel parchment carefully away. If bottoms are sticky, refrigerate the layers briefly and/or tear the parchment and peel it away in strips. Trim layers, if necessary, so that they fit easily inside the pan with $\frac{1}{16}$ to $\frac{1}{8}$ inch to spare all the way around. Place 1 layer in the bottom of pan. Set aside.

5. **Make the Mocha Mousse.** Pour half of the mousse over the layer in the pan. Tilt the pan to spread mousse and shake it back and forth and from side to side gently so that the mousse flows into the space between the layer and the pan. Place a second layer on top and cover with the remaining mousse. Tilt and shake the pan as before. Top with the third layer, right side up. Cover pan and refrigerate for at

WORK TIME: 1 HOUR 30 MINUTES
BAKE TIME: 15–20 MINUTES
CHILL TIME: AT LEAST 4 HOURS

INGREDIENTS

3/4 CUP SUGAR

1/2 CUP PLUS 2 TABLESPOONS CHOPPED BLANCHED AND TOASTED HAZELNUTS (PAGE 165) (2-1/4 OUNCES)

3 TABLESPOONS UNSWEETENED DUTCH PROCESS COCOA

1 TEASPOON INSTANT ESPRESSO OR COFFEE POWDER

2 TEASPOONS BRANDY

2 EGG WHITES

4 CUPS MOCHA MOUSSE (PAGE 143)

2 TEASPOONS POWDERED SUGAR OR COCOA, FOR DUSTING

LESS THAN 1/4 OUNCE FINE CHOCOLATE SHAVINGS (PAGE 162), FOR DECORATION

EQUIPMENT

1 OR 2 HEAVY BAKING SHEETS

8-INCH SPRINGFORM PAN OR CHEESE-CAKE PAN WITH REMOVABLE BOTTOM

NUTRITION INFORMATION

CALORIES PER SERVING: 187

FAT: 7.3 G

% CALORIES FROM FAT: 33%

PROTEIN: 4.7 G

CARBOHYDRATES: 28.5 G

CHOLESTEROL: 5.3 MG

least 4 hours, or until set. *Dessert may be completed to this point and refrigerated for up to 1 day before serving, or it may be tightly wrapped in plastic or foil or placed in an airtight container and frozen for up to 2 months. Torte may be served frozen.*

6. To serve: Wrap a hot wet and wrung out towel around the pan to melt the mousse slightly. Remove the sides of the pan. Set a decorative stencil or shapes cut out of paper on top and use a very fine strainer to sieve lightly with powdered sugar or cocoa. Remove stencil or shapes carefully. Use a metal spatula to pick up and press Chocolate Shavings only around the bottom edge of the torte. Refrigerate until ready to serve.

VARIATIONS

....

Brownie Mousse Torte: Use walnuts or pecans instead of hazelnuts for the layers and substitute Bittersweet Chocolate Truffle Mousse (page 142) for Mocha Mousse.

Chocolate Almond Mousse Torte: Substitute blanched almonds for the hazelnuts and Amaretto for the brandy or add a scant ⅛ teaspoon almond extract with the brandy. Stay with the Mocha Mousse or substitute Bittersweet Chocolate Truffle Mousse (page 142).

Frozen Chocolate Praline Torte

Here's a do-ahead fancy frozen party dessert with wonderful contrasting textures—crisp meringue, creamy cold frozen yogurt, and crunchy rich-flavored caramelized nuts. Change the yogurt flavor and type of nuts to create your own versions.

Serves 14 to 16. Make at least 1 day ahead.

1. Position rack in lower third of the oven and preheat to 225°F. Line baking sheet with parchment paper. Trace the parchment with two 8-inch circles. Turn it upside down so that the tracing can still be seen but pencil or ink will not transfer onto meringue.

2. Combine egg whites and cream of tartar in a mixer bowl. Beat at medium speed until soft peaks form. Gradually sprinkle in ¾ cup of the sugar, beating at high speed until meringue is very stiff. Scrape meringue into pastry bag. Starting from the center of each traced circle, pipe a spiral of meringue to fill the circle. Or spread meringue evenly over the circle with a metal spatula.

3. Bake for 1 to 2 hours, or until meringue layers are perfectly light, dry, and crisp. If possible, allow meringue to cool in the turned-off oven with the door closed. If meringues are not light, perfectly dry, and crisp, lower the heat to 200°F. and bake until they are. *Meringue layers should be made at least 1 day before assembling the torte. They may be made, cooled completely, and stored airtight at room temperature for up to 2 months.*

4. Have ready a baking sheet lined with foil or parchment paper for the walnut praline.

5. **Make the walnut praline.** Stir the remaining ½ cup of the sugar and ¼ cup water together in a medium saucepan, off the heat, until the sugar is completely moistened. Cover and bring to a simmer over medium heat. Simmer, covered, for 2 to 3 minutes. Uncover and wash down the sides of the pan with a wet pastry brush. Continue to cook, without stirring, until syrup is light amber. To check, spoon a drop or two of syrup onto a white plate from time to time until the color looks right. Add the nuts and stir gently with a wooden spoon to coat. Turn the nuts in

WORK TIME: 50 MINUTES
BAKE TIME: 1–2 HOURS
FREEZE TIME: AT LEAST 24 HOURS

INGREDIENTS

3 LARGE EGG WHITES, AT ROOM
   TEMPERATURE

1/8 TEASPOON CREAM OF TARTAR

1-1/4 CUPS SUGAR, PREFERABLY
   FINE GRANULATED OR SUPERFINE

3/4 CUP CHOPPED WALNUTS
   (3 OUNCES)

2 QUARTS CHOCOLATE FROZEN YOGURT
   (1 HALF GALLON)

EQUIPMENT

1 HEAVY BAKING SHEET

PASTRY BAG FITTED WITH A 1/2- OR
   9/16-INCH PLAIN TIP
   (ATECO #6 OR #7) (OPTIONAL)

9-INCH SPRINGFORM PAN OR CHEESE-
   CAKE PAN WITH REMOVABLE BOTTOM

NUTRITION INFORMATION

CALORIES PER SERVING: 209

FAT: 5.22 G

% CALORIES FROM FAT: 23%

PROTEIN: 4.86 G

CARBOHYDRATES: 33.5 G

CHOLESTEROL: 7 MG

the pan until the syrup is a medium-dark amber color. Remove from heat. Immediately scrape nut mixture onto the lined baking sheet and spread out. Or make praline in the microwave as described on page 80, using a 2-cup glass measure. Microwave on High for 7 to 8 minutes before adding the nuts, then for 30 to 60 seconds, or until the syrup is medium dark.

6. Let praline stand until completely cool and brittle. Break into pieces and coarsely chop. *Store airtight in the refrigerator for up to 2 months or freeze for up to 6 months.*

7. **Assemble the torte.** Lightly grease the inside of the springform and line with foil or plastic wrap. If frozen yogurt is rock hard, soften slightly in the refrigerator until it is easier to scoop but still very firm. (If in doubt, don't soften; frozen yogurt melts quickly.) Scoop nearly half of the yogurt into the pan and smooth it as flat as possible. Work quickly to prevent a meltdown. Sprinkle a third of the crushed praline over the yogurt. Press praline into yogurt with the back of the spoon.

8. Place a meringue layer carefully on the yogurt and gently nestle it into place. Cover the layer with flat scoops of all the remaining yogurt and half the remaining praline. Try to fill in the space between the meringue and the pan with yogurt so meringue will not show when dessert is unmolded. Smooth and press the surface gently and top with the second meringue layer. Reserve remaining praline. Cover torte with plastic wrap and freeze at least overnight. *Torte may be completed to this point several days in advance.*

9. **To serve:** Remove pan from freezer. Invert onto serving platter and remove sides and bottom of pan. Peel away foil or plastic liner. Texture sides, if desired, with a cake comb or serrated knife. Sprinkle top with the remaining praline. Serve immediately.

Bittersweet Chocolate Marquise with Praline Crème Anglaise

One of my favorite traditional desserts is the ultra-rich bittersweet chocolate mousse called Marquise au Chocolat. None of the lighter recipes I devised seemed rich enough to deserve the name—until I froze my best try. This will soon enter your repertoire too.

WORK TIME: 1 HOUR 20 MINUTES
FREEZE TIME: AT LEAST 12 HOURS

INGREDIENTS

4 CUPS BITTERSWEET CHOCOLATE
   TRUFFLE MOUSSE (PAGE 142)
5 TABLESPOONS SUGAR
3 TABLESPOONS CHOPPED WALNUTS,
   TOASTED BLANCHED HAZELNUTS
   (PAGE 165), OR TOASTED ALMONDS
   (3/4 OUNCE)
1 CUP LOW-FAT (1%) MILK
1 EGG
1/2 TEASPOON VANILLA EXTRACT
1 TEASPOON UNSWEETENED DUTCH
   PROCESS COCOA

EQUIPMENT

4- TO 5-CUP LOAF PAN
LARGE BAKING SHEET

NUTRITION INFORMATION

CALORIES PER SERVING: 219
FAT: 8.3 G
% CALORIES FROM FAT: 31%
PROTEIN: 5.9 G
CARBOHYDRATES: 34.8 G
CHOLESTEROL: 65.8 MG

Serves 10. Make 1 day ahead.

1. Oil the inside of the loaf pan with vegetable oil. Line the bottom and sides of the pan with a piece of plastic wrap large enough to hang over on all sides. Smooth the plastic lining as perfectly as possible, bunching or pleating primarily at the corners. Set aside.

2. **Make the Bittersweet Chocolate Truffle Mousse.** Scrape the mousse into the pan and smooth the top. Cover with the overhanging plastic wrap and freeze overnight. *Dessert may be prepared to this point and frozen for up to 2 months.*

3. **Make the praline for the crème anglaise.** Line a baking sheet with foil. Combine 3 tablespoons of the sugar with 1½ tablespoons water in a 1-cup microwavesafe glass measure. Cover tightly with plastic wrap. Microwave on High for 3½ to 4 minutes, or until mixture is pale amber. Reach into oven and puncture plastic wrap with a knife. Use a potholder to remove container. Use a fork to remove plastic wrap. Pour in the nuts and poke them down into the syrup with the tip of the knife (do not mix or stir). Cook, uncovered, on High for 20 to 30 seconds, or until syrup is medium dark. Use a potholder to remove container and immediately scrape mixture onto the lined baking sheet. Spread out with a metal spatula. Let stand until completely cool and brittle. Or make the praline in a saucepan as described on page 77.

4. Break the praline into pieces and pulverize in a food processor. Transfer to a tightly covered container. *Praline may be stored, airtight, in the refrigerator for up to 2 months or frozen for up to 6 months.*

5. **Make the crème anglaise.** Have a medium-fine strainer set over a medium bowl set in a larger bowl of ice water ready near the stove. In a nonreactive heavy saucepan, scald the milk. Meanwhile, in a small bowl, beat the egg and remaining 2 tablespoons sugar with a handheld mixer until pale and thick, 2 to 3 minutes. Gradually pour half the scalded milk over egg mixture, stirring constantly with a

wooden spoon or heatproof paddle. Scrape the mixture back into saucepan with remaining hot milk. Cook, stirring constantly, over medium heat without allowing the mixture to simmer. Reach all over the bottom of the pan to avoid burning. Remove from heat the moment the sauce coats a spoon lightly (175°–180°F.) and pour it immediately through the strainer. Stir in the vanilla and pulverized praline. Cool completely, stirring gently only once in a while. Refrigerate until needed. *Sauce may be refrigerated for up to 1 day.*

   6. To serve: Uncover the frozen mousse and invert onto a serving platter. Remove the pan and peel away plastic wrap. Sieve a little cocoa over the top. Slice about ½ to ¾ inch thick and serve frozen, with sauce.

Sorbet Basket

A crisp meringue basket turns ice creams and sorbets into a charming centerpiece. If you don't remember how good ice cream and meringue can be, remind yourself with this recipe.

Serves 10 to 12. Make at least 1 day ahead.

1. Make the basket templates. Cover each baking sheet with parchment paper. Use loaf pan to trace templates with a heavy pencil or marking pen, leaving space between each tracing. Trace the bottom of the pan for the base of the basket. Use the side and the end of the pan to trace 3 side panels and 3 end panels. (The third side and end are for practice piping, and to allow for breakage.) Turn parchment paper over; the tracing should be visible through the paper.

2. Position racks in the upper and lower third of the oven and preheat to 225°F.

3. Make the meringue. In a heatproof bowl, whisk the cream of tartar with the egg whites and ½ cup of the sugar. Set in a skillet of barely simmering water and stir briskly with a rubber spatula until very warm to the touch (110°-120°F.), about 45 seconds or longer. Transfer mixture to a large mixing bowl. Beat on high speed until stiff and glossy, about 2 minutes. Continue to beat, gradually sprinkling in the remaining sugar. Beat until stiff and cool. Transfer mixture to a pastry bag.

4. Meringue basket will be shaped like an upside-down loaf pan—wider at the bottom than the top—so the longest side of each tracing will always be the bottom edge of the basket. Pipe end and side panels first as follows: Start piping at the bottom (longer) edge of a tracing and pipe toward the opposite side. Pipe a short length of meringue, like a twig, pulling the meringue to a point. Start a second twig adjacent to and touching the first, also ending in a point. Twigs need not be perfectly parallel. Continue to fill in each end and side panel. Pipe a few twigs to make a second layer. Fill in the bottom panel by piping a single layer of meringue, in any pattern you like since it will not be seen. Sieve cocoa lightly over meringue panels, if desired.

5. Bake for 1½ to 2 hours, or until dry and crisp. Turn oven off and leave meringue inside to cool. Remove from oven. Carefully slide a very thin knife or metal spatula under each part to detach it from the parchment paper. *When*

WORK TIME: 1 HOUR 15 MINUTES
BAKE TIME: 1-1/2–2 HOURS
FREEZE TIME: AT LEAST 24 HOURS

INGREDIENTS

1/2 TEASPOON CREAM OF TARTAR

4 EGG WHITES

1 CUP SUGAR, PREFERABLY
    FINE GRANULATED OR SUPERFINE

2 TO 3 TEASPOONS UNSWEETENED
    DUTCH PROCESS COCOA (OPTIONAL)

4 PINTS ASSORTED SORBETS,
    SHERBETS, ICE CREAMS, AND/OR
    FROZEN YOGURT

MINT LEAVES OR NONTOXIC FRESH
    FLOWERS, FOR GARNISH (OPTIONAL)

EQUIPMENT

2 HEAVY BAKING SHEETS

5-CUP LOAF PAN

PASTRY BAG FITTED WITH A CLOSED
    STAR TIP (ATECO #3)

SMALL ROUND OR OVAL ICE CREAM OR
    SORBET SCOOP, 1-1/4 TO 1-1/2
    INCHES, OR A MELON BALLER

NUTRITION INFORMATION

CALORIES PER SERVING: 233

FAT: 2.43 G

% CALORIES FROM FAT: 10%

PROTEIN: 4.16 G

CARBOHYDRATES: 47.5 G

CHOLESTEROL: 9.37 MG

completely cool, basket parts may be stored in an airtight container for several weeks.

6. Mold the sorbets. At least 1 day before serving, place the loaf pan that was used for the templates in the freezer. Meanwhile, scoop 4 to 5 neat scoops, 1¼ to 1½ inches in diameter, of each flavor, for a total of 16 to 20 scoops. (If sorbet is too hard, refrigerate for 15 to 20 minutes until easier to scoop.) Place scoops in a shallow dish, cover, and freeze until needed. Line the loaf pan with plastic wrap so that wrap hangs over the sides of the pan. Scoop and press remaining sorbets firmly into pan in alternating layers. Fill the pan to about ⅜ inch from the top. Cover with overhanging wrap and freeze. Freeze any leftovers. *Sorbets may be prepared to this point up to 1 week ahead.*

7. Assemble the basket. Uncover the top of the molded ice cream. Use a serrated knife to trim the meringue base so that it fits inside the edges of the loaf pan, flush against the top of the ice cream. Invert the pan on a dish that fits into the freezer. The meringue base will be on the bottom. Slip off the loaf pan and remove the plastic wrap. Attach the basket side panels by gently sliding them against the ice cream. Attach the long panels first, then the end panels. If end panels need to be trimmed to fit, lay them on the counter and trim with a serrated knife, using a gentle sawing motion. Arrange the frozen scoops inside the top of the basket. Gently wrap the whole dessert in plastic wrap or slip it into a large plastic bag. Freeze until ready to serve.

8. To serve: Garnish with mint leaves or flowers, if desired. Slice the basket and its contents with a large sharp knife.

Notes

• About flavors: I like to intersperse sorbets with vanilla frozen yogurt, which provides a rich-tasting creaminess. I often use a very old-hat combo like strawberry or raspberry sorbet with vanilla and chocolate frozen yogurt. You may want to try tropical fruit combinations or go frozen yogurt all the way. Don't forget to choose pleasing color combinations. You might also like to drizzle chocolate sauce and/or sprinkle broken meringues or a few chopped nuts between the layers.

• Individual baskets? These fall into the extra-fuss-but-incredibly-cute department. Mold the sorbet in a square baking dish lined with plastic wrap. Cut into squares after frozen. Make dozens of little square meringue pieces and ease them against the sides of the sorbet squares. Top with a few little scoops.

Mocha Raspberry Charlotte

Everyone loves chocolate with raspberries and since I love ladyfingers, I put them all into a charlotte.

Use this recipe as a guide to making charlottes with other fruits and other mousses.

Serves 12.

1. Use a pastry brush to moisten the ladyfingers with the brandy. To do so, turn the pan on its side (ladyfingers should fit tightly enough to keep them from falling) and roll it slowly along the counter as you brush the interior. Moisten the top of 1 ladyfinger layer and fit it into the bottom of the pan, moist side up, trimming, if necessary. Trim the second layer to fit, remove it, and moisten both sides. Set aside until needed.

2. **Make the Mocha Mousse.** Scatter about a third of the berries into the mold. Immediately pour half the mousse over the berries. Top with the second ladyfinger layer. Scrape in remaining mousse. Cover charlotte with plastic wrap and refrigerate for at least 4 hours, or until set. Heap the remaining berries on top of the mousse. *Dessert may be completed to this point, covered, and refrigerated for up to 1 day.*

3. **To serve:** Remove the sides of the pan and transfer the charlotte to a serving platter. Sieve a little powdered sugar over berries before serving, if desired.

WORK TIME: 1 HOUR 15 MINUTES
BAKE TIME: 20–25 MINUTES
CHILL TIME: AT LEAST 4 HOURS

INGREDIENTS

LADYFINGER CHARLOTTE LINER (PAGE 150), BAKED AND COOLED

4 TO 5 TABLESPOONS BRANDY

4 CUPS MOCHA MOUSSE (PAGE 143)

2-1/2 TO 3 CUPS RASPBERRIES, RINSED AND WELL DRIED

1 TO 2 TEASPOONS POWDERED SUGAR, FOR DUSTING (OPTIONAL)

NUTRITION INFORMATION

CALORIES PER SERVING: 233

FAT: 6.16 G

% CALORIES FROM FAT: 23%

PROTEIN: 6.5 G

CARBOHYDRATES: 38.8 G

CHOLESTEROL: 59.2 MG

White Chocolate Charlotte with Strawberries

Tangy fruit may be the best partner of all for white chocolate. Let strawberries step aside for whatever is sensational in the market: sliced peaches or nectarines, raspberries or blackberries, or a combination.

Serves 10 to 12.

1. Rinse and hull the strawberries and spread out to dry on a clean dishtowel until needed.

2. Use a pastry brush to moisten the ladyfingers with the rum. Turn the pan on its side (ladyfingers should fit tightly enough to keep them from falling) and roll it along the counter as you brush the interior. Set the better looking layer aside. Moisten the top of the other layer and fit it into the bottom of the pan, moist side up, trimming if necessary. Reserve remaining liquor.

3. Place largest berries with pointed ends facing up in the bottom of the lined pan. Fit them as close together as possible. Reserve remaining berries.

4. **Make the White Chocolate Mousse.** Pour it over the berries. If the mousse does not fill the mold nearly to the top (leaving just enough room to fit in the second ladyfinger layer) fill in the mold with additional berries as follows: Cut large berries into quarters, turn pieces upside down, and push them into the mousse wherever you can between the first layer of berries; turn small berries upside down and push them into the mousse whole. When mold is nearly filled, moisten the back of the reserved ladyfinger layer and place it on top of the mousse, moistened side down, trimming to fit snugly, if necessary. Cover or place in a closed container and refrigerate for at least 5 hours. *Dessert may be kept covered and refrigerated for up to 1 day.*

5. **To serve:** Remove sides of pan and transfer dessert to a serving dish. Place an extra berry or two on top if desired. Sieve a little powdered sugar over the top.

WORK TIME: 1 HOUR 15 MINUTES
BAKE TIME: 20–25 MINUTES
CHILL TIME: AT LEAST 5 HOURS

INGREDIENTS

24 LARGE RIPE STRAWBERRIES OR
    2 PINTS SMALL BERRIES
LADYFINGER CHARLOTTE LINER (PAGE
    150), BAKED AND COOLED
4 TO 5 TABLESPOONS RUM
4-1/2 CUPS (1-1/2 RECIPES) WHITE
    CHOCOLATE MOUSSE (PAGE 144)
1 TABLESPOON POWDERED SUGAR

NUTRITION INFORMATION

CALORIES PER SERVING: 265
FAT: 9 G
% CALORIES FROM FAT: 31%
PROTEIN: 6 G
CARBOHYDRATES: 38.8 G
CHOLESTEROL: 75.8 MG

Primavera

Custard with rum-soaked sponge cake always tastes rich and somehow Italian to me, hence the choice of name.
Regardless of the springtime reference, I make this dessert clear through
autumn by switching to figs and seedless grapes. Make a seasonal bouquet of fruit—whatever
is best at the market—and have fun with the arrangement.

WORK TIME: 1 HOUR 10 MINUTES
BAKE TIME: 20–25 MINUTES

INGREDIENTS

GENOISE A, MADE WITH CAKE FLOUR
   (PAGE 152), BAKED AND COOLED
5 TO 6 TABLESPOONS DARK RUM
1-1/3 CUPS VANILLA PASTRY CREAM
   (PAGE 140)
2 TO 3 CUPS BERRIES OR FRESHLY
   SLICED SOFT FRUIT, SUCH AS KIWI,
   PEACH, PINEAPPLE, MANGO, ETC.
1/3 CUP STRAINED APRICOT JAM

EQUIPMENT

9-INCH CARDBOARD CAKE CIRCLE
   (OPTIONAL)

NUTRITION INFORMATION

CALORIES PER SERVING: 170
FAT: 4 G
% CALORIES FROM FAT: 22%
PROTEIN: 3.9 G
CARBOHYDRATES: 27 G
CHOLESTEROL: 84.8 MG

Serves 10 to 12.

1. Set the Genoise, right side up, on the counter in front of you. Using a 7-inch pot lid or plate as a guide, cut a smaller cake from the center of the Genoise. Carefully remove the outside ring of cake without breaking it. Set it on the cake circle or a serving platter.

2. Cut the small cake horizontally into 3 layers. Discard 1 layer or save it for another use. Place 1 layer back inside the ring of cake. Use a pastry brush to moisten the inner sides of the cake ring and the top of the cake layer liberally with the rum. Reserve ⅓ cup of the pastry cream. Scrape the remaining pastry cream inside the cake ring. Spread evenly over the bottom and thinly up the inner sides of the ring. Moisten the second cake layer with rum and fit it, moist side down, inside the cake ring over the pastry cream. Press with your fingers to make it level. Be sure the cake is still round; push it back into shape if necessary. Moisten top and sides of cake with rum. Spread reserved pastry cream evenly over top cake layer just up to the seam of the ring; do not spread on the ring. *Cake may be completed to this point, covered with plastic wrap, and refrigerated for up to 1 day.*

3. Arrange fruit abundantly on top of the cake, covering the pastry cream and the seam where the ring was cut. Leave a margin of about ½ inch of cake showing around the top edge to frame the arrangement. Simmer the apricot jam to make a glaze. Lightly brush hot glaze on fruit and exposed cake, including the sides. (Cover and refrigerate any leftover glaze for another use.) Refrigerate until ready to serve.

Summer Berry Tart

I like to say that I am a purist about fresh fruit tarts. Friends, including close members of my old staff at Cocolat, might say "fanatic" or "maniac." Here it is, the gospel according to Alice: A tart is not an American cream pie with a little fruit on top. A tart in the finest French tradition is about balance and restraint. It is a celebration of superb fruit and beautifully made pastry. I am very proud of my New Tart Crust, but you can also use phyllo for this tart and the tartlets that follow. Use a Phyllo Tart Shell (page 155) or Phyllo Tartlet Shells (page 155), baked and cooled. Take into account that the phyllo shells are somewhat deeper than the New Tart Crust, so you may want to increase the amount of filling and fruit.

WORK TIME: 45 MINUTES
BAKE TIME: 40–50 MINUTES

INGREDIENTS

1/3 CUP RED CURRANT JELLY

1 TABLESPOON SUGAR

9-1/2-INCH NEW TART CRUST (PAGE 153), BAKED AND COOLED

2 CUPS BERRIES, SUCH AS RASPBERRIES AND BLUEBERRIES, OR 4 TO 5 KIWIS, SLICED THIN

2/3 CUP VANILLA PASTRY CREAM (PAGE 140)

EQUIPMENT

9-1/2-INCH FLUTED TART PAN WITH REMOVABLE BOTTOM

NUTRITION INFORMATION

CALORIES PER SERVING: 142

FAT: 3.38 G

% CALORIES FROM FAT: 21%

PROTEIN: 3 G

CARBOHYDRATES: 25.6 G

CHOLESTEROL: 53.63 MG

Serves 6 to 8. Best served within 3 hours of assembling.

1. About 2 to 2½ hours before serving, assemble the tart. Simmer the jelly and sugar in a very small saucepan until slightly thickened and reduced, just a few minutes. Paint the entire top surface of the crust with a thin layer of glaze. Let it dry for a few minutes.

2. Arrange a neat single ring of berries ¼ inch in from the edge of crust. Spread the pastry cream evenly inside the ring of berries. Arrange or scatter berries over the pastry cream to cover. If you are scattering them, reserve a handful to arrange afterwards to fill in holes and otherwise create a beautiful tart. Reheat the remaining glaze. Use a pastry brush to dab glaze lightly on berries. (It is not necessary to use all the glaze; excess may be refrigerated indefinitely.) Let stand for about 2 hours before serving.

Notes

• See page 92 for other tart combinations

• Fresh fruit tarts should be eaten within a short time after they are assembled. Traditional tarts with a rich butter crust and those with a phyllo crust tarts may even be eaten immediately after they are assembled, but a tart with my light New Tart Crust is better about 2 hours later, to allow the pastry cream to moisten the crust ever so slightly.

• Fruit must be impeccably fresh and very flavorful, and it should be handled gently to avoid bruising. A tart should never be assembled with fruit still wet from rinsing. Avoid rinsing fragile bush berries at all, if possible; otherwise lay them out flat on a towel to dry. I use a fan or a hairdryer on cool to hasten drying.

• Glaze must be applied with a light hand or not at all. You should not find it necessary to use all of the glaze in the recipe.

• Custard (pastry cream) should be used with restraint. I glower at those who sigh with delight after tasting one of my tarts and then say, "Couldn't there be just a little more custard?" "A thousand times no!" say I. But just to be a little flexible, my pastry cream recipes make enough for two tarts "à la Alice" or only one tart if you absolutely must do it your way.

Fruit Tartlets

These are as stunning as jewels. Crusts can be made well in advance and the filling can be made a
day ahead as well. You need fuss only on serving day. Note that tartlets made with Chocolate or Cocoa Pastry Cream or Lemon
Curd are somewhat richer than those made with Vanilla Pastry Cream.

WORK TIME: 1 HOUR 15 MINUTES
BAKE TIME: 35—37 MINUTES

INGREDIENTS

1/3 CUP RED CURRANT JELLY OR
    STRAINED APRICOT JAM

1 TABLESPOON SUGAR

8 NEW TARTLET CRUSTS (PAGE 153),
    BAKED AND COOLED

1/2 CUP OR MORE VANILLA, CHOCOLATE,
    OR COCOA PASTRY CREAM (PAGES
    140—141) OR LEMON CURD
    (PAGE 141)

3 CUPS BERRIES OR FRESH OR
    POACHED FRUIT

2 TO 3 TABLESPOONS POWDERED
    SUGAR, FOR GARNISH (OPTIONAL)

CARAMEL SHARDS OR ROUNDS (PAGE
    158) OR SPUN SUGAR (PAGE 159),
    FOR GARNISH (OPTIONAL)

FINE CHOCOLATE SHAVINGS (PAGE
    162), FOR GARNISHING TART EDGES
    (OPTIONAL)

EQUIPMENT

EIGHT 3-1/2-INCH FLUTED TARTLET
    PANS

Serves 8. Best served within 3 hours.

1. Simmer the jelly and sugar in a very small saucepan until slightly thickened and reduced, just a few minutes. Use hot, reheating as necessary. Brush the tops of the crusts with glaze and let it dry.

2. Spread crust with 1 tablespoon (or more) filling to within about ¼ inch of the edges. If you are making berry tartlets, arrange a ring of berries around the edge first, then spread the filling inside the ring. Arrange fruit on top of filling. Berries or small fruit pieces may also be heaped by using a little extra pastry cream on top of first layer of fruit before piling on more.

3. Reheat the glaze and dab fruit lightly, if desired, or sieve a little powdered sugar on top. Or garnish with caramel or Spun Sugar. Chocolate tartlets look pretty with fine shavings on top or around the edges.

VARIATIONS
....

Lemon Berry Tart or Tartlets: Use red currant glaze and Lemon Curd (page 141) with blueberries and raspberries.

Banana Tart or Tartlets: Use apricot glaze and Chocolate or Vanilla Pastry Cream (pages 140-141) with ripe banana slices. Garnish with Caramel Shards or Rounds or Spun Sugar (pages 158-159) at the very last minute or—also last minute—a drizzle of hot caramel, followed by a few minutes in the refrigerator to harden it before serving.

Caramel Orange Tart or Tartlets: Use apricot glaze and Vanilla Pastry Cream (page 140) with drained slices of Caramel Oranges with Rum (page 62). Garnish with Caramel Shards or Rounds or Spun Sugar (pages 158–159) at the very last minute.

Chocolate Raspberry or Strawberry Tarts or Tartlets: Use red currant glaze and Chocolate Pastry Cream (page 141) with fresh raspberries or sliced strawberries. Dust with powdered sugar.

NUTRITION INFORMATION

CALORIES PER SERVING: 164.9

FAT: 3.35 G

% CALORIES FROM FAT: 18%

PROTEIN: 2.84 G

CARBOHYDRATES: 32.13 G

CHOLESTEROL: 47.25 MG

Black Bottom Banana Napoleons

This is an impressive fancy dinner party dessert that never even hints at being lean. If caramelizing the top pastry layer seems too fussy, omit it and sieve a little powdered sugar over the top like a classic millefeuille.

Serves 6.

1. Combine 3 tablespoons of the sugar with the flour and cornstarch in a small bowl. Add whole egg and yolk and beat with a handheld electric mixer until pale and thick, 1 to 2 minutes. Set aside.

2. Scald the milk in a medium nonreactive saucepan. Pour the hot milk gradually over egg mixture, beating until half the milk is added. Scrape egg mixture back in saucepan with remaining milk. Cook on medium heat, stirring constantly with a wire whisk, reaching all over the bottom and sides of the pan, until custard thickens and the first bubble is seen at the edge of the pan. Continue to cook and whisk vigorously for 30 to 45 seconds more. Scrape custard into a clean bowl. Whisk in the vanilla.

3. Measure a slightly heaped ½ cup of hot custard and transfer it to a small bowl with the chocolate. Stir until chocolate is completely melted. Cover both mixtures so that plastic wrap comes in direct contact with custard to prevent a skin from forming. Refrigerate. *Custards may be prepared to this point and refrigerated for up to 2 days.*

4. Position a rack in the center of the oven and preheat to 375°F. Line a heavy baking sheet with parchment paper.

5. Pile defrosted phyllo sheets on a tray. Cover with plastic wrap and a damp towel and keep well covered until each sheet is needed. Remelt clarified butter, if necessary.

6. Place 1 sheet of phyllo on the counter in front of you. Brush with 1 teaspoon melted clarified butter, making sure to cover sheet completely. Sprinkle sheet with ¾ to 1 teaspoon sugar. Place a second phyllo sheet on top. Brush with melted butter and sprinkle with sugar as before. Measure and cut the 2-layer pile in

WORK AND BAKE TIME:
1-1/2—2 HOURS

INGREDIENTS

5 TABLESPOONS SUGAR

4 TEASPOONS FLOUR

4 TEASPOONS CORNSTARCH

1 EGG

1 EGG YOLK

1 CUP LOW-FAT (1%) MILK

1 TEASPOON VANILLA EXTRACT

1-1/2 OUNCES BITTERSWEET OR SEMI-SWEET CHOCOLATE, CHOPPED FINE

4 PHYLLO SHEETS, DEFROSTED ACCORDING TO PACKAGE INSTRUCTIONS

4 TEASPOONS MELTED CLARIFIED BUTTER (PAGE 164)

2 TABLESPOONS CARAMEL POWDER (PAGE 159)

2 SMALL OR 1 LARGE BANANA, CUT INTO 30 ROUNDS 1/4 INCH THICK

EQUIPMENT

HEAVY BAKING SHEET

LIGHTWEIGHT BAKING SHEET

PASTRY BAG FITTED WITH A CLOSED STAR TIP (ATECO #3) (OPTIONAL)

thirds the long way. Stack the pieces on top of one another and neaten the edges. You now have a 6-layer strip about 4 inches wide and 17 to 18 inches long. Cut strip into 9 rectangles about 4 inches wide and nearly 2 inches long.

7. Slide a long metal spatula or knife under the rectangles and transfer them to the lined baking sheet; they can almost touch. Cover pastry with a sheet of parchment. Place the lightweight baking sheet directly on top of the parchment, to weight the pastry.

8. Bake for 5 minutes. Remove the weight and parchment. Rotate baking sheet from front to back for even baking. Bake, uncovered, for 3 to 5 minutes more, watching very carefully, until pastry is dark golden brown. Cool pastry on a rack. Let baking sheet cool completely.

9. Repeat Steps 6 and 7 with the remaining 2 sheets of phyllo. Bake with parchment and a weight. Bake for 5 minutes. Remove baking sheet from oven. Remove weight and parchment. Turn 6 of the rectangles upside down and separate them a little from one another and from the rest of the pastry pieces. Sprinkle each of the 6 pieces evenly with ¾ to 1 teaspoon Caramel Powder. (If it is a little too sticky to sprinkle, place it in a strainer and sieve it over the pastry by stirring with a spoon.) Return the pieces to the oven and bake 3 to 5 minutes more, or until the caramel is melted and all pieces are dark golden brown. Cool on a rack. Store all pastry pieces airtight between layers of parchment or wax paper. Take special care with the caramel-topped pieces; do not stack them. *Pastry may be prepared to this point and stored airtight at room temperature for up to 2 days.* A Krispy Kan (page 184) is handy if the weather is damp.

10. **Assemble the napoleons.** To assemble with a pastry bag: Scrape the chocolate custard into the pastry bag; do not stir or beat the custard before filling the bag, even if it seems stiff. Pipe 2 neat lines down the length of 1 pastry piece, equidistant from each other and from the edges of the pastry. Repeat this with 5 more pastry pieces. Embed 5 overlapping banana slices in the custard. Pipe 2 lines of custard next to each other on top of the bananas. Top each with a plain pastry piece; push down gently. Rinse and dry pastry bag; refit with tip. Scrape vanilla custard into bag. Pipe 3 lines of custard right next to each other, down the center of each pastry piece, leaving about ⅜ inch of bare pastry along the edges. Pipe another 2 lines of custard on top between the first 3 lines. *Napoleons may be assembled to this point, covered, and refrigerated for up to 2½ hours before serving. Keep the caramel-coated tops stored airtight until ready to serve.*

11. To serve: Top each napoleon with a caramel-coated pastry piece. Push gently into the custard. Serve immediately.

Notes

• The custard recipe is quite precise; there is just enough to make the 6 napoleons. This means no nibbling. It also means that if you choose to pipe the custard, as I always do, you must not use a wider pastry tube or take other liberties in piping, or you will run short of custard before you reach the sixth napoleon and have to spoon off bits of custard from the others. If you hate to operate on such a tight budget, increase the custard recipe by half and use the extra as an insurance policy. If you do so, don't use all the custard just because it's there—the napoleons are perfectly balanced as originally planned.

• To assemble without a pastry bag: Spread just 2 teaspoons of chocolate custard down the length of each of 6 pastry pieces, leaving ⅜ inch of bare pastry along each long edge. Embed 5 overlapping banana slices in the custard. Divide the remaining chocolate custard into 6 portions and spread each down the center of the bananas. Top each with a plain pastry piece; push down gently. Divide the vanilla custard into 6 portions; spread each with a small spatula or drop small dollops down the length of the pastry, leaving ⅜ inch of bare pastry along the edges.

VARIATIONS

....

Once you've made the napoleons with bananas and custard, you may want to try something else: raspberries or strawberries in place of bananas; very thick homemade pear or applesauce on the bottom layer with Vanilla Pastry Cream (page 140) on the top; sweetened chestnut puree or chopped candied chestnuts on the bottom with Maida's Cream (page 160) on top.

Apple Rose Tartlets

Baked apple halves are sliced and transformed into roses for these lovely tartlets. I learned to make apple roses over twenty years ago from Camille Cadier, one of my first French cooking teachers. The instructions seem endless but it takes less time to do than to read. Try some unusual antique apple varieties like spitzenburg, Northern Spy, or Jonathan at the peak of the season. Another time, replace the applesauce beneath the roses with Vanilla Pastry Cream (page 140).

WORK TIME: 2-1/2—3 HOURS

Serves 8.

1. Position the rack in lower third of the oven and preheat to 350°F.

2. Peel 4 apples, reserving the peels from two. Cut peeled apples in half lengthwise and neatly remove and discard cores. Place a peeled apple half cut side down on a cutting board and slice crosswise into slices ⅛ inch thick. Transfer to the baking dish, keeping slices together in the shape of the original apple half. Repeat with remaining halves. Sprinkle with 2 tablespoons rum and 3 to 4 tablespoons sugar, depending on tartness. Cover with foil and bake for 20 minutes. Uncover and baste apples. Cook, uncovered, for 10 to 20 minutes, or until tender when pierced with a fork. Cool completely before forming roses.

3. **Make the glaze.** In a small saucepan, combine reserved apple skins with the apple juice, the 3 tablespoons sugar, a pinch of cinnamon, and remaining 2 tablespoons rum. Simmer until liquid is reduced and thickened to a glaze. Pour into a strainer set over a bowl and press the solids to extract as much juice as possible. You should have about ¼ cup. Discard solids. Cool and refrigerate until needed. *Glaze may be refrigerated for 3 to 4 days.*

4. **Make the applesauce.** Cut remaining 6 unpeeled apples in quarters and remove the cores. Cut each quarter in four and place in a large saucepan with ¼ cup sugar, ⅛ teaspoon cinnamon, and 1 tablespoon water. Cover and cook over medium heat until apples are soft, at least 30 minutes. Mash apples with a fork or potato masher and continue to cook, uncovered, until liquid has completely evaporated and mixture is very thick, 5 to 10 minutes. Force through a strainer or ricer to remove peels. If mixture seems too runny at this point, return it to stove and cook a

INGREDIENTS

10 MEDIUM BAKING APPLES

4 TABLESPOONS RUM OR BRANDY, OR MORE TO TASTE

1/2 CUP PLUS 3 TABLESPOONS SUGAR, OR MORE TO TASTE

1 CUP APPLE JUICE

1/4 TEASPOON GROUND CINNAMON

8 PHYLLO NESTS (PAGE 156), BAKED

EQUIPMENT

9 X 13-INCH BAKING DISH

NUTRITION INFORMATION

CALORIES PER SERVING: 290

FAT 3.1 G

% CALORIES FROM FAT: 9%

PROTEIN: 1.3 G

CARBOHYDRATES: 67 G

CHOLESTEROL: 5.5 MG

little longer. Taste and adjust sugar and cinnamon; add a little more brandy or rum, if desired. Cool. *Applesauce may be prepared to this point, covered, and refrigerated for 3 to 4 days.*

   5. Make the apple roses. Place a baked apple half on a cutting board, flat side down. Separate the slices in the middle. Twist the center slice into a cone or spiral shape to form a bud. Wrap 1 or 2 adjacent slices partially around it like the center petals of a rose. Fan the outer slices to suggest the outer petals. Adjust and arrange the apple rose as much or as little as you like. Slide a spatula under the finished rose and transfer it to a dish large enough to hold 8 roses. Form the remaining baked apple halves into roses. *Apple roses may be prepared to this point, covered, and refrigerated for 3 to 4 days.*

   6. To assemble and serve: Ten minutes before serving, divide the applesauce among the phyllo nests, placing 2 to 3 tablespoons in each. Top each mound of sauce with an apple rose. Reheat the glaze until hot and brush each rose with it. Serve as soon as possible. *(If necessary, completed tartlets may wait, at room temperature, up to 2 hours.)*

Notes

• In a hurry? Omit Step 3 and substitute a little strained apricot jam, simmered with a pinch of cinnamon, for the apple glaze in Step 6. Shorten Step 4 by peeling the remaining 6 apples before cooking them so they need not be strained later.

• Here's a quick way to test and choose an apple variety for these tartlets. Buy a few kinds, even 1 apple of each. Do this within the week you plan to make and serve the tartlets, since some of the apples are great 1 week and not so good the next. Don't forget to label them. Halve, peel, and core, one of each of the apples. Slice it as described in Step 2 of the recipe. Place it, flat side down, in a ramekin or custard cup just big enough to hold it. Sprinkle with 1 to 1½ teaspoons sugar, cover with microwavesafe plastic wrap, and cook on High for 1 minute and 30 seconds. Puncture and remove the plastic wrap and let the apple cool and reabsorb its juice. Cook each apple in the same manner. Cool before tasting. You'll be amazed at the differences in sweetness and flavor. You'll also be able to judge how well the apple holds its shape, how much cooking it takes, and how much sugar it needs.

I love apples. And I don't consider apple cores to be garbage
either. I leave them in my purse, on the
dashboard, or on the bedside table. They dry out and become
very aromatic. This is not appreciated by everyone.

Apples are personal. I like mine tart and crisp.
Pippins and Granny Smiths are my
year-round favorites, raw and cooked, though cooked
Pippins have the edge. I also brake for Braeburns, Fujis,
and Jonathans, in their season. Sweet apples
appeal to me if they are very crisp and have tang.
Fall brings an astonishing array of apples with incredible
subtleties of flavor and perfume, sweetness
and tartness.

Pavé

By rights I should not call this dessert Pavé (paving stone in French), since it is round, not rectangular, in shape. But there's such a thing as being too literal minded. Serve this dessert on an elegant occasion with strong coffee or espresso. Use the same quantities of everything, but divide in half to make two smaller desserts six and a half inches in diameter. Serve one now, freeze one for later.

WORK AND BAKE TIME: 2 HOURS

Serves 12 to 14.

1. Position rack in lower third of the oven and preheat to 350°F. Cut 1 piece of parchment paper the exact size of baking sheet. Trace two 9-inch circles with a dark pencil. Place the paper upside down (tracing should show through) on baking sheet.

2. Make the batter for Cocoa Soufflé Pastry B. Divide batter evenly between the 2 traced circles and spread gently with a spatula to cover the circles, neatening the edges with your finger. Bake for 15 minutes. Cool on the parchment on a rack. Cut parchment between the pastry circles to separate them. Set aside.

3. Assemble the dessert. Select the best looking ladyfinger layer for the top. Brush the bottom side only with liqueur. Brush both sides of the second layer. Set both aside. Sieve some of the cocoa over a cardboard cake circle or on a plate or small cookie sheet. Place 1 cocoa pastry layer, upside down, on it. Peel parchment from the pastry. Set aside.

4. Make Bittersweet Chocolate Meringue Mousse. Scoop a third of the mousse on top of the cocoa pastry layer and spread nearly to the edge of the layer. Place the double-moistened ladyfinger layer on top; press gently to level. Scoop a little less than half of the remaining mousse on top of the ladyfinger layer and spread nearly to the edge. Repeat with second pastry layer and all but about ⅓ cup of the remaining mousse. Top with the remaining ladyfinger layer, placed moistened side down. Press gently on top of dessert to level it. Spread sides with remaining mousse. *Dessert may be covered with plastic wrap and refrigerated for up to 1 day or wrapped airtight and frozen for up to 6 weeks.*

5. To serve: Use a fine strainer to sieve just enough cocoa over dessert to highlight piping. Press Chocolate Shavings around sides. If desired, sieve powdered sugar through a stencil to decorate top.

INGREDIENTS

1 RECIPE COCOA SOUFFLÉ PASTRY B
(PAGE 149), BATTER ONLY

TWO 9-INCH LADYFINGER LAYERS A
(PAGE 149), BAKED AND COOLED

3 TO 4 TABLESPOONS GRAND MARNIER,
RUM, OR LIQUEUR OF CHOICE

2 TABLESPOONS UNSWEETENED DUTCH
PROCESS COCOA

5 CUPS BITTERSWEET CHOCOLATE
MERINGUE MOUSSE (PAGE 143)

3/4 OUNCE CHOCOLATE SHAVINGS OR
CHOCOLATE SPLINTERS (PAGES
162–163)

1 TO 2 TEASPOONS POWDERED SUGAR,
FOR DUSTING (OPTIONAL)

EQUIPMENT

LARGE HEAVY BAKING SHEET

PASTRY BAG FITTED WITH A ROUND TIP
(ATECO #7) OR CLOSED STAR TIP
(ALSO ATECO #7)

9-INCH CARDBOARD CAKE CIRCLE
(OPTIONAL)

PAPER STENCIL OR DOILY (OPTIONAL)

NUTRITION INFORMATION

CALORIES PER SERVING: 227

FAT: 7 G

% CALORIES FROM FAT: 27%

PROTEIN: 6 G

CARBOHYDRATES: 37 G

CHOLESTEROL: 90.9 MG

Triple Mousse Celebration Cake

With a fraction of the fat of my original Cocolat recipe, this frozen dessert is a blockbuster. It's triply worthwhile, especially if you have a crowd to feed. Or cut it in half to make two small dinner party desserts.

WORK TIME: 2 HOURS 30 MINUTES
BAKE TIME: 15 MINUTES
FREEZE TIME: 24 HOURS

INGREDIENTS

2 TO 3 TABLESPOONS UNSWEETENED
  DUTCH PROCESS COCOA

1 SHEET COCOA SOUFFLÉ PASTRY B
  (PAGE 149), BAKED AND COOLED IN
  THE PAN

2-1/2 CUPS (1/2 RECIPE) BITTERSWEET
  CHOCOLATE MERINGUE MOUSSE
  (PAGE 143)

2 CUPS (1/2 RECIPE) MILK CHOCOLATE
  MOCHA MOUSSE (PAGE 145)

2 CUPS (1/2 RECIPE) WHITE CHOCOLATE
  MOUSSE (PAGE 144)

1 TABLESPOON UNSWEETENED DUTCH
  PROCESS COCOA, FOR DUSTING

1 TABLESPOON NATURAL (NONALKA-
  LIZED) COCOA (SEE NOTE) OR 1
  TABLESPOON POWDERED SUGAR,
  FOR STENCILING (OPTIONAL)

EQUIPMENT

SMALL BAKING SHEET OR TRAY

TWO 5 X 3-INCH PIECES CORRUGATED
  CARDBOARD

TWO 10 X 3-INCH PIECES CORRUGATED
  CARDBOARD

Serves 14 to 16. Make at least 1 day ahead.

1. Tear off and place an 18-inch sheet of wax paper or foil on the counter in front of you. Sieve cocoa liberally over paper. Run a knife around the edges of the pastry to release it from pan. Invert pan on the cocoa-dusted surface. Remove pan and peel away paper. Cut pastry crosswise into 3 equal pieces, 5 x 10 inches. Transfer one to a small baking sheet or tray that will fit in the freezer. Set aside.

2. **Make a mold for the cake.** If pastry pieces are smaller than 5 x 10 inches, measure and trim cardboard lengths to match. Place each cardboard piece on a slightly larger piece of foil, fold foil up around edges of cardboard, and secure with tape. Line cardboards up end to end on the counter, foil side down, alternating long and short pieces. Use tape to "hinge" each piece loosely to the next piece. Pick up the whole assembly, bend it at the hinges (readjust tape if hinges are too tight to bend or too loose), and set it around the pastry piece, foil sides facing inward, like 4 walls. Tape the last 2 edges together. Tape walls to baking sheet.

3. **Make the Bittersweet Chocolate Meringue Mousse.** Scrape mousse immediately into mold on top of pastry. Smooth surface. Place second pastry piece on top of mousse and press to level.

4. **Make the Milk Chocolate Mocha Mousse.** Scrape mousse immediately into mold on top of pastry. Smooth surface. Place third pastry piece on top of mousse and press to level.

5. **Make the White Chocolate Mousse.** Scrape mousse immediately into mold on top of pastry. Smooth surface of mousse as perfectly as possible. Cover mold with plastic wrap and freeze overnight or until ready to serve.

6. When frozen, remove the cake. Cut through the tape hinges and remove cardboards. Dip a long sharp knife into hot water and wipe it dry. Trim each of the 4 sides of the cake neatly with the knife. Dip and wipe after each cut. If you wish to make 2 smaller square cakes to serve at different times, cut the cake in half. Place cake(s) in a covered container and keep frozen until ready to serve. *Cake may be frozen for 2 months.*

7. To serve: Remove cake from freezer. Use a fine strainer to sieve Dutch process cocoa evenly over the top of the dessert. If desired, set a paper stencil, doily, or strips of stiff paper over the cocoa and sieve again with natural cocoa or powdered sugar. Remove stencil carefully. Transfer dessert to serving platter. Serve frozen.

Notes

• After freezing, the cake sometimes settles in the center, leaving raised edges. This can be remedied before dusting the cake with cocoa, as follows: Dip a knife in hot water and wipe dry. Trim edges level. Proceed with Step 7.

• Natural cocoa is usually a lighter color than Dutch process cocoa. I like to dust a dessert with the darker cocoa and then stencil the surface with the lighter color. If you do not have both types of cocoa on hand, stencil with powdered sugar instead.

NUTRITION INFORMATION

CALORIES PER SERVING: 182

FAT: 7 G

% CALORIES FROM FAT: 33%

PROTEIN: 5.5 G

CARBOHYDRATES: 27 G

CHOLESTEROL: 56 MG

Mocha Bûche de Noël

Several years ago I made a bûche de Noël (Yule log cake) that was more like a Baked Alaska—with a rich frozen interior
and a warm toasted meringue topping. Since freezing adds body and a perception of richness to lighter mousses,
it's a great technique for making a light bûche. Here Cocoa Soufflé Pastry is rolled up around a Milk Chocolate Mocha Mousse.
All is frozen, then covered with toasted safe meringue before serving.

Serves 12 to 14. Make at least 1 day ahead.

1. Line the bottom and sides of the jelly-roll pan with foil. Make sure that you'll have room for it in your freezer.

2. Make Milk Chocolate Mocha Mousse. Scrape the mousse into the pan and spread evenly. Cover with plastic wrap and freeze until soft-firm, 3 hours or longer.

3. Take frozen mousse from the freezer and remove plastic wrap. Use the foil liner at one end of the pan to fold 2 inches of mousse over onto itself. Press on the foil to flatten the folded mousse a little, then unfold the foil. Run a knife around the edges of the pastry to loosen it from the pan. Lift pastry by grasping the parchment liner and place it, pastry side down, over the mousse, lining it up within the 4 sides of the pan. Peel the paper from the pastry. Sieve cocoa evenly over pastry and cover with a sheet of foil. Holding foil securely to pan at both ends, invert onto the counter. Remove pan and peel foil off the frozen mousse. You should see 2 inches of exposed pastry at 1 end of the mousse.

4. Starting at the end opposite the exposed pastry, use the foil to help roll the pastry and the mousse together to form a roll 11 or 12 inches long. Wrap roll with foil and return to freezer overnight. *Bûche may be completed to this point and frozen for up to 1 week.*

5. Make the safe meringue. Bring 1 inch of water to a simmer in a large skillet. Combine the cream of tartar and 3 teaspoons of water in a 6- to 8-cup stainless steel bowl. Whisk in the egg whites and sugar. Place thermometer near stove in a mug of very hot tap water. Set bowl in skillet. Stir mixture briskly and constantly with a rubber spatula, scraping the sides and bottom often to avoid scrambling the whites. After 1½ minutes, remove bowl from skillet. Quickly insert thermometer, tilting bowl to cover stem by at least 2 inches. If less than 160°F., rinse thermometer in

WORK TIME: 1 HOUR 30 MINUTES
BAKE TIME: 20 MINUTES
FREEZE TIME: 3 PLUS 24 HOURS

INGREDIENTS

4-1/2 CUPS (1-1/2 RECIPES) MILK
   CHOCOLATE MOCHA MOUSSE
   (PAGE 145)
1 SHEET COCOA SOUFFLÉ PASTRY A
   (PAGE 148), BAKED AND COOLED
1 TO 2 TABLESPOONS UNSWEETENED
   DUTCH PROCESS COCOA
SCANT 1/4 TEASPOON CREAM OF
   TARTAR
3 EGG WHITES
1/2 CUP SUGAR
2 TABLESPOONS POWDERED SUGAR
CHOCOLATE BUTTERMILK GLAZE
   (PAGE 147) (OPTIONAL)

EQUIPMENT

11 X 17- OR 12 X 16-INCH JELLY-ROLL
   OR HALF SHEET PAN
CORRUGATED CARDBOARD 14 X 4
   INCHES, WRAPPED IN FOIL
INSTANT-READ THERMOMETER

NUTRITION INFORMATION

CALORIES PER SERVING: 246

FAT: 9 G

% CALORIES FROM FAT: 31%

PROTEIN: 7.2 G

CARBOHYDRATES: 37.7 G

CHOLESTEROL: 95.3 MG

skillet water and return it to mug. Replace bowl in skillet. Stir as before until temperature reaches 160°F. when bowl is removed. Beat on high speed until cool and stiff. (For more details on safe meringue, see pages 138-140.)

6. Remove frozen roll from freezer; unwrap and place on foil-wrapped cardboard. Use a spatula to cover the roll completely with meringue, leaving no bare cake showing. Meringue should also touch the foiled cardboard everywhere along the base of the roll. Texture with a fork to resemble tree bark and stumps, if desired. Place in freezer until ready to bake. *Bûche may be completed to this point, tented carefully with foil, and frozen for up to 1 day.*

7. To toast and serve: Preheat oven to 425°F. Sieve powdered sugar over the bûche. Transfer the bûche, on its cardboard base, to a baking sheet. Bake just until golden brown, 4 to 6 minutes. Transfer to a serving platter. Serve immediately. Sauce each serving with glaze if desired.

VARIATIONS

....

Black Forest or Chestnut Bûche de Noël: Substitute 1 quart of slightly softened vanilla frozen yogurt for the mousse. Sprinkle yogurt evenly with 1 cup or more coarsely chopped drained amareno cherries or cherries in brandy or pieces of candied chestnuts in syrup (page 179). Cover with plastic wrap and press pieces into yogurt before freezing.

Customized Bûche de Noël: Create your own bûche by using 1 quart of your favorite frozen yogurt for the filling. Press in pieces of candied or brandied fruits, candied citrus peels, crushed praline, or chopped nuts. Or, fill with 4 cups of any other mousse (pages 142-146).

Bittersweet Chocolate Truffles

A few days after the frozen truffle cookie discovery (see Beryl's Walnut Truffle Cookies), I woke in the middle of the night.
If there could be frozen truffle cookies, why not frozen truffles? These have fewer than half the calories of the
pure chocolate and heavy cream truffles that made Cocolat famous. The truffles must be served directly from the freezer. Because they
are so special and because they have this rather unusual requirement, they will certainly end up a conversation piece.

Makes about 45 truffles. Make at least 1 day ahead.

1. **Make the mousse.** Transfer to a bowl, cover, and freeze until firm enough to scoop, 5 hours or longer.

2. **Form truffle centers.** Have ready a bowl of hot water, a melon baller, a pan lined with wax paper, and the firm mousse. Dip the melon baller into the water and wipe dry. Form a scant 1-inch ball. Place it on the pan. Dip, wipe, and scoop centers until the mixture is used up. Freeze centers overnight. *Centers may be prepared to this point and frozen for up to 2 weeks.*

3. **Coat the truffles.** Melt chocolate in the top of a double boiler over barely simmering water, stirring frequently to hasten melting and prevent overheating. Or microwave on Medium (50% power) for about 3 minutes, stopping to stir several times. Chocolate is ready when it is completely melted and smooth and between 115° and 120°F.

4. Pour cocoa into shallow dish. Have ready another shallow dish for the completed truffles. Remove a third to a half of the frozen centers from the freezer and place them in a shallow dish next to the container of melted chocolate.

5. With your right hand (left if you are left-handed), fingers together and slightly cupped, scoop a large handful of melted chocolate into your left hand. Rub both hands together to coat them with a thick layer of melted chocolate. Quickly pick up a frozen center with your left hand and roll it gently between your hands with a circular motion and as little pressure as possible, just long enough to cover it with a coating of chocolate. Add chocolate to your hands as necessary. Immediately place the coated center in the cocoa dish. If you see any uncoated spots, dip a finger into

WORK TIME: 1 HOUR 30 MINUTES
FREEZE TIME: 5 PLUS 12 HOURS

INGREDIENTS

2 CUPS (1/2 RECIPE) BITTERSWEET
CHOCOLATE TRUFFLE MOUSSE
(PAGE 142)

16 OUNCES BITTERSWEET OR SEMI-
SWEET CHOCOLATE, CHOPPED

1/3 CUP UNSWEETENED DUTCH
PROCESS COCOA

EQUIPMENT

A CHILD OR OTHER FRIEND TO HELP IN
STEP 5

NUTRITION INFORMATION

CALORIES PER TRUFFLE: 47

FAT: 2.7 G

CALORIES FROM FAT: 46%

PROTEIN: .9 G

CARBOHYDRATES: 6.2 G

CHOLESTEROL: 4.9 MG

the chocolate and patch the truffle. Have your friend shake the dish back and forth to roll the truffle in cocoa and then transfer it to another dish. Repeat until all the frozen centers are coated, adding chocolate to your hands between each one. Truffles may spring small leaks where the chocolate coating is imperfect or cracked, although your technique will improve with practice. In any case, the cocoa will cover all, and the traditional chocolate truffle is a rustic-looking delicacy in the first place. (Absent a friend, divide the cocoa between 2 dishes. Place 2 or 3 truffles in cocoa before stopping to shake the dish. Continue to add truffles and shake until the first cocoa dish is crowded with truffles, then start on the second.) *Truffles may be stored in a tightly covered container in the freezer for up to 6 weeks.*

6. **To serve:** Place in fluted paper candy cups. Serve frozen.

Notes

• This hand-coating method is for people who love to get their hands in chocolate. Professional chocolatiers use it when a very thin chocolate coating is desired. It's good to have a friend to help with the cocoa; he or she can also fetch and replace things in the freezer, since both of your hands will be covered with melted chocolate.

• You need to work quickly to keep the melted chocolate from hardening on your hands as you handle the frozen centers. The trick is to keep the center moving— never let it rest in one place in your hands—and get it out of your hands as fast as possible.

• You will have both chocolate and cocoa left over because the dipping technique requires that you work with more than you need. Place leftover ingredients in small plastic bags (strain the cocoa first). Store in the freezer (since cocoa and chocolate may contain a little of the melted truffle mixture) until needed for another recipe.

Mocha Truffles: Use 2 cups (1/2 recipe) Mocha Mousse (page 143) for truffle centers. Coat in milk chocolate or white chocolate. Roll in cocoa or powdered sugar.

Liqueur Truffles: Reduce the quantity of milk in the Bittersweet Chocolate Truffle Mousse to 6 tablespoons. Add 1 to 1½ tablespoons of your favorite liqueur with the vanilla in Step 3.

Petite Sweets

....

Sometimes, what is wanted is just a little something sweet to go with the coffee. Not to mention cookies in the lunch box, cookies in bed, and cookies with ice cream. I admit to a preference for crisp cookies over soft ones—except when it comes to lemon bars, brownies, and macaroons. And, when I'm not eating chocolate, I choose flavors that are assertive like lemon and ginger or rich like caramel. Here are some of my favorites.

Chocolate Macaroons

Chewy dark chocolate. I love the crackled tops.

WORK TIME: 20 MINUTES
REST TIME: 30 MINUTES
BAKE TIME: 20–25 MINUTES

INGREDIENTS

2/3 CUP BLANCHED ALMONDS
   (3 OUNCES)
1 CUP SUGAR
2 TABLESPOONS UNSWEETENED DUTCH
   PROCESS COCOA
3/8 TEASPOON ALMOND EXTRACT
1 TO 2 EGG WHITES

EQUIPMENT

HEAVY COOKIE SHEETS
PASTRY BAG FITTED WITH A 1/2-INCH
   PLAIN TIP (ATECO #6) (OPTIONAL)

NUTRITION INFORMATION

CALORIES PER COOKIE: 42
FAT: 1.5 G
% CALORIES FROM FAT: 30%
PROTEIN: .76 G
CARBOHYDRATES: 6.9 G
CHOLESTEROL: 0 MG

Makes 30 to 32 cookies.

1. Line cookie sheets with parchment paper.

2. Grind the almonds with the sugar and cocoa in a food processor until fine. Add the almond extract and pulse to combine. With the motor running, slowly add just enough of the egg white to form a thick sticky paste that barely holds its shape when dropped from a spoon.

3. Transfer mixture to the pastry bag, if you are using one. Pipe mounds about 1¼ inches in diameter and ⅜ inch high on cookie sheets. Or drop slightly rounded teaspoons of batter about 1½ inches apart onto the sheets. Let stand at room temperature for 30 minutes before baking.

4. Position the racks in upper and lower third of the oven and preheat to 300°F.

5. Bake macaroons for 20 to 25 minutes. They will puff and be slightly crisp and crackled on top; centers will still be moist but not completely gooey. Cool completely on a rack before peeling off the parchment paper. *Macaroons may be stored, airtight, at room temperature for up to 3 days or frozen for up to 2 months.*

VARIATION
....

Chestnut Macaroons: Increase the sugar to 1½ cups, substitute ½ cup unsweetened chestnut puree (page 179) for the cocoa, and substitute 1 teaspoon vanilla extract for the almond extract. In Step 2, process the almonds and sugar until fine. Add the chestnut puree and vanilla and pulse to combine. Continue with the recipe.

Aunt Tillie's Cornflake Cookies

This American coconut and cornflake classic is updated with much less sugar and a few minor changes to reduce the fat. My friend Joan dropped in one day to taste and chat. Her parting words were, "How about some tangy apricots?" Indeed.

WORK TIME: 15 MINUTES
BAKE TIME: 20—25 MINUTES

Makes 40 cookies.

1. Position the rack in lower third of the oven and preheat to 300°F. Line the baking sheet with parchment paper or foil.

2. Beat the egg whites with the cream of tartar on medium speed until soft peaks form. Gradually sprinkle in the sugar and beat at high speed until very stiff but not dry. Use a rubber spatula to gently fold in the cornflakes, coconut, walnuts, and dried apricots. Fold until the cornflakes are coated with egg white.

3. Drop by slightly rounded teaspoons about 1½ inches apart on baking sheet. Bake for 20 to 25 minutes, or until delicately brown. Cool on a rack. *Cookies may be stored, airtight, for 3 to 4 days or frozen for up to 2 months.*

INGREDIENTS

2 EGG WHITES, AT ROOM TEMPERATURE

1/8 TEASPOON CREAM OF TARTAR

1/2 CUP SUGAR, PREFERABLY FINE
   GRANULATED OR SUPERFINE

2-1/2 CUPS CORNFLAKES

2/3 CUP (LOOSELY PACKED) SWEET-
   ENED SHREDDED COCONUT
   (1-3/4 OUNCES)

1/3 CUP COARSELY CHOPPED WALNUTS
   (1-1/2 OUNCES)

1/4 CUP CHOPPED DRIED APRICOTS
   (1 OUNCE)

EQUIPMENT

HEAVY BAKING SHEET

NUTRITION INFORMATION

CALORIES PER COOKIE: 31

FAT: 1.1 G

% CALORIES FROM FAT: 31%

PROTEIN: .5 G

CARBOHYDRATES: 5 G

CHOLESTEROL: 0 MG

Sweet Corn Lace

Maida Heatter's savory corn lace recipe is the direct ancestor of these thin, crisp cinnamon cookies. Include them on a cookie tray or with fresh berries. They will disappear instantly.

WORK AND BAKE TIME:
1 HOUR 15 MINUTES

INGREDIENTS

7 TABLESPOONS SUGAR

1/4 TEASPOON GROUND CINNAMON

4 TEASPOONS UNSALTED BUTTER,
    CUT INTO SMALL PIECES

3/8 TEASPOON SALT

1 CUP YELLOW CORNMEAL

EQUIPMENT

2 HEAVY BAKING SHEETS

NUTRITION INFORMATION

CALORIES PER COOKIE: 18

FAT: .33 G

% CALORIES FROM FAT: 16%

PROTEIN: .22 G

CARBOHYDRATES: 35.9 G

CHOLESTEROL: .76 MG

Makes about 54 cookies.

1. Position the racks on bottom and top third of the oven and preheat to 350°F. Cut several pieces of aluminum foil the same size as the baking sheets and spray with vegetable oil spray or butter well. Cut several sheets of plastic wrap the same size.

2. Combine 2 tablespoons of the sugar with the cinnamon and set aside.

3. In a medium saucepan over medium heat, bring 1⅔ cups water to a simmer with the remaining sugar, butter, and salt. Remove from heat. Pour in the cornmeal all at once. Stir cornmeal mixture until smooth and thick. Batter will look like stiff cornmeal mush.

4. Place 6 rounded teaspoons of the cornmeal mixture evenly spaced on each sheet of foil. Place a piece of plastic wrap on top and press down on each lump using the heel of your hand. Use your fingers to smooth and flatten cookies until they are 3½ to 4 inches in diameter and less than 1/16 inch thick. Peel the plastic wrap off the cookies. If it sticks, chill the sheets. Sprinkle each cookie with the cinnamon sugar. Slide foil onto baking sheets. Bake 1 sheet first to check cookie size, thickness, and timing. Cookies will be done in 10 to 15 minutes depending on how thick they are. Cookies are done when they are evenly golden brown all over. Rotate sheets from back to front and from top to bottom about halfway through baking time so that cookies bake evenly. They will seem very fragile and may have

lacy holes in them. Use a wide metal spatula to transfer cookies to a paper towel. Cool cookies completely. *Cookies may be stored, airtight, for 3 to 4 days.*

Notes

• These cookies can be made almost paper thin and quite large or nearly as thick as 1/16 inch—your choice—but be sure to bake until they are colored all over. Underbaked cookies will be tough instead of fragile and crisp.

• The good news is that these take just seconds to mix. But they take a while to complete since you can bake only 2 sheets or 12 cookies at a time. You can, however, get all of the cookies ready on foil sheets while the first batch is baking.

• If your cookies are too fragile to pick up, you've made them too thin!

Cornmeal Cookies

Almost austere in their simplicity, yet so so good. When Jackie Jones dropped in to show me her preliminary design for this book, cornmeal cookies were everywhere in the kitchen, and I had lost all perspective. Jackie's immediate approval rallied my spirits. After a few days' vacation from corn cookies, I realized again just how delicious they are.

Makes about 75 cookies.

1. Stir flour, cornmeal, and salt together with a wire whisk to combine. Set aside.

2. In a medium mixing bowl, beat butter until creamy. Add sugar and beat at high speed for about 1 minute, or until mixture loses its crumbly texture and begins to form a mass. Beat in the egg yolk, yogurt, and vanilla. Add dry ingredients and beat on low speed just until combined. Scrape bowl and beater. Knead the mixture briefly with your hands to mix thoroughly.

3. Tear off a piece of wax paper about 14 inches long. Gather the dough together and form it, lengthwise on the paper, into a neat 9- to 10-inch cylinder about 1¾ inches in diameter. Wrap securely in the paper. Fold or twist the ends of

WORK TIME: 10 MINUTES
CHILL TIME: 1 HOUR
BAKE TIME: 30 MINUTES

INGREDIENTS

1-1/2 CUPS SIFTED ALL-PURPOSE
   FLOUR (6 OUNCES)
1/2 CUP YELLOW CORNMEAL
1/8 TEASPOON SALT
4 TABLESPOONS UNSALTED BUTTER,
   AT ROOM TEMPERATURE
2/3 CUP SUGAR
1 EGG YOLK
2 TABLESPOONS NONFAT YOGURT
1/2 TEASPOON VANILLA EXTRACT

EQUIPMENT

HEAVY COOKIE SHEETS

NUTRITION INFORMATION

CALORIES PER COOKIE: 25

FAT: .7 G

% CALORIES FROM FAT: 26%

PROTEIN: .38 G

CARBOHYDRATES: 4.2 G

CHOLESTEROL: 4.49 MG

the paper, trying not to pinch or flatten the ends of the log. Chill for at least 1 hour, or until needed. *Dough may be prepared to this point and refrigerated for up to 3 days or rewrapped in foil or plastic and frozen for up to 3 months.*

4. Position the racks in the upper and lower third of the oven and preheat to 350°F. Line the cookie sheets with parchment paper or aluminum foil.

5. Use a sharp knife to slice dough into rounds about ⅛ inch thick. Place slices 1 inch apart on the cookie sheets. Bake for 10 to 12 minutes, or until golden brown at the edges. Rotate sheets from top to bottom and front to back about halfway through the baking time. Use a metal spatula to transfer cookies to a rack. Cool cookies completely before stacking or storing. *Cookies may be stored, airtight, for up to 2 weeks or frozen for up to 2 months.*

···

Hot Ginger Hearts

I think of these as blond ginger cookies because though they are very gingery, they are not flavored with dark wintery spices like the cinnamon and clove that normally keep company with ginger. Try them with a fruit compote.

WORK TIME: 15 MINUTES

CHILL TIME: 1 HOUR

BAKE TIME: 30–45 MINUTES

INGREDIENTS

1-1/2 CUPS SIFTED ALL-PURPOSE
   FLOUR (6 OUNCES)

1/8 TEASPOON SALT

2/3 CUP SUGAR

4 TEASPOONS MINCED CRYSTALLIZED
   GINGER

Makes 40 cookies.

1. Stir flour and salt together with a whisk to combine. Set aside. Place sugar and minced ginger in a bowl. Use the tips of your fingers to rub the ginger and sugar together just until the bits of ginger are separate from one another. Set aside.

2. In a medium mixing bowl, beat the butter until creamy. Add gingered sugar, ground ginger, and pepper. Beat on high speed for about 1 minute. Beat in the egg yolk, yogurt, and vanilla. On low speed, beat in the flour just until combined. Gather the dough into a mass, wrap, and chill until firm enough to roll, 1 hour or more.

3. Position the racks in upper and lower third of the oven and preheat to 350°F. Line the cookie sheets with parchment paper.

4. Roll out the dough between 2 sheets of wax paper until a scant ¼ inch thick. Cut with a cookie cutter, leaving as little space between cuts as possible. Reroll the dough scraps. If the dough becomes too soft to work with at any time, slide a cookie sheet under the wax paper and transfer the rolled dough to the refrigerator until firm. Transfer hearts to the cookie sheets, placing them about 1 inch apart. Bake for 12 to 14 minutes. Rotate sheets from top to bottom and from front to back about halfway through the baking time. Cookies are done when they are golden brown around the edges and on the bottom but still pale in the center. Use a metal spatula to transfer cookies to a rack. Cool completely before storing or stacking. *Cookies may be stored, airtight, for up to 2 weeks or frozen for up to 2 months.*

Note

Simple round cookies may be made by shaping the dough into a log and slicing it, as described in Step 3 on pages 117–118. Bake as above.

4 TABLESPOONS UNSALTED BUTTER

1 TEASPOON GROUND GINGER

2 PINCHES GROUND WHITE PEPPER

1 EGG YOLK

2 TABLESPOONS NONFAT YOGURT

1/2 TEASPOON VANILLA EXTRACT

EQUIPMENT

HEAVY COOKIE SHEETS

HEART-SHAPE COOKIE CUTTER,
  2-1/4 INCHES

NUTRITION INFORMATION

CALORIES PER COOKIE: 41

FAT: 1.3 G

% CALORIES FROM FAT: 28%

PROTEIN: .56 G

CARBOHYDRATES: 6.9 G

CHOLESTEROL: 8.4 MG

Lemon Crisps

Wanting a low-fat cookie that was crisp and tender like a butter cookie or sugar cookie,
I tried an old Shaker recipe that was low in fat to start with. Alas, it was hard rather than crisp. Racking my brain for tenderizing
strategies, I remembered that acidic dairy products are tenderizers. The addition of a little yogurt made a big difference
and gave birth to Cornmeal Cookies and Hot Ginger Hearts. When it came time for this lemon cookie, lemon juice with low-fat milk
gave the same result. An additional trick for tenderness is to make these cookies fairly thin.

WORK TIME: 10 MINUTES
CHILL TIME: 1 HOUR
BAKE TIME: 30–45 MINUTES

INGREDIENTS

1-1/2 CUPS SIFTED ALL-PURPOSE
FLOUR (6 OUNCES)
1/8 TEASPOON SALT
1 LEMON
4 TABLESPOONS UNSALTED BUTTER,
AT ROOM TEMPERATURE
3/4 CUP SUGAR
1/2 TEASPOON VANILLA EXTRACT
1/4 TEASPOON LEMON EXTRACT
1 EGG YOLK
2 TABLESPOONS LOW-FAT (1%) MILK

EQUIPMENT

HEAVY COOKIE SHEETS

NUTRITION INFORMATION

CALORIES PER COOKIE: 42
FAT: 1.3 G
% CALORIES FROM FAT: 28%
PROTEIN: .56 G
CARBOHYDRATES: 7.1 G
CHOLESTEROL: 8.4 MG

Makes 40 cookies.

1. Stir flour and salt together with a whisk to combine. Set aside.

2. Grate lemon directly over a medium mixing bowl until there is enough zest to measure 2 packed teaspoons. Cut lemon in half and squeeze enough juice to measure 1 tablespoon. Add the juice to the zest. Add the butter and beat until creamy. Add the sugar and extracts. Beat on high speed for about 1 minute. Beat in the egg yolk and milk. On low speed, beat in the flour just until combined. Dough will be sticky. Form into a 9-inch log and wrap in wax paper as described on pages 117-118. Chill until firm enough to slice, 1 hour or longer. *Dough may be prepared to this point and refrigerated for up to 3 days before baking or rewrapped in foil or plastic and frozen for up to 3 months.*

3. Position the racks in the upper and lower third of the oven and preheat to 350°F. Line the cookie sheets with parchment paper.

4. Use a sharp knife to slice dough into cookies a scant ¼ inch thick. Place 1 inch apart on the cookie sheets. Bake for 12 to 14 minutes. Rotate sheets from top to bottom and front to back about halfway through baking time. Cookies are done when they are golden brown around the edges and on the bottom but still pale in the center. Use a metal spatula to transfer cookies to a rack. Cool completely before storing or stacking. *Cookies may be stored, airtight, for up to 2 weeks or frozen for up to 2 months.*

VARIATIONS
....

Lemon Poppy Seed Crisps: Roll dough log in about 3 tablespoons poppy seeds until well coated. Slice and bake as described.

Lemon Walnut Crisps: Add ⅓ cup finely chopped walnuts to flour in Step 1. Make dough log 9½ to 10 inches long. This makes about 45 cookies.

Marbled Hearts: See pages 122-123.

....

Plain Chocolate Cookies

These cookies are irresistible! I use crushed ones to coat the sides of my Chocolate Marble Cheesecake (page 44).
Mint and chocolate are a familiar duo, but you may not have thought of pairing chocolate with pepper and cinnamon, as they do in Mexico.
The combination also shows up in a German cookie called Wienerstube.

Makes 40 to 45 cookies.

1. Combine the flour, cocoa, baking soda, and salt in a medium bowl and mix thoroughly with a whisk. Set aside. Combine the sugars in a small bowl and mix well with your fingers, pressing out any lumps. (If lumps are stubborn, process in a food processor for a few seconds.) Set aside.

2. In a medium mixing bowl, beat the butter and margarine until creamy. Add the sugar mixture and vanilla. Beat on high speed for about 1 minute. Beat in the egg white. On low speed, beat in the flour mixture just until incorporated. Gather the dough together with your hands and form it into a neat 9- to 10-inch log. Wrap in wax paper as described on pages 117-118 and chill for at least 45 minutes, or

---

WORK TIME: 20 MINUTES
CHILL TIME: AT LEAST 45 MINUTES
BAKE TIME: 12—14 MINUTES

INGREDIENTS

1 CUP ALL-PURPOSE FLOUR (5 OUNCES)

1/2 CUP PLUS 1 TABLESPOON UNSWEETENED DUTCH PROCESS COCOA

1/4 TEASPOON BAKING SODA

1/4 TEASPOON SALT

1/2 CUP PLUS 1 TABLESPOON LIGHT
   BROWN SUGAR

1/2 CUP PLUS 1 TABLESPOON
   GRANULATED SUGAR

3 TABLESPOONS UNSALTED BUTTER,
   AT ROOM TEMPERATURE

3 TABLESPOONS STICK MARGARINE

1 TEASPOON VANILLA EXTRACT

1 EGG WHITE

EQUIPMENT

HEAVY COOKIE SHEETS

NUTRITION INFORMATION

CALORIES PER COOKIE: 46

FAT: 1.8 G

% CALORIES FROM FAT: 33%

PROTEIN: .64 G

CARBOHYDRATES: 7.6 G

CHOLESTEROL: 2.1 MG

until needed. *Cookies may be prepared to this point and refrigerated for up to 3 days or rewrapped in foil or plastic and frozen for up to 3 months.*

3. Place the racks in the upper and lower third of the oven and preheat to 350°F. Line the cookie sheets with parchment paper or aluminum foil.

4. Use a sharp knife to slice rounds of chilled dough a scant ¼ inch thick. Place 1 inch apart on the cookie sheets. Bake for 12 to 14 minutes. Rotate baking sheets from top to bottom and front to back about halfway through. Cookies will puff and crackle on top, then begin to settle down slightly when done. Use a metal spatula to transfer cookies to a rack. Cool cookies completely before storing or stacking. *Cookies may be stored, airtight, for up to 2 weeks or frozen for up to 2 months.*

Notes

• Cookies baked for a little less time will be crisp on the outside and slightly soft within; those baked a little longer will be dry, crisp, and tender throughout. The softer ones dry out after a day or so.

• Homemade slice-and-bake frozen cookies are the ultimate in high-quality convenience food. Double the recipe and stash 1 log in the freezer. It need not be totally defrosted before slicing, just enough to slice easily. You can even refreeze the unused portion.

VARIATIONS

....

Mint Chocolate Cookies: Prepare Plain Chocolate Cookies, adding ¼ teaspoon peppermint extract with the butter in Step 2.

Mexican Chocolate Cookies: Prepare Plain Chocolate Cookies, adding ½ teaspoon ground cinnamon, a generous pinch of pepper, and a generous pinch of cayenne to the sugars in Step 1.

Marbled Cookies or Hearts: Prepare 1 batch of Plain Chocolate Cookies dough and one batch of Lemon Crisps (page 120) or Hot Ginger Hearts dough (page 118). Gather each dough into 2 equal balls; wrap and chill just until firm but malleable, 30 to 60 minutes in the refrigerator, or less time in the freezer. (The lemon dough is much softer than the chocolate—put it in the freezer for part of the time until it is about the same consistency as the chocolate dough.) Remove 1 ball of each flavor. Squish the doughs together with your hands. Fold and knead a few times, turning the dough in a different direction each time. Cut through the dough with a knife to check the pattern. Knead until you like the pattern; do not blend thoroughly. For round cookies, form the dough into a 9- to 10-inch log and wrap it in wax paper as described on pages 117–118. Repeat with the remaining dough. For heart-shape cookies, form the log into a heart shape. Chill, slice, and bake as in Steps 2, 3, and 4.

Chocolate Biscotti

*These are crisp, dry, super crunchy, not too sweet Italian chocolate nut cookies made especially for dipping in
wine or coffee. Crushed biscotti are also superb topping for vanilla frozen yogurt. Or serve a small scoop of the yogurt in a really pretty
coffee cup. Pour half a cup of extra-strong black coffee around it and serve with Chocolate Biscotti.*

WORK AND BAKE TIME:
1 HOUR 30 MINUTES

INGREDIENTS

2/3 CUP WHOLE ALMONDS OR
   HAZELNUTS (3-1/3 OUNCES)

1-3/4 CUPS ALL-PURPOSE FLOUR
   (9 OUNCES)

1/3 CUP UNSWEETENED DUTCH
   PROCESS COCOA

1 TEASPOON BAKING SODA

1/4 TEASPOON SALT

1 TABLESPOON INSTANT ESPRESSO
   OR COFFEE POWDER (OPTIONAL)

1/3 CUP SEMISWEET CHOCOLATE
   MORSELS

2 EGGS

2 EGG WHITES

1 CUP SUGAR

1 TEASPOON VANILLA EXTRACT

1/2 TEASPOON ALMOND EXTRACT
   (OPTIONAL)

Makes 50 to 60 cookies. Make at least 2 days ahead.

1. Position the racks in lower and upper third of the oven and preheat to 350°F.

2. Toast the nuts in a shallow pan for 10 to 15 minutes on lower rack. Cool
completely. Coarsely chop. Set aside.

3. Reduce oven temperature to 300°F. Line 1 baking sheet with parchment
paper.

4. Place the flour, cocoa, baking soda, salt, and instant espresso powder, if
using, in a small bowl. Stir with a whisk to combine.

5. In a food processor fitted with the steel blade, process the chocolate
morsels with about a quarter of the flour mixture until the chocolate is reduced to
crumbs. Combine with remaining flour mixture. Set aside.

6. In a medium mixing bowl, beat the eggs and egg whites with the sugar,
vanilla, and almond extract, if using almonds, until well combined. Stir in the flour
mixture. Stir in the nuts. Mixture will be thick and sticky.

7. Use a large spoon to scoop batter onto the lined baking sheet, dividing it
evenly into 3 long skinny rope-shape loaves, each 12 inches long, or 2 loaves 16 to

17 inches long, depending on your baking sheet. Loaves must be at least 2½ inches apart. Use the back of the spoon or a spatula to even up the ropes of batter and neaten the edges.

8. Bake for 45 minutes on the lower rack. Remove from the oven and cool the loaves for 10 minutes on the pan. Leave the oven turned on.

9. Carefully peel the parchment from the loaves and remove them to a bread board. Use a sharp serrated knife to slice loaves into ½-inch slices. Arrange the slices on oven racks and bake for about 20 to 25 minutes, or until cookies are crisp and dry. Or arrange slices on 2 baking sheets and bake for 12 minutes, rotating sheets from top to bottom and back to front about halfway through. Turn cookies over and bake for additional 12 to 15 minutes, rotating sheets as before.

10. Cool biscotti completely, on racks, before storing. *Biscotti may be stored, airtight, for several weeks at room temperature.*

Notes

• Toasting slices directly on oven racks saves time and the trouble of turning them over.

• Biscotti stay crisp and dry but become tender after aging for a few days.

• Biscotti usually don't seem completely dry and crisp until they are cooled. After 20 minutes of toasting I remove a cookie and let it cool, while the rest continue to bake. I test the slice once it's cool. If it is dry and crisp, or nearly so, then I assume that the others are done. If in doubt, I test another slice, leaving the rest in a little longer.

• Traditional biscotti recipes use whole nuts, which, of course, end up getting cut when the loaves are sliced. In this lower-fat version fewer nuts are used—chopping the nuts just a little bit makes them go farther!

• Crushed Chocolate Biscotti (with or without the nuts) may be pressed against the sides of a cheesecake in place of a crust.

EQUIPMENT

2 LARGE HEAVY BAKING SHEETS OR
JELLY-ROLL PANS

NUTRITION INFORMATION

CALORIES PER COOKIE: 47

FAT: 1.5 G

% CALORIES FROM FAT: 27%

PROTEIN: 1.2 G

CARBOHYDRATES: 7.7 G

CHOLESTEROL: 7 MG

Chocolate Chip Biscotti

These are for my husband, Elliott, who usually hates biscotti. They taste like super-crunchy chocolate chip cookies. It was hard to keep him away from the canister, even though I was trying to see how many weeks they would keep.

WORK AND BAKE TIME:
1 HOUR 30 MINUTES

INGREDIENTS

2 CUPS SIFTED ALL-PURPOSE FLOUR
　(8 OUNCES)
1/2 TEASPOON BAKING SODA
1/4 TEASPOON SALT
2 EGGS
3/8 CUP SUGAR
3/8 CUP LIGHT BROWN SUGAR
1 TEASPOON VANILLA EXTRACT
1/2 CUP CHOPPED WALNUTS
　(2 OUNCES)
2/3 CUP SEMISWEET CHOCOLATE CHIPS

EQUIPMENT

LARGE HEAVY BAKING SHEET

NUTRITION INFORMATION

CALORIES PER COOKIE: 42
FAT: 1.5 G
% CALORIES FROM FAT: 30%
PROTEIN: .8 G
CARBOHYDRATES: 6.7 G
CHOLESTEROL: 7 MG

Makes 50 to 60 cookies. Make at least 2 days ahead.

1. Preheat the oven to 300°F. Line the baking sheet with parchment paper.

2. Place the flour, baking soda, and salt in a small bowl. Stir with a whisk to combine. Set aside.

3. In a medium mixing bowl, beat the eggs with the sugars and vanilla until well combined. Beat in the flour just until combined. Stir in the nuts and chocolate chips. Mixture will be thick and sticky.

4. Use a large spoon to scoop batter onto the baking sheet, dividing it evenly into 3 long skinny rope-shape loaves, each 12 inches long, or 2 loaves 16 to 17 inches long, depending on your baking sheet. Loaves must be at least 2½ inches apart. This will be a slightly messy process. Use the back of the spoon or a spatula to even up the ropes of batter and neaten the edges. Bake for 35 minutes. Remove from oven and cool loaves for 10 minutes on the pan. Leave the oven turned on.

5. Carefully peel the loaves from the parchment paper and remove them to a bread board. Use a sharp serrated knife to slice the loaves on the diagonal into ½-inch slices. Arrange the slices directly on the oven racks. Bake for 20 to 25 minutes, or until the cookies are crisp and dry. Or arrange the cookies on 2 baking sheets. Bake for 12 minutes, rotating the sheets from top to bottom and back to front about

halfway through the baking time. Turn cookies over and bake for 12 to 15 minutes, rotating sheets as before.

6. Cool biscotti completely on racks before stacking or storing. They become more tender after 2 or 3 days stored in an airtight container. *Biscotti may be stored, airtight, at room temperature for several weeks. They will remain dry and very crunchy.*

··

Double Chocolate "Mandelbrot"

This recipe is adapted from my great-aunt Martha Finkelstein's Mandelbrot. I wanted lots of chocolate so I eliminated the Mandel *(almond)! The Wondra flour makes these cookies very tender. These also have a sweeter chocolate flavor and more delicate texture than my Chocolate Biscotti, so despite apparent similarities, I cannot choose between them.*

Makes about 50 cookies.

1. Position oven racks in lower and upper third of the oven and preheat to 350°F. Line 1 baking sheet with aluminum foil.

2. Stir the flour, cocoa, and baking powder with a whisk to combine. Set aside.

3. Beat the eggs with the sugar and vanilla for 2 to 3 minutes until light and thickened. Beat in the oil, then the flour mixture. Stir in the chocolate chips.

4. Spoon or pour batter in 2 long strips the length of the pan. Batter will spread a little. Use a rubber spatula to neaten and separate the strips as much as possible. Bake for 25 minutes on the lower oven rack, turning the pan from front to back about halfway through the baking time. Remove and allow to cool for 5 to 10 minutes.

5. Turn oven down to 325°F.

6. Carefully peel away the foil. Remove loaves to a bread board and cut into ½-inch slices. Place the pieces on 2 baking sheets. Bake for 12 minutes, rotating baking sheets from top to bottom and front to back about halfway through the

WORK AND BAKE TIME:
1 HOUR 30 MINUTES

INGREDIENTS

1-3/4 CUPS WONDRA FLOUR

1/3 CUP UNSWEETENED DUTCH
PROCESS COCOA

1 TEASPOON BAKING POWDER

3 EGGS

1 CUP SUGAR

1 TEASPOON VANILLA EXTRACT

3 TABLESPOONS CORN OIL

1/3 CUP SEMISWEET CHOCOLATE
MORSELS

EQUIPMENT

HEAVY BAKING SHEETS OR
JELLY-ROLL PANS

baking time. Turn cookies over. Bake for 12 to 15 minutes, rotating sheets as before. Cool completely before storing. *Cookies may be stored, airtight, for several weeks at room temperature.*

Note

These cookies are more fragile than biscotti. If you handle them very carefully, you may bake the slices directly on oven racks as described on page 125, to save time.

Chocolate Hazelnut Meringues

My mother-in-law, Libby Medrich, is a sculptor who normally works in bronze. She occasionally switches to egg whites in order to make these cookies for us.

WORK TIME: 30 MINUTES
BAKE TIME: 2 HOURS
COOL TIME: 1 HOUR

INGREDIENTS

3 EGG WHITES, AT ROOM TEMPERATURE

1/8 TEASPOON CREAM OF TARTAR

1/2 TEASPOON VANILLA EXTRACT

2/3 CUP SUGAR

1/4 CUP SEMISWEET CHOCOLATE MINI MORSELS, OR REGULAR MORSELS, COARSELY CHOPPED

1/4 CUP CHOPPED TOASTED BLANCHED HAZELNUTS (PAGE 165) (1 OUNCE)

Makes 50 to 60 cookies.

1. Preheat oven temperature to 200° or 300° F. (See Note.) Position racks in the upper and lower third of the oven. Line baking sheets with parchment paper.

2. In a medium-large mixing bowl, combine the egg whites with the cream of tartar and vanilla. Beat at medium-high speed until soft peaks form. Add the sugar

slowly, about 1 tablespoon at a time, until all is added and the mixture is very stiff and glossy. Beat on high speed for several more seconds.

3. Use a large rubber spatula to fold in the chocolate chips and nuts. Drop by slightly rounded tablespoons at least 1 inch apart on the baking sheets. Bake for 2 hours at 200°F. Or bake at 300°F. for 30 minutes. Turn the oven off and leave the cookies in the oven for 1 hour or longer until perfectly dry and crisp. Cool cookies on a rack. *Cookies may be stored, airtight, for several weeks at room temperature.*

Note

Libby bakes her cookies at 300°F. for 30 minutes; I bake mine at 200°F. for 2 hours. Her cookies turn out slightly golden, which is nice. Mine remain pure white and are less fragile. Both are good.

EQUIPMENT

HEAVY BAKING SHEETS

NUTRITION INFORMATION

CALORIES PER COOKIE: 16

FAT: .6 G

% CALORIES FROM FAT: 30%

PROTEIN: 27 G

CARBOHYDRATES: 2.68 G

CHOLESTEROL: 0 MG

··

Chocolate Nut Logs

Crunchy and satisfying. These were "rediscovered" as cookies in photographer Michael Lamotte's studio as we nibbled the extra "fairy fingers" from the Chocolate Haystack (page 73).

Makes 50 to 60 cookies.

1. Position the racks in upper and lower third of the oven and preheat to 200°F. Line the baking sheets with parchment paper.

2. Combine ¼ cup of the sugar, the almonds, cocoa, and cornstarch in a food processor and process until mixture resembles a fine meal. Set aside.

3. Combine the egg whites, cream of tartar, vanilla, and almond extract in a medium mixing bowl. Beat at medium speed until soft peaks form. Gradually sprinkle in the remaining ½ cup sugar, beating on high speed until very stiff but not dry.

4. Fold dry ingredients into meringue with a large rubber spatula. Scrape the mixture into a pastry bag. Pipe logs 2½ to 3 inches thick or pipe long straight strips of meringue from edge to edge across the length or width of the baking sheets.

WORK TIME: 20 MINUTES
BAKE TIME: 1 HOUR 30 MINUTES
COOL TIME: 1 HOUR

INGREDIENTS

3/4 CUP SUGAR, PREFERABLY FINE
    GRANULATED OR SUPERFINE

1/2 CUP PLUS 2 TABLESPOONS
    ALMONDS (3 OUNCES)

3 TABLESPOONS UNSWEETENED
    DUTCH PROCESS COCOA

4 TEASPOONS CORNSTARCH

1/2 CUP EGG WHITES, AT ROOM
    TEMPERATURE (3 TO 4)

1/4 TEASPOON CREAM OF TARTAR
1 TEASPOON VANILLA EXTRACT
1/8 TEASPOON ALMOND EXTRACT

EQUIPMENT

2 HEAVY BAKING SHEETS
PASTRY BAG FITTED WITH AN OPEN
   STAR TIP (ATECO #7)

NUTRITION INFORMATION

CALORIES PER COOKIE: 20
FAT: .8 G
% CALORIES FROM FAT: 33%
PROTEIN: .5 G
CARBOHYDRATES: 3.1 G
CHOLESTEROL: 0 MG

Leave about ½ inch between each length. Use up all of the meringue.

5. Bake for 1½ hours. Turn the oven off and allow meringue to cool in the oven for at least 1 hour. Cool completely before using or storing. If you have piped long strips, break them into pieces about 2½ to 3 inches long. *Chocolate Nut Logs may be stored, airtight, for several weeks at room temperature.*

Note

If your pastry bag tip is a closed star (with the metal points bent inward), nut granules will clog the tip and ruin your piping. To transform a closed star tip into an open star tip, straighten the metal points by bending each one with your fingers or by pushing a wooden spoon handle through the tip. Or simply make the cookies with a plain round tip with a ⅝-inch opening.

VARIATION
....

Substitute pecans, walnuts, or hazelnuts for the almonds. Omit the almond extract.

....

Faux Florentines

These fanciful fakes were inspired by Maida Heatter's wonderful crisp Oatmeal Wafers. Caramelized and fragrant with orange, they fool the palate. Are those rolled oats or almonds? The bittersweet chocolate is pure indulgence; the cookies are also excellent—and much leaner—without it. In a hurry? Try the Faster Faux variation that follows.

WORK AND BAKE TIME:
60 MINUTES

Makes 45 to 50 cookies. Best eaten within 2 days.

1. Position the racks in upper and lower third of the oven and preheat to 350˚ F. Line the cookie sheets with parchment paper or aluminum foil, even if they are nonstick.

2. In a medium mixing bowl, beat the eggs with the sugars, extracts, zest, and salt at high speed until very thick and light, about 3 minutes. Beat in the melted butter, then the baking powder, just until mixed. Stir in the oatmeal and candied orange peel.

3. Drop level teaspoons of batter about 2 inches apart on baking sheets. Bake for about 10 to 12 minutes, or until cookies are dark brown all over. Rotate pans from top to bottom and front to back halfway through and watch carefully to avoid burning. When cookies are done, slide paper liners onto the counter to cool for a few minutes until cookies can be peeled easily from the paper. Cool cookies completely on a rack before stacking, storing, or filling.

4. Melt the chocolate in a heatproof bowl placed in a pan of barely simmering water, stirring frequently, until almost melted. Remove from the heat and continue to stir until melted and smooth. Or microwave on Medium (50% power) for about 2½ to 3 minutes, stirring twice. Use a small plastic zipper bag as a disposable pastry bag. Scrape the melted chocolate into a corner of the bag, twist the bag, and cut off the tip of the corner to make a tiny opening. Pipe a random drizzle or crosshatch over the top of all of the cookies. *Store airtight until serving to retain crispness. Cookies may be frozen for up to 2 months.*

INGREDIENTS

3 EGGS

3/4 CUP SUGAR

3/4 CUP LIGHT BROWN SUGAR

3/4 TEASPOON VANILLA EXTRACT

1/8 TEASPOON ALMOND EXTRACT

FINELY GRATED ZEST OF 1 ORANGE

1/2 TEASPOON SALT

2 TABLESPOONS UNSALTED BUTTER, MELTED

4 TEASPOONS BAKING POWDER, STRAINED IF LUMPY

3-1/2 CUPS OATMEAL, PREFERABLY QUAKER OLD-FASHIONED, NOT INSTANT

3/4 CUP DICED CANDIED ORANGE PEEL (PAGE 175)

6 OUNCES BITTERSWEET CHOCOLATE, CUT INTO TINY PIECES

EQUIPMENT

BAKING SHEETS

NUTRITION INFORMATION

CALORIES PER COOKIE: 77

FAT: 2.3 G

% CALORIES FROM FAT: 26%

PROTEIN: 1.5 G

CARBOHYDRATES: 13.5 G

CHOLESTEROL: 14 MG

VARIATIONS

....

Faux Florentine Sandwich Cookies: Drop batter by level half teaspoons. Bake and cool. Spread melted chocolate on the back of half of the cookies and sandwich them with the remaining cookies.

Faster Faux Florentines: Add 1 cup (6 ounces) semisweet chocolate chips to the batter with the candied peel. Omit the bittersweet chocolate and eliminate Step 4. Less dressy but very yummy and fast.

Beryl's Walnut Truffle Cookies

My friend Beryl Radin asked one day about the little puddles of batter on my cookie sheets. I told her they were a mistake but I was planning to bake them anyhow, just in case they turned into something. Indeed, they were delicious baked but somehow incomplete. Beryl said, "Sandwich them with something and eat them frozen." They are wonderful.

WORK AND BAKE TIME:
   2 HOURS 30 MINUTES
FREEZE TIME:
   4 HOURS PLUS OVERNIGHT

INGREDIENTS

1-1/2 CUPS SUGAR

1 CUP PLUS 2 TABLESPOONS CHOPPED
   WALNUTS (4-1/2 OUNCES)

1/3 CUP UNSWEETENED DUTCH
   PROCESS COCOA

2 TEASPOONS INSTANT ESPRESSO
   OR COFFEE POWDER

1 TABLESPOON PLUS 1 TEASPOON
   BRANDY

3 EGG WHITES

2 CUPS (1/2 RECIPE) BITTERSWEET
   CHOCOLATE TRUFFLE MOUSSE (PAGE
   142), MADE AND FROZEN AT LEAST
   4 HOURS IN ADVANCE

COCOA, FOR DUSTING (OPTIONAL)

EQUIPMENT

HEAVY BAKING SHEETS

NUTRITION INFORMATION

CALORIES PER COOKIE: 54

FAT: 2.1 G

% CALORIES FROM FAT: 33%

PROTEIN: 1 G

CARBOHYDRATES: 8.7 G

CHOLESTEROL: 3.96 MG

Makes 50 to 55 cookies. Make at least 1 day ahead.

   1. Position the racks in the lower and upper third of the oven and preheat to 300°F. Line the baking sheets with parchment paper.

   2. Combine the sugar, walnuts, cocoa, espresso powder, and brandy in a food processor and process until fine. With the motor running, slowly add just enough egg white to form a thick sticky mixture that flows slowly from a spatula.

   3. Drop the batter by the scant level teaspoon about 2 inches apart on baking sheets. Bake for 15 to 18 minutes, rotating pans from back to front and top to bottom about halfway through. Cookies will puff and crackle slightly. Cool sheets on a rack. When cookies are completely cool, carefully peel away the parchment paper. *Cookies may be completed to this point and stored, airtight, for up to 2 days before using.*

   4. Assemble cookies. Sort and pair up cookies of similar size and shape. Using a melon baller or miniature ice cream scoop dipped in hot water and wiped dry, scoop up about ¾-inch balls of frozen truffle mixture. Sandwich the scoop between 2 cookies and press together gently. Repeat to form sandwiches of the remaining cookies. Remember to dip the scoop in hot water and blot it dry between each scoop. Try not to get chocolatey fingerprints on the surface of the cookies. Freeze the sandwiches in an airtight container until serving. *Truffle cookie sandwiches may be frozen for up to 2 months (less any extended period that you may have kept the truffle mixture already frozen).*

5. To serve: Sieve cocoa lightly over sandwiches, if desired. Place each in a fluted paper candy cup. Serve immediately.

....

Michael's Fudge Brownies

I think it's pretty nervy to call something a brownie unless it's darn chocolatey and just a little gooey inside. That should tell you how good these are. One of the great pediatric nurses at Cedars-Sinai Medical Center in Los Angeles decided that a little boy who had undergone a liver transplant and couldn't tolerate fat should still have a great birthday cake. Since she is married to my brother, Michael, and he is the chief baker at their house, he called me late one night to ask if I had a good low-fat recipe. Now the medical staff is hooked and these are known as "Michael's Brownies"—which is also pretty nervy.

WORK TIME: 15 MINUTES
BAKE TIME: 20–25 MINUTES

INGREDIENTS

1 CUP SIFTED ALL-PURPOSE FLOUR
(4 OUNCES)
1/2 CUP PLUS 1/2 TABLESPOON
UNSWEETENED DUTCH PROCESS
COCOA
1/4 TEASPOON SALT
1/4 TEASPOON BAKING POWDER
5 TABLESPOONS BUTTER OR STICK
MARGARINE
1-1/4 CUPS SUGAR

1 EGG

2 EGG WHITES

1 TEASPOON VANILLA EXTRACT

1 TEASPOON INSTANT ESPRESSO
   OR COFFEE POWDER, DISSOLVED
   IN 1 TEASPOON HOT WATER

EQUIPMENT

8-INCH SQUARE PAN

NUTRITION INFORMATION

CALORIES PER BROWNIE: 134

FAT: 4.6 G

% CALORIES FROM FAT: 29%

PROTEIN: 2.2 G

CARBOHYDRATES: 22.8 G

CHOLESTEROL: 23 MG

Makes sixteen 2-inch brownies.

1. Position the rack in lower third of the oven and preheat to 350°F. (325°F. if using a glass pan). Spray the pan with vegetable oil spray.

2. Stir together the flour, cocoa, salt, and baking powder with a whisk. Set aside.

3. Melt the butter in a medium saucepan. Off the heat, stir in the sugar until combined (texture will remain sandy). Add the egg, egg whites, vanilla, and dissolved espresso powder. Beat with a wooden spoon about 40 strokes, scraping the sides of the pan as necessary. Add the dry ingredients and beat for another 40 strokes, or just until completely mixed.

4. Scrape mixture into prepared pan. Spread evenly. Bake for 20 to 25 minutes, or until a toothpick inserted into the center comes out a little gooey. Cool on a rack. Cut into 16 squares. *Brownies may be stored, well wrapped, for about 2 days at room temperature or frozen for up to 2 months.*

Note

I originally did this recipe with a handheld mixer, and that works fine also. Just don't overdo the mixing.

···

Lemon Bars

Traditionally the tart/sweet lemon topping rests on a crumbly buttery shortbread base. Sometimes, despite the quantity of lemon, the bars can be too sweet. Mine sit on a crunchy cornmeal cookie crust and the lemon topping is almost puckery—just the way I like them.

WORK AND BAKE TIME: 1 HOUR

Makes sixteen 2-inch squares. Best served the same day.

1. Position the rack in lower third of the oven and preheat to 350°F. Spray pan lightly with vegetable oil spray.

2. Make the crust. Stir the ¾ cup of flour, the cornmeal, salt, and baking soda together with a whisk to combine. Set aside. In a medium mixing bowl, beat the butter until creamy. Add ⅓ cup of the sugar and beat at high speed for about 1 minute, or until mixture begins to form a mass. Beat in the egg yolk, yogurt, and vanilla. Add the dry ingredients and beat on low speed just until combined. Scrape bowl and beater. Knead the mixture briefly with your hands to mix thoroughly.

3. Press the dough evenly into the pan and prick all over with a skewer or fork. If pan is lightweight, place on baking sheet. Bake until brown on top, 20 to 25 minutes.

4. Make the topping. Whisk eggs and the egg white with the remaining sugar until combined. Whisk in the lemon juice and zest. Whisk in the ¼ cup of flour. When crust is brown, turn oven temperature down to 300˚F. Pour topping mixture over hot crust and bake for 15 to 20 minutes, or until topping barely jiggles in the center when you shake the pan gently back and forth. Cool on a rack. Chill before cutting into squares.

5. Serve cold or at room temperature (I like them cold) dusted with powdered sugar. *Bars may be stored in the refrigerator for 2 or 3 days. Do not freeze.*

INGREDIENTS

3/4 CUP SIFTED ALL-PURPOSE FLOUR
   (3 OUNCES)
1/4 CUP YELLOW CORNMEAL
PINCH OF SALT
1/8 TEASPOON BAKING SODA
2 TABLESPOONS UNSALTED BUTTER,
   AT ROOM TEMPERATURE
1 CUP SUGAR
1 EGG, SEPARATED
1 TABLESPOON NONFAT YOGURT
1/4 TEASPOON VANILLA EXTRACT
2 EGGS
1/2 CUP STRAINED LEMON JUICE
GRATED ZEST OF 1 LARGE LEMON
1/4 CUP ALL-PURPOSE FLOUR
POWDERED SUGAR, FOR DUSTING

EQUIPMENT

8-INCH SQUARE PAN
BAKING SHEET (OPTIONAL)

NUTRITION INFORMATION

CALORIES PER BAR: 121
FAT: 2.5 G
% CALORIES FROM FAT: 18%
PROTEIN: 2.4 G
CARBOHYDRATES: 22.6 G
CHOLESTEROL: 43.6 MG

The New Basics

....

These are the sponge cakes,
pastry, mousses, fillings, layers,
frostings, sauces, and
garnishes from which dozens of
desserts can be made. A few
are simply classics, lightened
just a little. Others are
considerably revised, brand-new
ideas, even breakthrough
concepts such as Safe Meringue
and New Tart Crust. You
will use them over and over
again in my recipes. And,
ultimately, you will build your
own repertoire of new desserts
from these New Basics.

SAFE MERINGUE

Concern about salmonella poisoning from raw eggs has been especially problematic for those of us who make dessert. Many of the world's greatest desserts include uncooked or partially cooked egg yolks and/or egg whites. Fabulous mousses and Bavarian creams, silky fillings, even chocolate truffles, not to mention soft meringue pie toppings, baked Alaska, and frozen ice creams and parfaits are all victims of the Raw Egg Taboo. We may be personally willing to take our chances on eating some of these delicacies, but conscience dictates that I not disseminate recipes that include raw or partially cooked eggs.

I hated the idea of giving up my favorite traditional recipes because of egg safety. I also knew that meringue could play an important role in new desserts with less fat because meringue can be used both to stretch or replace part of the cream in a recipe and to add lightness, volume, and creaminess without adding fat. Meringue is too valuable an element in dessert making to give up without a fight.

We know that salmonella bacteria are destroyed when eggs (whites or yolks) are either heated to a temperature of 140°F. and held at that temperature for at least five minutes or heated to 160°F. The challenge is to heat the eggs without scrambling them and to incorporate them into a recipe without diminishing the quality of the dessert.

Revising older recipes so that they are safe can be done, but it is not always straightforward. It is often possible to bring whole eggs or egg yolks to the safe temperature of 160°F. by heating them with other liquids in the recipe. Indeed, I have done this in all of the recipes in this book. Egg whites, though, are another story!

Egg whites are usually incorporated into dessert recipes in the form of uncooked meringue. Many chefs have responded to the raw egg challenge by converting uncooked meringue to Italian meringue. To make Italian meringue, the sugar is made into a syrup and cooked to 242°F. before it is beaten into the egg whites. If there is enough syrup (and it takes a lot) the egg whites will be heated to a safe 160°F. The problem is that many recipes don't have enough sugar to make a syrup, or they have only enough to make a little bit of syrup— not enough to heat the whites to 160°F. Many recipes using the Italian meringue technique are still not safe because of this. In addition, many home dessert makers are wary of sugar syrups, fearful of sugar crystallization, and uncomfortable with the tricky timing and thermometers involved. Even I don't like making Italian meringue.

I wanted a simpler and more reliable method than Italian meringue. I used up hundreds of egg whites trying to precook them before beating. I tried over and over to heat the egg whites on a stove burner and in a double boiler, stirring furiously. I was never able to heat them sufficiently without scrambling them. Ultimately, inspired by Harold McGee's experiments with egg yolks and hollandaise sauce, I realized that I could

successfully heat egg whites if I first combined them with the sugar and cream of tartar, which are normally beaten in later, plus a little water. These simple additions prevent the egg whites from coagulating (scrambling) until they are much hotter than 160°F. At first I devised an elaborate way of doing this in the microwave oven—it worked, but it was complicated enough to intimidate even my best friends. I finally realized that having cracked the concept of combining the egg whites with sugar, cream of tartar, and water first, I could simply heat the mixture on the stove in a hot water bath while stirring briskly. I was excited to have found a more reliable alternative than Italian meringue and one that was so easy to do.

My new and simpler method for Safe Meringue is incorporated into each recipe where it applies. I include the following recipe for making Safe Meringue separately, with two egg whites, in order to explain the procedure more fully.

THE NEW SAFE MERINGUE

INGREDIENTS

2 TEASPOONS WATER

1/8 TEASPOON CREAM OF TARTAR

2 EGG WHITES

4 TABLESPOONS SUGAR (SEE NOTES)

EQUIPMENT

INSTANT-READ THERMOMETER

Work time: 7 minutes

1. Bring 1 inch of water to a gentle simmer in a large skillet. Combine the 2 teaspoons water with the cream of tartar in a 4- to 6-cup stainless steel bowl. Add the egg whites and sugar and whisk together briskly to combine ingredients thoroughly and break up the egg white clots (which have a tendency to scramble first). Place thermometer near the stove in a mug of very hot tap water.

2. Set bowl of egg whites in skillet. Stir mixture briskly and constantly with a rubber spatula, scraping the sides and bottom often to avoid scrambling the whites. After 1 minute, remove bowl from skillet. Quickly insert thermometer, tilting bowl to cover stem by at least 2 inches. If less than 160°F., rinse thermometer in skillet water and return it to mug. Replace bowl in skillet. Stir as before until temperature reaches 160°F. when bowl is removed. Beat on high speed until cool and stiff.

Notes

• Safe Meringue can be made with a minimum of 1 tablespoon sugar per egg white rather than the 2 tablespoons per white in this recipe. It takes 25 to 30 percent less time to reach 160°F. and you need to be extra careful to avoid overcooking. The greater ratio of sugar adds greater protection from scrambling and yields a stabler, stiffer, smoother, and creamier meringue. You may even use up to ¼ cup sugar per egg white, should your recipe call for it.

• Egg whites will scramble if you heat them too long or let them get much hotter than 175°F. or if you do not stir briskly and constantly during the heating process. You need to stir very briskly with a rubber spatula instead of whisking or beating with a whisk during the heating process because excess foam scrambles easily at low temperatures. Overcooked whites will not beat up to a stiff meringue.

• A stainless steel bowl heats up quickly and shortens the time it takes to heat the whites. If you use a glass or crockery bowl, it will take a little longer.

• Safe Meringue is firmer and less easily deflated than ordinary meringue. This dictates a slight change in the conventional procedure for folding meringue together with another mixture such as a mousse base, which is often fairly loose or semiliquid. Rather than folding a small amount of the meringue into the mousse base first, reverse the procedure: Fold a small quantity of the mousse base into the meringue to loosen the meringue before folding everything together.

• Safe Meringue is relatively foolproof. It produces a consistently stiff and voluminous meringue unlike conventional meringue where volume and stiffness depend on knowing when and how fast to add the sugar and having the egg whites at room temperature before beating.

• Safe Meringue is great for baked meringues too. Heating egg whites with sugar makes such a beautifully stable and foolproof meringue that I sometimes do it even in recipes where the meringue will be baked anyway, such as meringue baskets, meringue mushrooms, decorations, etc. Just combine egg whites with cream of tartar and sugar (water is unnecessary) and heat, as described, but only until whites are nice and warm to the touch (160°F. is not necessary when meringue is thoroughly baked afterwards). Beat until stiff and shape according to the recipe. This method is convenient because the meringue stays stiff much longer than ordinary meringue, giving you plenty of time to pipe perfect shapes.

• You can also fold Safe Meringue into whipped cream to stretch it, fold Safe Meringue into stiff pastry cream to make a softer, creamier, and lighter custard filling, and replace all or part of the whipped cream in mousse recipes with Safe Meringue.

• Safe Meringue can be used in place of ordinary meringue in old recipes. These include uncooked desserts such as mousse, Bavarian cream, and ice cream as well as soft meringues for pie topping and baked Alaska where a short baking or browning period may not be enough to heat the meringue thoroughly.

To convert an old recipe: Use the amount of sugar that would normally have been beaten into the raw egg whites and/or borrow sugar from elsewhere in the recipe. If possible, try to use at least 2 tablespoons sugar per egg white. Mousses and Bavarian creams other than chocolate usually have plenty of sugar to work with so there is no problem. If your favorite chocolate mousse recipe does not have enough sugar to meet the minimum 1 tablespoon sugar per egg white, much less 2 tablespoons, you will have to fudge a little. If the recipe has 3 egg whites and only 2 tablespoons of sugar, chances are that adding 1 more (or even 2) tablespoons won't hurt. If you usually use semisweet chocolate, you might switch to bittersweet to offset the added sugar. Another approach is to substitute a small quantity of unsweetened chocolate for a little of the semisweet and then go ahead and add some additional sugar to your egg whites. A little playing around usually solves the problem.

OLD-FASHIONED UNCOOKED MERINGUE

If eggs are known to be safe in your area and you wish to substitute traditional uncooked meringue for Safe Meringue in one of my recipes, proceed as follows. Use the same quantities of egg whites, cream of tartar, and sugar as for Safe Meringue but omit the water. Combine the whites, at room temperature, with the cream of tartar in a clean and dry mixer bowl. Beat at medium speed until soft peaks form. Sprinkle sugar in gradually, continuing to beat at high speed until meringue is stiff but not dry. Use in place of Safe Meringue.

THE NEW PASTRY CREAMS

Pastry cream, or starch-thickened vanilla custard, is a staple of the classic dessert repertoire. It is used under fresh or cooked fruit in tarts; it fills cakes, napoleons and eclairs; it combines with butter to make buttercreams; and it is folded into whipped cream on numerous occasions. The New Pastry Cream is lightened up just a tad. I eliminated one quarter of the fat and lowered the percentage of calories from fat from 34 percent (or more) to 25 percent by using low-fat milk in place of whole milk (or cream!) and a mixture of yolks and whites in place of the traditional yolks-only. The New Pastry Cream is excellent and rich tasting with as many uses as ever.

For lighter desserts, I pair pastry creams with phyllo pastry and with my New Tart Crust. I make dressier layered desserts by alternating pastry cream with chocolate mousse between layers of sponge cake, Genoise, or Ladyfingers. You will yourself trying your own variations on all of these recipes in addition to your own.

◎ ◎ ◎

VANILLA PASTRY CREAM

The recipe for Vanilla Pastry Cream is followed by bittersweet chocolate and cocoa variations. The latter is lower in fat than the chocolate but delectably dark and richer in color; the former is richer in flavor but paler in color. Pastry cream may also be flavored to taste with instant coffee powder, orange or lemon zest, liqueurs, or crushed caramelized nuts.

INGREDIENTS

3 TABLESPOONS SUGAR
4 TEASPOONS FLOUR
4 TEASPOONS CORNSTARCH
1 WHOLE EGG
1 EGG YOLK
1 CUP LOW-FAT (1%) MILK
3/4 TEASPOON VANILLA EXTRACT

NUTRITION INFORMATION

CALORIES PER 1/3 CUP: 115
FAT: 3.2 G
% CALORIES FROM FAT: 25%
PROTEIN: 4.7 G
CARBOHYDRATES: 17 G
CHOLESTEROL: 108.5 MG

MAKES ABOUT 1-1/3 CUPS, ENOUGH FOR TWO 9-1/2-INCH FRUIT TARTS, OR ONLY ONE IF YOU LOVE CUSTARD

Work time: 10 minutes

1. Combine the sugar, flour, and cornstarch in a small bowl. Add the egg and egg yolk and beat with a handheld mixer until mixture is pale and thick, 1 to 2 minutes. Set aside.

2. Scald the milk in a medium nonreactive saucepan. Pour hot milk gradually over yolk mixture, whisking constantly until all of the milk is added.

3. Return mixture to saucepan and cook on medium heat, stirring constantly with a whisk, reaching all over the bottom and sides of the pan, until custard thickens considerably. Continue to cook and whisk for 30 to 45 seconds more. Scrape custard into a clean bowl. Whisk in the vanilla. Cool. Cover and refrigerate. *Custard may be refrigerated for up to 2 days.*

CHOCOLATE PASTRY CREAM

MAKES 1-2/3 CUPS

Proceed as for Vanilla Pastry Cream. Stir 4 ounces of bittersweet or semisweet chocolate, chopped medium fine, into hot Vanilla Pastry Cream with the vanilla in Step 3. Stir until chocolate is melted and mixture is smooth. *Custard may be refrigerated for up to 2 days.*

COCOA PASTRY CREAM

MAKES 1-1/2 CUPS

Complete Step 1 as for Vanilla Pastry Cream. In Step 2, combine ¼ cup cocoa with ¼ cup additional sugar in a small nonreactive saucepan. Whisk in just enough of the milk to form a smooth paste. Stir in the remaining milk. Scald milk mixture over medium heat. Pour it gradually over the yolk mixture, whisking constantly until all of the milk is added. Complete Step 3 as for Vanilla Pastry Cream. *Custard may be refrigerated for up to 2 days.*

LEMON CURD

Here is a very tart and tangy lemon cream that I use under fresh fruit in tarts and tartlets and to marble into or spread on top of cheesecake. You'll find yourself using it to replace the more traditional curd that's laden with butter and egg yolk: Spread it on toast, roll it up in a sponge cake jelly roll, sandwich it between cookies, use it as a cake filling.

INGREDIENTS

GRATED ZEST OF 1/2 LEMON
1/3 CUP STRAINED LEMON JUICE
5 TABLESPOONS SUGAR
1 EGG
1/2 TEASPOON VANILLA EXTRACT

NUTRITION INFORMATION

CALORIES PER 1/3 CUP: 168
FAT: 2.51 G
% CALORIES FROM FAT: 13%
PROTEIN: 3.3 G
CARBOHYDRATES: 35.2 G
CHOLESTEROL: 106 MG

MAKES 2/3 CUP

Work time: 15 minutes

1. Combine the lemon zest, juice, and sugar in a small saucepan and bring to a simmer. In a small bowl, beat the egg until light.

2. Beat some of the hot lemon mixture into the egg. Scrape the egg mixture back into the saucepan. Cook, stirring constantly and reaching all over the bottom and sides of the pan, until the mixture barely starts to simmer around the edges. Continue to cook and stir for about 15 seconds. Pour through a strainer set over the bowl. Stir in the vanilla. Cool. *Lemon Curd may be refrigerated, covered, for at least 1 week.*

THE NEW MOUSSES

Mousse is French for foam, but the best mousses are creamy and flavorful as well as foamy. In low-fat mousses the challenge is to find the right balance of creaminess, foam, and depth of flavor. And, of course, the mixture must set without seeming rubbery or like Jello-O. In place of the usual heavy cream, Safe Meringue (page 138) provides foam and some creaminess. I like rich mousses best, so with the exception of Lemon Mousse, the mousses in this collection are all chocolate. Chocolate does triple duty by supplying flavor, rich texture, and some stiffening. Judicial amounts of gelatin are also used except in Bittersweet Chocolate Meringue Mousse, which contains enough chocolate to set on its own. The substantial amount of fat (cocoa butter) in chocolate dictates that we use no egg yolks, cream, or butter in mousses made entirely of chocolate rather than cocoa. This is how we balance the fat budget!

You can serve mousses in pretty glasses with a spoon or use them to create myriad desserts by substituting one mousse for another as in Lemon Mousse Cake, Mocha Raspberry Charlotte, and Chocolate Grand Marnier Cake. And since mousses often seem even richer when frozen, they are included in frozen desserts such as Bittersweet Chocolate Marquise, Mocha Bûche de Noël, Triple Mousse Celebration Cake, and even Bittersweet Chocolate Truffles.

BITTERSWEET CHOCOLATE TRUFFLE MOUSSE

This will become an important part of your new repertoire. It is very chocolatey and satisfying to eat simply from a dish with a spoon. You will find it throughout this book used as a filling, served as a frozen dessert, or made into truffles.

INGREDIENTS

1-3/4 TEASPOONS GELATIN
2 EGGS, SEPARATED
1/2 CUP UNSWEETENED DUTCH PROCESS COCOA
1/2 CUP PLUS 1/3 CUP SUGAR
1-1/4 CUPS LOW-FAT (1%) MILK
4 OUNCES BITTERSWEET OR SEMISWEET CHOCOLATE, CHOPPED FINE
1 TEASPOON VANILLA EXTRACT
1/8 TEASPOON CREAM OF TARTAR

EQUIPMENT

INSTANT-READ THERMOMETER
6 TO 8 INDIVIDUAL DESSERT GLASSES OR
5- TO 6-CUP SERVING BOWL

NUTRITION INFORMATION

CALORIES PER SERVING: 203
FAT: 7.7 G
% CALORIES FROM FAT: 31%
PROTEIN: 5.3 G
CARBOHYDRATES: 33.6 G
CHOLESTEROL: 54.5 MG

**MAKES ABOUT 4 CUPS,
ENOUGH TO SERVE 6 TO 8**

Work time: 45 minutes
Chill time: at least 4 hours

1. Sprinkle the gelatin over ¼ cup cold water in a small cup. Let stand, without stir-ring, for at least 5 minutes, or until needed.

2. Place egg yolks in a medium to large bowl near the stove and have ready a small whisk. Combine the cocoa with ⅓ cup of sugar in a 1- to 1½-quart saucepan. Stir in enough milk to form a paste. Stir in the remaining milk. Bring mixture to a simmer over medium heat, stirring frequently with a wooden spoon, reaching all over the bottom and sides of the pan to prevent scorching. Stir the chocolate mixture continuously once it begins to simmer. Simmer gently, stirring, for about 1½ minutes.

3. Remove from the heat and whisk a small amount of the hot mixture into the egg yolks. Scrape the mixture back into the pot and whisk well to combine. It will be hot enough to be safe. It will thicken without further cooking. Stir in the softened gelatin, chopped chocolate, and vanilla. Let stand a minute or so and whisk again until chocolate is completely melted and the mixture is perfectly smooth.

4. Set the saucepan in a large bowl of ice water to cool and thicken. Stir and scrape the sides from time to time. If mixture begins to set before needed, remove from ice bath, whisk and set aside. Should mixture actually set, place the pan in a bowl of hot water and stir just until resoftened.

5. **Make the safe meringue.** Bring 1 inch of water to a simmer in a large skillet. Combine cream of tartar and 2 teaspoons of water in a 4- to 6-cup stainless steel bowl. Whisk in the egg whites and ½ cup of sugar. Place thermometer near stove in a mug of very hot tap water. Set bowl in skillet. Stir mixture briskly and constantly with a rubber

spatial, scraping the sides and bottom often to avoid scrambling the whites. After 1 minute, remove bowl from skillet. Quickly insert thermometer, tilting bowl to cover stem by at least 2 inches. If less than 160°F., rinse thermometer in skillet water and return it to mug. Replace bowl in skillet. Stir as before until temperature reaches 160°F. when bowl is removed. Beat on high speed until cool and stiff. (For more details on safe meringue, see pages 138–140.)

5. Fold about a quarter of the cooled chocolate mixture into the beaten egg whites. Scrape egg white mixture back into the remaining chocolate mixture. Fold to combine. Scrape mixture into dessert glasses or a serving bowl, cover, and refrigerate for at least 4 hours, or until set. Or use immediately to finish another dessert. *Mousse may be refrigerated, covered, for up to 1 day.*

Note

For an even more bittersweet mousse, use only ⅓ cup sugar in Step 4.

BITTERSWEET CHOCOLATE MERINGUE MOUSSE

This alternative to Bittersweet Chocolate Truffle Mousse is simpler to make, contains no gelatin, and takes its flavor from bittersweet and unsweetened chocolates rather than cocoa. Eat it with a spoon or include it in another dessert.

INGREDIENTS

1 TEASPOON INSTANT ESPRESSO
OR COFFEE POWDER
1 OUNCE UNSWEETENED CHOCOLATE,
CHOPPED FINE
4 OUNCES BITTERSWEET OR SEMISWEET
CHOCOLATE, CHOPPED FINE
SCANT 3/8 TEASPOON CREAM OF TARTAR
5 EGG WHITES
10 TABLESPOONS SUGAR
1 TEASPOON VANILLA EXTRACT

EQUIPMENT

INSTANT-READ THERMOMETER

NUTRITION INFORMATION

CALORIES PER SERVING: 127
FAT: 5.4 G
% CALORIES FROM FAT: 35%
PROTEIN: 2.8 G
CARBOHYDRATES: 19.7 G
CHOLESTEROL: 0 MG

MAKES ABOUT 5 CUPS, ENOUGH TO SERVE 8 TO 10

Work time: 20 minutes
Chill time: at least 4 hours

1. In a small heatproof bowl, dissolve the espresso powder in 5 tablespoons of water. Add all the chocolate and vanilla. Set the bowl in a pan of barely simmering water and stir frequently until chocolate is melted and smooth. Or microwave on Medium (50% power) for about 1 minute 15 seconds. Stir until smooth.

2. Make the safe meringue. Bring 1 inch of water to a simmer in a large skillet. Combine the cream of tartar and 5 teaspoons of water in a 6- to 8-cup stainless steel bowl. Whisk in the egg whites and the sugar. Place thermometer near stove in a mug of very hot tap water. Set bowl in skillet. Stir mixture

briskly and constantly with a rubber spatula, scraping the sides and bottom often to avoid scrambling the whites. After 2 minutes, remove bowl from skillet. Quickly insert thermometer, tilting bowl to cover stem by at least 2 inches. If less than 160°F., rinse thermometer in skillet water and return it to mug. Replace bowl in skillet. Stir as before until temperature reaches 160°F. when bowl is removed. Beat on high speed until cool and stiff. (For more details on safe meringue, see pages 138–140.)

3. Fold about a quarter of the meringue into the chocolate mixture. Fold in the remaining meringue and use immediately to complete another dessert, or scrape into serving dishes. Cover and refrigerate for at least 4 hours, or until set. *Mousse may be refrigerated, covered, for up to 1 day.*

MOCHA MOUSSE

A little cream cheese and milk chocolate make a creamy mocha-flavored mousse suitable for eating with a spoon or filling a more elaborate dessert.

INGREDIENTS

1-3/4 TEASPOONS GELATIN
4 EGG WHITES
1/4 CUP UNSWEETENED DUTCH PROCESS COCOA
2-1/2 TEASPOONS INSTANT ESPRESSO
OR COFFEE POWDER
10 TABLESPOONS SUGAR
1-1/4 CUPS LOW-FAT (1%) MILK
4 OUNCES MILK CHOCOLATE, CHOPPED FINE
2 OUNCES LIGHT CREAM CHEESE
1/8 TEASPOON CREAM OF TARTAR

EQUIPMENT

INSTANT-READ THERMOMETER

NUTRITION INFORMATION

CALORIES PER SERVING: 187

FAT: 7 G

% CALORIES FROM FAT: 32%

PROTEIN: 6.2 G

CARBOHYDRATES: 27.5 G

CHOLESTEROL: 9.4 MG

**MAKES ABOUT 4 CUPS, ENOUGH
TO SERVE 6 TO 8**

Work time: 45 minutes

Chill time: at least 4 hours

1. Sprinkle the gelatin over ¼ cup cold water in a small cup. Let stand, without stirring, at least 5 minutes, or until needed. Place two of the egg whites in a small bowl near the stove and have ready a small whisk.

2. Combine the cocoa with the espresso powder and 4 tablespoons of the sugar in a small saucepan. Stir in enough milk to form a paste. Stir in the remaining milk. Bring mixture to a simmer over medium heat, stirring frequently with a wooden spoon, reaching all over the bottom and sides of the pan to prevent scorching. Stir the chocolate mixture constantly once it begins to simmer. Simmer gently, stirring, for about 1½ minutes.

3. Remove from the heat and whisk a small amount of the hot mixture into the egg whites. Scrape the mixture back into the pot and whisk well to combine. It will be hot enough to be safe. It will thicken without further cooking. Stir in the softened gelatin and chopped chocolate. Let stand a minute or so and whisk again until chocolate is completely melted and mixture is perfectly smooth.

4. Microwave the cream cheese on High for about 10 seconds, or until smooth and creamy. Stir a small amount of the chocolate mixture into the cheese, just until combined. Add the mixture to the remaining chocolate and whisk until combined.

5. Set the saucepan in a large bowl of ice water to cool and thicken. Stir and scrape the sides from time to time. If mixture begins to set before needed, remove from the ice bath, whisk, and set aside. Should mixture actually set, place the pan in a bowl of hot water and stir just until resoftened.

6. Make the safe meringue. Bring 1 inch of water to a simmer in a large skillet. Combine the cream of tartar and 2 teaspoons of water in a 4- to 6-cup stainless steel bowl. Whisk in the remaining 2 egg whites and the remaining 6 tablespoons of sugar. Place thermometer near stove in a mug of very hot tap water. Set bowl in skillet. Stir mixture briskly and constantly with a rubber spatula, scraping the sides and bottom often to avoid scrambling the whites. After 1 minute, remove bowl from skillet. Quickly insert thermometer, tilting bowl to cover stem by at least 2 inches. If less than 160°F., rinse thermometer in skillet water and return it to mug. Replace bowl in skillet. Stir as before until temperature reaches 160°F. when bowl is removed. Beat on high speed until cool and stiff. (For more details on safe meringue, see pages 138–140.)

7. Fold about a quarter of the chocolate mixture into the egg whites. Scrape the mixture back into the remaining chocolate.

Fold to combine. Use to complete a dessert or immediately pour into serving dishes, cover, and refrigerate for at least 4 hours, or until set. *Mousse may be refrigerated, covered, for up to 1 day.*

WHITE CHOCOLATE MOUSSE

This delicate mousse is only as good as the white chocolate you use. You must use a quality brand like Valrhona, Lindt, Callebaut, Tobler, or Suchard, that lists cocoa butter as its only fat, not so-called white chocolate made of palm kernel oil or other vegetable fats. Enjoy this mousse simply with fresh berries or use it in a more elaborate dessert.

INGREDIENTS

1-1/2 TEASPOONS GELATIN

6 OUNCES WHITE CHOCOLATE, FINELY CHOPPED

3/4 CUP LOW-FAT (1%) MILK

1/8 TEASPOON CREAM OF TARTAR

2 EGG WHITES

4 TABLESPOONS SUGAR

EQUIPMENT

INSTANT-READ THERMOMETER

NUTRITION INFORMATION

CALORIES PER SERVING: 199

FAT: 9.5 G

% CALORIES FROM FAT: 41%

PROTEIN: 4.9 G

CARBOHYDRATES: 26 G

CHOLESTEROL: 6.89 MG

**MAKES ABOUT 3 CUPS, ENOUGH
TO SERVE 5 TO 6**

Work time: 45 minutes

Chill time: at least 4 hours

1. Sprinkle the gelatin over 2 table-spoons cold water in a small cup. Let soften for at least 5 minutes, without stirring. Place the chocolate in a medium bowl.

2. Scald the milk in a small saucepan. Remove from the heat and stir in the gelatin. Pour the milk over the chocolate and stir until the chocolate is completely melted and the mixture is smooth. Set the bowl in a larger bowl of ice water to cool and thicken. Stir and scrape the sides from time to time. If mixture begins to set before needed, remove from ice bath, whisk, and set aside. Should mixture actually set, place the bowl in a bowl of hot water and stir until resoftened.

3. **Make the safe meringue.** Bring 1 inch of water to a simmer in a large skillet. Combine the cream of tartar and 2 teaspoons of water in a 4- to 6-cup stainless steel bowl. Whisk in the egg whites and sugar. Place thermometer near stove in a mug of very hot tap water. Set bowl in skillet. Stir mixture briskly and constantly with a rubber spatula, scraping the sides and bottom often to avoid scrambling the whites. After 1 minute, remove bowl from skillet. Quickly insert thermometer, tilting bowl to cover stem by at least 2 inches. If less than 160°F., rinse thermometer in skillet water and return it to mug. Replace bowl in skillet. Stir as before until temperature reaches 160°F. when bowl is removed. Beat on high speed until cool

and stiff. (For more details on safe meringue, see pages 138-140.)

4. Fold about a quarter of the chocolate mixture into the meringue. Scrape meringue back into the remaining chocolate. Fold to combine. Use immediately to finish another dessert or scrape into dessert glasses or a serving bowl. Refrigerate for at least 4 hours to set. *Mousse may be refrigerated, covered, for up to 1 day.*

WHITE CHOCOLATE MINT MOUSSE

Add a scant ¼ teaspoon mint extract to the chocolate mixture in Step 2.

WHITE CHOCOLATE ORANGE MOUSSE

Add ½ teaspoon freshly grated orange zest to the chocolate mixture in Step 2.

MILK CHOCOLATE MOCHA MOUSSE

Substitute 6 ounces milk chocolate for white chocolate. Add 1 tablespoon instant espresso or coffee powder to chocolate in Step 1.

LEMON MOUSSE

Every dessert chef needs a lemon mousse recipe. This light mousse is extra lemony and possibly even more appealing than my old classic rich one. Serve it forth in a dessert glass or use it in a cake or as a filling.

INGREDIENTS

1-1/2 TEASPOONS GELATIN

GRATED ZEST OF 1 LEMON

1/2 CUP STRAINED LEMON JUICE

3/4 CUP SUGAR

1 WHOLE EGG

1 EGG YOLK

3/4 TEASPOON VANILLA EXTRACT

4 EGG WHITES

1/4 TEASPOON CREAM OF TARTAR

1/3 CUP HEAVY CREAM

EQUIPMENT

INSTANT-READ THERMOMETER

NUTRITION INFORMATION

CALORIES PER SERVING: 109

FAT: 3.9 G

% CALORIES FROM FAT: 31%

PROTEIN: 2.8 G

CARBOHYDRATES: 16.6 G

CHOLESTEROL: 53.2 MG

MAKES 6 CUPS, ENOUGH TO SERVE 8 TO 10

Work time: 30 minutes

Chill time: at least 4 hours

1. Sprinkle the gelatin over 3 tablespoons cold water in a small bowl or cup. Set aside to soften, without stirring, for at least 5 minutes. Set a strainer over a large bowl.

2. Combine the lemon zest, juice, and ¼ cup of the sugar in a medium saucepan and bring to a simmer. Beat the whole egg and egg yolk in a small bowl until light. Beat some of the hot lemon mixture into the eggs. Scrape back into the saucepan. Cook and stir constantly, reaching all over the bottom and sides of the pan to prevent burning, until barely starting to simmer around the edges. Pour the mixture through the strainer set over a bowl. Stir in the softened gelatin and vanilla. Set the bowl in a larger bowl of ice water. Stir and scrape the sides from time to time until mixture is cool and beginning to thicken. If it begins to set before needed, remove from the ice bath, whisk, and set aside. If it actually sets, place in a bowl of hot water and stir until softened again.

3. **Make the safe meringue.** Bring 1 inch of water to a simmer in a large skillet. Combine the cream of tartar and 4 teaspoons of water in a 6- to 8-cup stainless steel bowl. Whisk in the egg whites and the remaining sugar. Place thermometer near stove in a mug of very hot tap water. Set bowl in skillet. Stir mixture briskly and constantly with a rubber spatula, scraping the sides and bottom often to avoid scrambling the whites. After 1½ minutes, remove bowl from skillet. Quickly insert thermometer, tilting bowl to cover stem by at least 2 inches. If less than 160°F., rinse thermometer in skillet water and return it to mug. Replace bowl in skillet. Stir as before until temperature reaches 160°F. when bowl is removed. Beat on high speed until cool and stiff. Set aside. (For more details on safe meringue, see pages 138-140.)

4. Beat the cream until it holds its shape but is not too stiff. Set aside. Fold half the lemon mixture into the beaten egg whites. Scrape back on top of the remaining lemon mixture. Scrape whipped cream on top. Fold all together. Turn into dessert glasses or use immediately in a dessert recipe. Cover and refrigerate for at least 4 hours, or until set. *Mousse may be refrigerated, covered, for up to 1 day.*

THE NEW CHOCOLATE FROSTINGS, GLAZES, AND SAUCES

Three chocolate toppings are included in this book. All of them work as frosting, glaze, or sauce. Each has different flavor characteristics, from a tangy sharp bittersweet to a softer, sweeter chocolate flavor. I have paired them appropriately with my recipes—you will learn more about them as you try them with other desserts or fruit.

CREAM CHEESE FUDGE GLAZE AND FROSTING

A little sweeter and less bittersweet than either Chocolate Buttermilk or Rich Chocolate Glaze and Frosting, which follow, this is a good glaze for my Chocolate Chestnut Torte or frosting for an old-fashioned devil's food cake. Warmed, it is an excellent sauce for vanilla frozen yogurt.

INGREDIENTS

1 CUP POWDERED SUGAR
1/4 CUP UNSWEETENED DUTCH PROCESS COCOA
3 OR 4 TABLESPOONS LOW-FAT (1%) MILK
4 OUNCES LIGHT CREAM CHEESE
1/4 TEASPOON VANILLA EXTRACT

MAKES 1-1/3 CUPS

Work time: 10 minutes

1. Whisk the sugar, cocoa, and milk together in a 4-cup glass measuring cup until smooth. (Use 3 tablespoons of milk for frosting, 4 tablespoons for a glaze or sauce.) Cover with plastic wrap and microwave on High for 2 minutes, or until the mixture comes to a boil and rises to the top of the container. Set aside.

2. Place the cream cheese in a microwavesafe 2-cup measure or small bowl. Microwave on High for 10 to 20 seconds to soften. It should be creamy and smooth when you stir it with a rubber spatula. Pour a little of the chocolate over the cream cheese and stir in with the rubber spatula to combine. Do not whip or beat. Continue to add chocolate gradually to the cheese, stirring until smooth after each addition. Stir in the vanilla. Cool until desired consistency for sauce or glaze or chill until stiff enough to spread. *Frosting may be refrigerated, covered, for up to 1 week and reheated in the microwave.*

◎ ◎ ◎

CHOCOLATE BUTTERMILK GLAZE AND FROSTING

This frosting is very bittersweet and a little tangy. I like it for Double Chocolate Layer Cake and Kahlúa Fudge Ring. Some who find it just a little too tangy eaten on its own declare it perfectly delicious on and between chocolate layers. It is also an excellent sauce for ice cream and frozen yogurt.

INGREDIENTS

1 CUP SUGAR

1 CUP UNSWEETENED DUTCH PROCESS COCOA

1-1/4 CUPS LOW-FAT (1%) BUTTERMILK

1 TEASPOON VANILLA EXTRACT

MAKES ABOUT 2-1/8 CUPS

Work time: 20 minutes

1. Combine the sugar and cocoa in a heavy-bottomed medium saucepan. Use a wire whisk to stir in just enough buttermilk to form a smooth paste. Stir in the remaining buttermilk. Cook over medium heat until the mixture simmers and begins to boil, stirring constantly with a wooden spoon, scraping the sides and bottom of the saucepan. Boil gently for 3 minutes (or 2 minutes if you are making only half the recipe), stirring constantly to prevent burning. Remove from the heat and stir in the vanilla.

2. Pour through a fine strainer. Allow to cool. Cover, placing plastic wrap directly on the surface to prevent a skin from forming. Chill for several hours or overnight. Frosting will thicken as it cools. *May be refrigerated, covered, for at least 1 week.*

Note

The boiling time is important here. This glaze makes a thick smooth covering for a cake or torte, but it is not stiff enough to frost with swirls and peaks. If you cheat on the boiling time, it will not thicken enough (even after chilling) to coat a cake without dripping mostly off the sides, nor will it have the intensity of flavor it needs to be a great chocolate sauce.

RICH CHOCOLATE GLAZE AND FROSTING

Less tangy than Chocolate Buttermilk Glaze, this is also a richer alternative for Double Chocolate Layer Cake and Kahlúa Fudge Ring.

MAKES 2-1/4 CUPS

Substitute low-fat (1%) milk for the buttermilk. Proceed as for Chocolate Buttermilk Glaze through the addition of vanilla. Cool 5 minutes. Add 2½ ounces finely chopped milk chocolate. Stir until completely melted. Strain and store as in Step 2.

Note

As with Chocolate Buttermilk Glaze and Frosting, the boiling time is important. Be sure to boil gently for the time directed in Step 1.

THE NEW CHOCOLATE PASTRIES

These longtime-favorite pastries take on a brand new life when paired with low-fat mousses and sauces. They are more like chocolate soufflé mixtures than pastries, baked in thin sheets to be cut into layers or rolled up around fillings. Here is the fat-budget concept at work. Cocoa Soufflé Pastry can afford whole eggs since there is not much fat in cocoa. Chocolate Soufflé Pastry spends the fat budget—and then some—on the chocolate itself, thus no yolks are allowed.

CHOCOLATE SOUFFLÉ PASTRY

This is adapted from cookbook author Paula Peck's egg-whites-only pastry. It is very chocolatey. It exceeds our targeted percentage of calories from fat, so I use it with lighter fillings as in Chocolate Roulade, except when planning a splurge.

INGREDIENTS

6 OUNCES SEMISWEET OR BITTERSWEET
CHOCOLATE, CUT INTO SMALL PIECES
1 TEASPOON INSTANT ESPRESSO
OR COFFEE POWDER, DISSOLVED IN
3 TABLESPOONS WATER
1 TEASPOON VANILLA EXTRACT
2/3 CUP EGG WHITES,
AT ROOM TEMPERATURE (5 TO 6)
1/4 TEASPOON CREAM OF TARTAR
1/2 CUP SUGAR

EQUIPMENT

JELLY-ROLL OR HALF SHEET PAN,
11 X 17 OR 12 X 16 INCHES

NUTRITION INFORMATION

CALORIES PER SERVING: 111
FAT: 4.9 G
% CALORIES FROM FAT: 37%
PROTEIN: 2.6 G
CARBOHYDRATES: 16.3 G
CHOLESTEROL: 0 MG

**MAKES ONE 11 X 17- OR
12 X 16-INCH SHEET CAKE**

Work time: 20 minutes
Bake time: 15–17 minutes

1. Position the rack in lower third of the oven and preheat to 375°F. Line the pan with a piece of wax or parchment paper long enough to hang over the ends.

2. Melt the chocolate with the dissolved espresso and the vanilla in a small bowl set in a pan of barely simmering water or microwave on Medium (50% power) for about 1 minute 10 seconds. Stir until completely melted and smooth.

3. Beat the egg whites with the cream of tartar on medium speed until soft peaks form. Gradually sprinkle in the sugar and continue to beat at high speed until whites are stiff but not dry.

4. Fold a quarter of the whites completely into the chocolate mixture to lighten it. Fold the remaining whites gently but completely into the batter.

5. Spread batter evenly in the pan and bake for 10 minutes. Reduce heat to 350°F. and bake for 5 to 7 minutes, or until the pastry is firm to the touch. Set pan on a rack to cool completely before using or storing. *Pastry may be stored, covered, at room temperature for up to 1 day.*

COCOA SOUFFLÉ PASTRY A

I use this tender and moist cocoa sheet for roulades, like my Mocha Bûche de Noël.

INGREDIENTS

6 EGGS, SEPARATED
1 TEASPOON VANILLA EXTRACT
3/4 CUP SUGAR
1/4 TEASPOON CREAM OF TARTAR
1/4 CUP UNSWEETENED DUTCH
PROCESS COCOA
COCOA, FOR DUSTING

EQUIPMENT

JELLY-ROLL OR HALF SHEET PAN,
11 X 17 OR 12 X 16 INCHES

NUTRITION INFORMATION

CALORIES PER SERVING: 91
FAT: 3 G
% CALORIES FROM FAT: 28%
PROTEIN: 3.6 G
CARBOHYDRATES: 14.2 G
CHOLESTEROL: 106 MG

**MAKES ONE 11 X 17- OR
12 X 16-INCH SHEET CAKE**

Work time: 15 minutes
Bake time: 15 minutes

1. Position the rack in lower third of the oven and preheat to 350˚F. Line the pan with a piece of wax or parchment paper long enough to hang over the ends.

2. Beat the egg yolks with vanilla and ½ cup sugar until pale and thick. Set aside.

3. In a separate mixing bowl, beat the egg whites and cream of tartar on medium speed until soft peaks form. Gradually sprinkle in the remaining sugar, continuing to beat at high speed until stiff but not dry. Fold a quarter of the egg whites into the yolk mixture to lighten it. Scrape the remaining whites into the bowl and sift the cocoa over them. Fold until completely incorporated.

4. Spread the batter evenly into the pan and bake for about 12 to 15 minutes, or until pastry springs back when gently pressed with fingertips. Cool completely in the pan on a rack. *Pastry may be refrigerated, covered, in pan for 1 day or frozen for up to 2 months.*

5. Unmold according to instructions in the dessert recipe. Otherwise, run a small knife or metal spatula around the edges of the pastry to release it from the pan. Invert the pan onto a piece of foil dusted with cocoa. Remove pan and peel off the paper.

COCOA SOUFFLÉ PASTRY B

For layered desserts, like the Triple Mousse Celebration Cake and my unconventional Pavé, you can make a smaller batch of the cocoa pastry.

**MAKES ONE 10 X 15-INCH
SHEET CAKE**

Using only 4 eggs, ¾ teaspoon vanilla extract, ½ cup sugar, a scant ¼ teaspoon cream of tartar, and 2 tablespoons plus 2 teaspoons unsweetened Dutch process cocoa, prepare the batter as described in Steps 2 and 3 of Cocoa Pastry A. Line a 10 x 15-inch jelly-roll pan with parchment paper and bake as described in Step 4. Use as directed in the dessert recipe.

LADYFINGERS

Ladyfingers are not just "fingers" anymore. The batter, very light to begin with, is extraordinarily versatile. You will use it to make round layers as for the Lemon Mousse Cake, Mini Misùs, and my new Pavé, as well as traditional ladyfingers for such desserts as Mocha Raspberry Charlotte. With this recipe, your ladyfingers will always be plump and shapely—never flat and spreading.

LADYFINGER LAYERS A

INGREDIENTS

3 EGGS, SEPARATED
1 TEASPOON VANILLA EXTRACT
7 TABLESPOONS GRANULATED SUGAR
1/8 TEASPOON CREAM OF TARTAR
3/4 CUP SIFTED CAKE FLOUR (2-2/3 OUNCES)
1 TO 2 TABLESPOONS POWDERED SUGAR

EQUIPMENT

2 HEAVY BAKING SHEETS
PASTRY BAG WITH 9/16-INCH PLAIN TIP
(ATECO #7) OR CLOSED STAR TIP
(ATECO #7)

NUTRITION INFORMATION

CALORIES PER SERVING: 64
FAT: 1.16 G
% CALORIES FROM FAT: 16%
PROTEIN: 1.84 G
CARBOHYDRATES: 11.6 G
CHOLESTEROL: 47.1 MG

**MAKES EIGHTEEN TO TWENTY
3-INCH DISKS, TWO 9-INCH ROUND
LAYERS, OR FOUR 6-1/2-INCH
ROUND LAYERS**

Work time: 20 minutes

Bake time: 8–12 minutes

1. Position the racks in lower and upper thirds of the oven and preheat to 400°F. Trace parchment paper with either twenty 3-inch circles, two 9-inch circles, or four 6½-inch circles, leaving at least 1 inch between circles. Turn the paper upside down to line the baking sheets.

2. In a small or medium bowl, beat the egg yolks with the vanilla and slightly less than half of the granulated sugar for 2½ to 3 minutes until very thick and pale. (Do not skimp on the beating time or your ladyfingers will deflate and spread in the oven.) Scrape into a large bowl. Set aside.

3. In a clean dry mixing bowl, beat the egg whites with the cream of tartar at high speed until soft peaks form. Gradually beat in the remaining granulated sugar until mixture is very stiff but not dry.

4. Using a large rubber spatula, fold a third of the egg whites into the yolk mixture. Scrape half of the remaining whites on top and sift half of the flour over them. To fold effectively without deflating the batter, cut down through the center of the mixture to the bottom of the bowl with the spatula. Scrape a large scoop of batter up the side of the bowl. Lift it above the rest and let it fall gently back on top. Rotate the bowl and continue to cut, scrape, and lift batter without mixing, stirring, or smoothing. It may seem as if the parts will never come together, but they will. Scrape around the sides of the bowl from time to time and scrape the batter off the spatula with another spatula. Fold

until barely combined. Scrape the remaining whites on top of the batter and sift the remaining flour over them. Fold again, as described, until combined.

5. Scrape the batter into a pastry bag. Pipe disks or layers as follows: Start in the center of a circle and pipe a spiral of batter to the edge of the circle. Sieve powdered sugar on top.

6. Bake until golden brown, 8 to 10 minutes for 3-inch or 6½-inch layers, 10 to 12 minutes for 9-inch layers. Rotate sheets from upper to lower rack and from front to back about halfway through the baking time. Remove from the oven and cool in the pan on a rack. Invert and peel away the paper. *Layers may be stored, well wrapped, at room temperature for up to 2 days.*

░░░

LADYFINGER LAYERS B

INGREDIENTS

2 EGGS, SEPARATED
4-1/2 TABLESPOONS GRANULATED SUGAR
3/4 TEASPOON VANILLA EXTRACT
1/8 TEASPOON CREAM OF TARTAR
1/2 CUP SIFTED CAKE FLOUR (1-3/4 OUNCES)
1 TO 2 TABLESPOONS POWDERED SUGAR

EQUIPMENT

HEAVY BAKING SHEET, 12 X 16 INCHES

NUTRITION INFORMATION

CALORIES PER SERVING: 48
FAT: .9 G
% CALORIES FROM FAT: 16%
PROTEIN: 1.4 G
CARBOHYDRATES: 8.7 G
CHOLESTEROL: 35.3 MG

MAKES TWO 8-INCH LAYERS

Work time: 15 minutes

Bake time: 8–10 minutes

1. Preheat the oven to 400°F. Position the rack in lower third of the oven. Trace two 8-inch circles on parchment, leaving 1 inch betweem them. Turn paper upside down to line the baking sheet.

2. Make a batter as described above. Divide it between the 2 circles. Spread evenly. Sieve powdered sugar over batter. Bake for 8 to 10 minutes, or until golden brown. Rotate the sheet from back to front about halfway through the baking time. Remove from the oven and cool in the pan on a rack. Turn upside down and peel away the parchment. *Layers may be stored, well wrapped, at room temperature for up to 2 days.*

░░░

LADYFINGER CHARLOTTE LINER

Following this convenient procedure, you can easily line a mold with hot ladyfingers; they will turn dry and crisp as they cool.

INGREDIENTS

4 EGGS, SEPARATED
1/4 CUP PLUS 1/3 CUP GRANULATED SUGAR
1-1/2 TEASPOONS VANILLA EXTRACT
1/4 TEASPOON CREAM OF TARTAR
1 CUP SIFTED CAKE FLOUR (3-1/2 OUNCES)
2 TO 3 TABLESPOONS POWDERED SUGAR

EQUIPMENT

1 LARGE BAKING SHEET, AT LEAST 14 X 16
INCHES, OR 2 SMALLER ONES
PASTRY BAG FITTED WITH A 9/16-INCH
PLAIN TIP (ATECO #7) OR CLOSED
STAR TIP (ATECO #7)
8-INCH SPRINGFORM PAN

NUTRITION INFORMATION

CALORIES PER SERVING: 96
FAT: 1.74 G
% CALORIES FROM FAT: 16%
PROTEIN: 2.76 G
CARBOHYDRATES: 17.3 G
CHOLESTEROL: 70.7 MG

**MAKES A LINER WITH LAYERS FOR
AN 8-INCH CHARLOTTE MOLD**

Work time: 20 minutes

Bake time: 22–24 minutes

1. Position the racks in lower and upper third of the oven. Preheat the oven to 375°F. Trace two 7-inch circles and two 12 x 3-inch rectangles on parchment paper. It will be a tight fit. The circles can touch, but the rectangles must have at least 1 inch space between them and the circles. If you are using 2 baking sheets, trace the circles on 1 parchment liner and the rectangles on the second. Turn the paper upside down to line the pan.

2. Make batter as described on page 150. Scrape the batter into the pastry bag and pipe a series of straight or S-shaped ladyfingers 3 inches long and only ¼ inch apart within a rectangular guide. They will puff and attach together as they bake.

Repeat in the second rectangle. Pipe the ladyfinger layers as follows: Start in the center of a circle and pipe a spiral of batter to the edge of the circle. Sieve powdered sugar over the piped batter.

3. Bake in the lower third of the oven if you are using 1 baking sheet. Bake for 12 to 14 minutes, or until golden brown. Rotate sheets from back to front and upper to lower racks about halfway through the baking time. Turn the oven temperature down to 300°F. and leave the oven door open for about 1 minute. Close the door and bake for 10 minutes more. Remove from the oven. Immediately lift or slide the parchment paper off the baking sheet and turn it upside down. Peel away the paper from the rectangles. Bend one to fit around the inside of the springform with the flat sides facing inside. Repeat with the second rectangle, trimming to fit snugly against the first. Set aside to cool completely in the pan. Place layers on the paper on a rack to cool completely. *Liner may be stored, well wrapped, at room temperature for up to 1 day.*

GENOISE

Genoise is a traditional French whole-egg sponge cake used as the base for a million different desserts. The traditional version is not overly rich, but I was able to lighten it a little anyway, to allow the use of richer fillings and creams.

In addition to decreasing the amount of butter to lighten the Genoise, I have also improved on my old technique. Instead of clarifying the butter (to rid it of excess moisture) I brown it slightly in a saucepan. Browning provides more flavor from less butter while cooking away the excess moisture.

I have included two recipes for Genoise: Genoise A is for a single nine-inch cake; Genoise B is for two eight-inch cakes. Many recipes call for a single eight-inch Genoise. Do not divide the recipe in half—this will just drive you nuts. Make the full recipe and freeze the second cake. The frozen cake will provide a nice incentive for making another dessert again, easily and soon.

If you are interested, read about the differences between cake and all-purpose flour (pages 177–178). In any event, note that my recipes for Genoise give measurements for both kinds. Which flour to use is specified in each dessert recipe.

GENOISE A

INGREDIENTS

2-1/2 TABLESPOONS SWEET UNSALTED BUTTER
1 CUP SIFTED CAKE FLOUR OR
1 CUP LESS 2 TABLESPOONS SIFTED
ALL-PURPOSE FLOUR (3-1/2 OUNCES)
1/2 CUP PLUS 2 TABLESPOONS SUGAR
3 WHOLE EGGS
2 EGG WHITES
1 TEASPOON VANILLA EXTRACT

EQUIPMENT

9 X 2-INCH ROUND CAKE PAN

NUTRITION INFORMATION

CALORIES PER SERVING: 113
FAT: 3.7 G
% CALORIES FROM FAT: 30%
PROTEIN: 2.8 G
CARBOHYDRATES: 17 G
CHOLESTEROL: 60 MG

**MAKES ONE 9-INCH CAKE, 1-1/2
TO 1-3/4 INCHES TALL**

Work time: 20 minutes
Bake time: 20–25 minutes

1. Preheat the oven to 350°F. Line the bottom of the pan with parchment paper. Spray the sides with vegetable oil spray.

2. Place a strainer lined with a paper towel (not a coffee filter) or 4 single layers of cheesecloth over a 3- to 4-cup heatproof bowl near the stove. Melt the butter in a heavy-bottomed small saucepan and simmer until the loudest sizzling noises subside, butter turns golden brown, and particles brown. Pour through the strainer and keep hot until needed or reheat quickly before using at the end of Step 5.

3. Combine the flour with 2 tablespoons of the sugar and sift together twice. Return to the sifter and set aside.

4. In a large heatproof mixing bowl, use a whisk to combine the whole eggs, egg whites, and remaining sugar. Place bowl in or over a saucepan containing 1 to 2 inches of barely simmering water. Heat the eggs to lukewarm (check by touching), whisking occasionally. Or place the bowl directly on the stove burner and whisk constantly and vigorously for about 1 minute, until the eggs are warm. (This is the quickest, easiest way, but you must whisk eggs continuously to keep them from starting to scramble.)

5. Remove from the heat and beat on high speed, preferably with a stand mixer, until the mixture has cooled, tripled in bulk, and resembles softly whipped cream. When it is nearly ready, reheat the butter briefly, if necessary, and add the vanilla to it. Set aside.

6. Sift about a third of the flour mixture over the eggs. Use a large rubber spatula to fold the mixture quickly but gently until combined. Fold in half the remaining flour, then fold in the rest. Scoop 1 heaping cup of batter into the bowl containing the butter and vanilla. Fold together with a small rubber spatula. When combined, scrape over the remaining batter and fold with the large spatula until well incorporated. Turn the batter into the pan.

7. Bake until the cake shrinks slightly from the edges and the top springs back when pressed, 20 to 25 minutes. Cool the cake in the pan on a rack. Slide a small knife or metal spatula around the edges of the cake to release it from the pan. Unmold cake. *Cake may be stored, well wrapped, at room temperature for up to 1 day or frozen for up to 3 months.*

GENOISE B

INGREDIENTS

3-1/2 TABLESPOONS UNSALTED BUTTER
1-1/2 CUPS SIFTED CAKE FLOUR OR 1-1/3 CUPS
SIFTED ALL-PURPOSE FLOUR (5-1/4 OUNCES)
3/4 CUP PLUS 3 TABLESPOONS SUGAR
5 WHOLE EGGS
2 EGG WHITES
1-1/2 TEASPOONS VANILLA EXTRACT

EQUIPMENT

TWO 8 X 1-1/2- OR 2-INCH ROUND CAKE PANS

**MAKES TWO 8-INCH CAKES,
1-1/2 INCHES TALL**

Proceed as for Genoise A, combining the flour with 3 tablespoons of sugar in Step 3 and dividing the batter between 2 pans in Step 6.

THE NEW TART CRUST

My early attempts to make a "light" butter tart crust resembled cardboard. A leap of imagination was needed—an entirely different crust that when combined with custard and fruit would still capture the essence of my favorite fresh fruit tarts. The leap was provided when my great-aunt Martha Finkelstein gave me her recipe for the most tender crisp Mandelbrot either of us had ever tasted. The secret ingredient is, of all things, Wondra flour!

NEW TART CRUST

INGREDIENTS

1/2 CUP WONDRA FLOUR
1/4 TEASPOON BAKING POWDER
1 EGG
1/4 CUP SUGAR
1/4 TEASPOON VANILLA EXTRACT
FINELY GRATED ZEST OF 1/4 LEMON
1 TABLESPOON CORN OIL

EQUIPMENT

9-1/2-INCH FLUTED TART PAN WITH
REMOVABLE BOTTOM

NUTRITION INFORMATION

CALORIES PER SERVING: 77
FAT: 2.4 G
% CALORIES FROM FAT: 28%
PROTEIN: 1.6 G
CARBOHYDRATES: 12.3 G
CHOLESTEROL: 26.5 MG

MAKES ONE 9-1/2-INCH TART CRUST

Work time: 15 minutes
Bake time: 50 minutes

1. Position the rack in lower third of the oven and preheat to 350°F. Spray the bottom and sides of the pan with vegetable oil spray.

2. Whisk the Wondra together with the baking powder in a small bowl. Set aside.

3. Beat the egg, sugar, vanilla, and zest together for 2½ to 3 minutes (don't cheat—this is important) on high speed until thick. Beat in the oil, then the flour mixture, beating just until combined. Mixture will resemble a thick batter more than a dough.

4. Scrape batter into the pan. Spread evenly, making sure that the edges are at least as thick as the center. Bake on a cookie sheet for 15 to 20 minutes, or just until crust is slightly colored and has pulled away from the sides of the pan. Remove from oven.

5. Turn oven down to 325°F. Slip the rim off the tart pan while still hot. Slide a metal spatula carefully under the crust to release it from the bottom of the pan. Crust will be spongy and flexible. Use the spatula to slide crust onto a wire cooling rack. Cool for 10 minutes. Place crust, still on the rack, on a cookie sheet and bake until golden brown, 15 to 20 minutes. Cool completely on the rack before storing. Crust will crisp completely as it cools. *Crust may be stored, wrapped airtight, at room temperature for a few weeks.*

NEW TARTLET CRUST

EQUIPMENT

EIGHT 3-1/2-INCH FLUTED TARTLET PANS

MAKES EIGHT 3-1/2-INCH
TARTLET CRUSTS

1. Position the rack in lower third of the oven and preheat to 350°F. Spray the bottom and sides of the pans with vegetable oil spray.

2. Using the same ingredients as for New Tart Crust, follow Steps 1 through 3 of the recipe.

3. Divide the batter equally among tartlet pans. Spread evenly with the back of a spoon. Bake on a cookie sheet for 15 to 17 minutes, or until the crust is lightly colored and has pulled away from pan sides. Remove from oven.

4. Turn oven down to 325°F. While still hot, pry each crust from its pan with the tip of a paring knife. Crusts will be spongy and flexible. Cool for 10 minutes on a rack. Place the rack on a cookie sheet and bake only until golden brown, about 10 minutes. Cool completely on the rack before storing. Crusts will crisp completely as they cool. *Crusts may be stored, wrapped airtight, at room temperature for a few weeks.*

PHYLLO

Phyllo is ultra-thin sheets of the pastry used to make strudel and baklava. It is readily available and versatile, and it can be used to make hundreds of other desserts as well. It has tremendous possibilities for lightening traditional and new dessert recipes. Crisp and flaky phyllo shells can stand in for much richer stuff. I use baked unfilled shells in place of puff pastry, short dough, and traditional pie pastry for tarts, pies, and pastries. Phyllo also makes freeform nests, which can be filled with pumpkin pudding or frozen yogurt, or poached pears and chocolate sauce. Anytime you want more flakiness, add more sheets of phyllo.

Phyllo has to be brushed with oil or butter between each layer. This may seem like a lavish fat expenditure, but the total amount of butter or oil used in a crisp, flaky nine-inch tart shell is less than one ounce. Compare this to the three or four ounces necessary for a classic short pastry tart shell.

Packages of readymade phyllo are found in the frozen food section of most good supermarkets. Read the package for defrosting instructions and other general handling information. The sheets are either twelve by seventeen or fourteen by eighteen inches. In San Francisco we are lucky to have a small artisanal manufacturer of fresh phyllo dough, the Shaharazad Bakery. Check your own area for a similar treasure. Otherwise, rest assured that the recipes in this book were tested with widely available brands of frozen phyllo.

Phyllo dough is easy to use. Keep the package frozen until the day before or several hours before you want to use it. Most recipes call for only three to eight sheets; defrost the entire package anyway. Thawed phyllo keeps in the refrigerator for four to five weeks. You can also refreeze it.

The most critical thing to remember when working with phyllo is that it dries out quickly when left uncovered. During use, keep the sheets covered with plastic wrap and a damp towel. Make sure that the damp towel does not come in direct contact with the phyllo or the pastry will dissolve into paste. Remove the sheets one by one and cover the rest until needed. If one sheet gives you trouble, you can always toss it out and use another. For the rest, follow the individual recipe instructions.

Choosing the fat: Phyllo pastries can be made by using as little as one teaspoon of fat per sheet of phyllo. You may use oil or melted clarified or softened unsalted butter between phyllo layers. Each has its advantages. Choose oil if cholesterol is the major deciding factor; otherwise use butter. I use melted clarified butter. It's easy to spread very little over the sheet, and the absence of moisture produces a crisp pastry.

Making a little go a long way: Each time you take out a new phyllo sheet, put one teaspoon of clarified butter or oil into a small custard cup. Place your left hand (if you are right-handed) flat in the center of the phyllo to anchor it. Hold a pastry brush nearly vertical and using very firm dabbing strokes, spread the melted fat. Dab and brush until no more fat seems to be coming off. Dip

the brush into the fat only when necessary; make it last as long as possible. Move your hand around as necessary to anchor the pastry. With each new phyllo sheet, start brushing in a different area; don't forget the edges. You may run out of fat—and have to cheat a little— before you've finished the first sheet, but then you'll know how to pace yourself. Eventually you'll get good enough to use even less than one teaspoon of fat per sheet.

To save time, spray clarified butter (or oil) instead of brushing it on the phyllo. Use a small (two-ounce) plastic mister or spray bottle from the drugstore. You will need extra butter to start with. Fill the bottle just above the level of the spray tube first, then add the amount required in the recipe. To help pace yourself, add butter 1 teaspoon at a time and mark the bottle after each addition. The extra butter will be left in the bottom when you are done. Butter must be quite warm but not hot enough to melt the plastic. If spray is uneven, reheat butter, or simply brush lightly across the pastry afterward to spread; this is still much faster than using the brush for the entire job.

Baking the phyllo: Chefs disagree on the temperature at which to bake phyllo. I bake unfilled phyllo napoleon layers and tart shells at 375°F., despite advice to the contrary. I don't like the flavor or appearance of pale pastry so I bake it long enough to turn the phyllo a rich brown gold color, watching carefully to avoid burning.

PHYLLO TART SHELL

INGREDIENTS

4 PHYLLO SHEETS, DEFROSTED
4 TEASPOONS CLARIFIED BUTTER, MELTED
1 TABLESPOON SUGAR

EQUIPMENT

9-1/2-INCH FLUTED TART PAN WITH
REMOVABLE BOTTOM

NUTRITION INFORMATION

CALORIES PER SERVING: 45
FAT: 2.1 G
% CALORIES FROM FAT: 41%
PROTEIN: .8 G
CARBOHYDRATES: 6.1 G
CHOLESTEROL: 5.5 MG

MAKES ONE 9-1/2-INCH
TART SHELL

Work time: 25 minutes
Bake time: 15 minutes

1. Position the rack in lower third of the oven and preheat to 375°F.

2. Unroll and stack phyllo sheets on a tray and keep them well covered with plastic wrap covered with a damp towel.

3. Place 1 sheet of phyllo on a dry pastry board or the counter in front of you. Transfer 1 teaspoon of the butter into a small cup and brush the phyllo evenly with all of the butter in the cup. Sprinkle with ¾ teaspoon of the sugar. Place a second sheet of phyllo on top, butter it, and sprinkle with sugar. Continue with the remaining phyllo, butter, and sugar.

4. Trim the phyllo stack into a square about 11 or 12 inches in size by cutting off about 5½ to 6 inches from 1 end of the rectangle. It doesn't have to be exactly square. Peel off and set aside two of the square pieces of phyllo, leaving two stacked in front of you. Place two of the smaller pieces, side by side, on top of the square stack. Place the 2 remaining smaller pieces on top, side by side, but with the seam going in the opposite direction. Cover with the 2 remaining pieces. Pick up the stack, center it in the tart pan, and press it neatly into the bottom and up the sides. Use scissors to trim the edges even with the rim of the pan. *Unbaked tart shell may be refrigerated, well wrapped, for up to 1 day.*

5. Place the tart pan on a cookie sheet. Prick the bottom of the pastry all over with a fork. Place a round of wax or parchment paper on the pastry and set a lightweight cake pan on it to keep the pastry from puffing as it bakes. Bake for 5 minutes. Remove the weight and paper. Bake for 8 to 10 minutes, or until pastry is a deep golden brown. If pastry puffs up, prick again and press down with the pan that was used as a weight. Cool completely on a rack before filling or storing. *Shell may be stored, well wrapped, at room temperature for up to 1 day.*

PHYLLO TARTLET SHELLS

EQUIPMENT

TWELVE 3-1/2-INCH FLUTED TARTLET PANS

NUTRITION INFORMATION

CALORIES PER SERVING: 30
FAT: 1.4 G
% CALORIES FROM FAT: 41%
PROTEIN: .5 G
CARBOHYDRATES: 4 G
CHOLESTEROL: 3.6 MG

MAKES TWELVE
3-1/2-INCH TARTLETS

Work time: 45 minutes
Bake time: about 15 minutes

1. Complete Steps 1, 2, and 3 as for Phyllo Tart Shell.

2. Cut phyllo stack into 3 equal strips lengthwise. Cut each strip in four to make 12 small nearly square stacks. Fit stacks neatly into the bottom and up the sides of tartlet pans. Trim the edges with scissors. (For extra-flaky layers, sandwich trimmings between the layers of phyllo, dividing them evenly.)

3. Place the pans on a cookie sheet. Set small custard cups on top of the phyllo to keep it from puffing as it bakes. Or use paper muffin pan liners filled with 2 to 3 tablespoons of raw rice or beans for weights. Bake for 5 minutes. Remove weights. Bake for 8 to 10 minutes, or until the pastry is a deep golden brown. Cool completely before filling. *Shells may be stored, well wrapped, at room temperature for up to 1 day.* Cool completely on a rack before filling or storing. *Shell may be stored, well wrapped, at room temperature for up to 1 day.*

PHYLLO NESTS

EQUIPMENT

EIGHT 4-1/2- TO 5-INCH DISPOSABLE FOIL PIE
PANS OR SHALLOW OVENPROOF BOWLS

NUTRITION INFORMATION

CALORIES PER SERVING: 45
FAT: 2.1 G
% CALORIES FROM FAT: 41%
PROTEIN: .75 G
CARBOHYDRATES: 6 G
CHOLESTEROL: 5.5 MG

MAKES 8 NESTS

Work time: 25 minutes
Bake time: 16–24 minutes

1. Spray the pans lightly with veg-etable oil spray. Complete Steps 1, 2, and 3 as for Phyllo Tart Shell.

2. Cut phyllo stack into 6 squares, as follows: Cut the stack in half lengthwise, then cut each half crosswise in three. Peel off 1 square of phyllo and place it in a pie pan, pressing so that the pastry is flat in the bottom of the pan and gently ruffled up the sides. Peel off a second square and place it in the pan on top of the first with the points offset. Place a third the same way, rotating it a little more. Adjust the points and folds to make a freeform nest. Repeat to make the remaining 7 nests, always using 3 phyllo per nest.

3. Bake the nests, four at a time, on a heavyweight baking sheet for 8 to 12 min-utes, rotating the pan from front to back halfway through baking time, or until the pastry is a deep golden brown all over. Cool baking sheet before baking the remaining 4 nests. Cool nests thoroughly before filling.

TUILES

These are the caramelized sugar tuiles Tra Vigne Chef Michael Chiarello originally devised as a sugar crust topping for his divine Panna Cotta. Placed on the surface of a custard or pudding just before serving, they take the place of the trickier brulée crust. They also make rich sweet lace cook-ies, flat or curved, and superb citrus-laced cups for ice cream or frozen yogurt sundaes sauced with Chocolate Buttermilk Glaze (page 147).

SUGAR TUILES

INGREDIENTS

1/2 CUP ALL-PURPOSE FLOUR
1/2 CUP SUPERFINE SUGAR
1/4 CUP LIGHT CORN SYRUP
4 TABLESPOONS UNSALTED
BUTTER, MELTED

EQUIPMENT

HEAVY BAKING SHEETS

NUTRITION INFORMATION

CALORIES PER TUILE: 31.4
FAT: 1.17 G
% CALORIES FROM FAT: 33%
PROTEIN: .17 G
CARBOHYDRATES: 5.22 G
CHOLESTEROL: 3.1 MG

MAKES ABOUT FORTY
3-INCH TUILES

Work time: 25 minutes
Bake time: 30–60 minutes

1. Combine the ingredients in a mixer or food processor. Beat or process until well blended. Transfer dough to a container and cover airtight. *Dough may be refrigerated for several days or frozen for several months. If frozen, dough may be partially thawed, scooped as needed, and refrozen.*

2. Position the rack in lower third of the oven and preheat to 375°F. Line a baking sheet with parchment paper.

3. To make regular tuiles: Scoop level ½ teaspoons of dough and place about 3½ inches apart on the baking sheet. Bake for 9 to 12 minutes, or until deep mahogany brown, rotating the pan about halfway through the baking period and watching carefully toward the end. While 1 sheet of tuiles is baking, scoop remaining dough and place on additional sheets of parchment.

4. To make extra-thin tuiles: Place a sheet of wax paper or plastic wrap over the lumps of dough. Press or roll each lump as thin as possible, to a diameter of 3¼ inches or more. Freeze for 1 to 2 minutes before peeling away the wax paper or plastic. Bake and rotate pans until tuiles are deep mahogany as before; extra-thin tuiles will take only 6 to 8 minutes.

5. Slide the parchment paper with baked tuiles from the baking sheet. Cool completely, without removing tuiles, before using or storing. Slide parchment with unbaked tuiles onto the hot sheet. Bake as before, but for less time since the baking sheet was hot. Repeat until the desired num-ber of tuiles are baked. *Tuiles may be stored, airtight, for at least 1 week or frozen, layered between sheets of wax paper, for several weeks.*

GINGER TUILES

Add 1½ teaspoons ground ginger to ingredients in Step 1.

LEMON OR LIME CARAMEL TUILES

Add 1¼ teaspoons grated lemon or lime zest and 1½ teaspoons lemon or lime juice to the ingredients in Step 1.

CURVED TUILES

MAKES ABOUT 40 TUILES

Shape and bake the tuiles as for Sugar Tuiles (plain, ginger, lemon, or lime). Extra-thin are nice. While still piping hot, pick up parchment by the edges without detaching the tuiles and roll it up, tuiles inside, like a diploma. Secure with paper clips or wedge between heavy objects to prevent unrolling. Unroll when cool.

DESSERT CUPS

NUTRITION INFORMATION

CALORIES PER SERVING: 124
FAT: 4.7 G
% CALORIES FROM FAT: 33%
PROTEIN: .7 G
CARBOHYDRATES: 20.9 G
CHOLESTEROL: 12.4 MG

MAKES ABOUT 10 CUPS

Work time: 20 minutes
Bake time: 30–60 minutes

Invert 2 custard cups on work surface. Cover each with a paper towel, tucking it under the cup to secure it. Make large tuiles (plain, ginger, lemon, or lime), using the extra-thin method, each with 2 teaspoons of dough pressed or rolled out to a diameter of 5 inches. Form and bake only 2 tuiles at a time. Cool a few seconds or just long enough that you can slide a thin metal pancake turner underneath each tuile without deforming it. Quickly lift each tuile and invert it over a cup. Or cut the paper apart between tuiles and invert over the cup. Press down gently. Repeat with the remaining batter. Remove when cool. Peel parchment when tuile has cooled. *Dessert cups may be stored, airtight, for at least 1 week or frozen for several weeks.*

TUILE CAKE DECORATIONS

Line a baking sheet with parchment paper. Place a large piece of dough in the middle, cover with a sheet of wax paper, and press or roll out as thin as possible to the desired diameter; circle doesn't have to be perfectly even. Freeze for 1 or 2 minutes before peeling away the wax paper. Bake as a single large tuile. While still hot, cut into a perfect round top for a cheesecake, or cut into wedges or into decorative shapes with lightly oiled cookie cutters. Crushed or broken tuile pieces can also be pressed against the sides of a dessert. Do this shortly before serving so they retain their crunch.

CARAMEL

Caramel is a wonderful way to dress up desserts. You can use it with custards that are to be unmolded, on top of custards and puddings in place of a brulée top, in pastry creams and cheesecake as a flavoring. Caramel powder sprinkled on partly baked pastry will harden into a crisp glaze. And Spun Sugar is the stuff of dream desserts. You can make caramel in the microwave or in a saucepan on top of the stove. If using a saucepan, use a very small, lightweight one; it gives you better control than the heavy copper pot made expressly for the purpose. If despite all your care the sugar crystallizes, cover the pan, turn down the heat, and cook on low heat for three to four minutes, or until the crystals have remelted. Uncover and cook on medium heat until amber.

BASIC CARAMEL

INGREDIENTS

1/2 CUP SUGAR
1/4 CUP WATER

1. If making caramel for immediate use in Spun Sugar, do so only in a saucepan on the stovetop, not the microwave. Have a shallow pan or bowl filled with ice water ready. If making caramel to line soufflé or custard cups, have the cups ready. For all other purposes, have a foil-lined baking sheet ready.

2. Microwave method: Place sugar and water in a 2-cup glass measure. Stir to combine. Cover tightly with microwavesafe plastic wrap and cook on High for 7 to 9 minutes, or until caramel is a medium amber color. Reach into oven and pierce the plastic wrap with a sharp knife. Use a potholder to remove container carefully from oven. Use a fork to peel wrap off the container.

3. Stovetop method: Combine sugar and water in a lightweight 3- to 4-cup saucepan. Stir until the sugar is moistened. Do not stir again during the cooking. Cover and bring sugar and water to a simmer over medium heat. Uncover and wipe down the sides of the pan with a wet pastry brush or a wad of paper towel dipped in water. Cover and cook for 2 minutes, or until the sugar is completely dissolved. Uncover and cook until the syrup turns a pale amber. Test by spooning a drop or two of the syrup onto a white saucer. Swirl the pan gently, continuing to cook and test the color, until the syrup darkens to a medium amber color.

4. To use caramel to line custard cups: Divide the caramel among the cups, tilting to cover the sides and bottom.

5. To use caramel for shards, shapes, or powder or to reheat later for Spun Sugar: Pour the caramel immediately onto the lined baking sheet. Tilt sheet to spread caramel as thinly as possible.

6. To use caramel to spin sugar right away: Plunge the bottom of the saucepan in the pan of ice water for a minute to stop the boiling. (Do not do this if you have made caramel in the microwave; the hot glass will crack on contact with the ice water.) Allow to cool until it is thick and sticky. Proceed with instructions for Spun Sugar, starting with Step 3.

CARAMEL SHAPES OR ROUNDS

Make the caramel as described in Basic Caramel and spread on a foil-lined baking sheet. As soon as the caramel has begun to set, cut out as many shapes as you can with an oiled cookie cutter or sharp knife. Work quickly before caramel hardens completely. *Shapes or rounds may be stored in an airtight container or Krispy Kan (page 184) with a double thickness of wax paper between the layers.* Use to garnish custards or puddings in place of a brulée top.

CARAMEL SHARDS

Make the caramel as described in Basic Caramel and spread on a foil-lined baking sheet. Allow the caramel to cool and harden completely. Break into pieces. *Shards may be stored in an airtight container or Krispy Kan (page 184) with a double thickness of wax paper between the layers.* Use to garnish custards or puddings, to decorate cakes, or reheat for Spun Sugar.

CARAMEL POWDER

Make the caramel as described in Basic Caramel and spread on a foil-lined baking sheet. Allow the caramel to cool and harden completely. Break into pieces and pulverize in a perfectly dry food processor bowl fitted with the steel blade. *Powder may be stored indefinitely in an airtight container in the refrigerator or freezer.*

SPUN SUGAR

Usually associated with the great chefs of Europe, world-class desserts, and expensive restaurants, Spun Sugar is my favorite awesome feat in the kitchen. The classic procedure is surrounded by considerable mystique and is a deterrent to most home cooks. Who would guess that you could prepare the caramel in advance to reheat later and spin quickly at the last minute to create a dessert masterpiece?

EQUIPMENT
IMPROVISED SPINNING TOOL SUCH AS
A HANDFUL OF WOODEN OR METAL SKEWERS OR
A SNIPPED-OFF WIRE WHISK

1. To make caramel for spinning sugar immediately: Prepare Basic Caramel in a saucepan according to Steps 1, 3, and 6 of that recipe. Skip to Step 3 of this recipe.

2. To make caramel in advance for spinning sugar later: Prepare and store Caramel Shards until needed. When ready to spin, remelt shards (or any leftover hardened caramel) in a heatproof glass jar or glass measuring cup or a small saucepan. Microwave on Medium (50% power) for 1 minute. Continue to cook, 15 seconds at a time, just until most of caramel has melted into a very thick sticky syrup and it is just starting to boil in the center. Use a knife or small metal spatula to push some of the unmelted caramel at the edges toward the center as necessary. In a saucepan, melt the caramel over very low heat. It is not necessary for all of the caramel to melt.

3. Dip the spinning tool into the hot caramel and lift it about 12 inches above the container. The caramel thickens as it cools. At first it flows from the tips of the tool in very fine threads. The caramel must cool a little bit more in order to spin. Continue to dip and raise the tool, watching the threads. Caramel is ready to spin when threads become slightly thicker and more golden and flow more slowly. You will be able to grasp the threads in your bare hand and pull them aside, stretching them and coiling them onto your dessert. The threads of caramel are not hot, but the caramel in the container is *very* hot and so are the droplets and globs that fall from above. Each time you dip the tool, hold it high and wait until the heaviest flow of caramel has subsided into threads before you touch it. Pull threads to the side immediately, out from under the tool so that any drops of caramel that fall can not burn you. Continue to dip and wait for the threads, pulling them aside and on to the dessert. If the caramel gets too cool to spin, reheat gently, using Medium in the

microwave or a very low flame on the stove. Spun sugar lasts a very short time. Serve immediately.

4. Leftover caramel may be stored for reuse. Reheat the caramel, pour onto a sheet of foil, and allow to harden. Break into shards or pulverize into powder. *Caramel may be stored airtight in the refrigerator or freezer indefinitely.*

BRULÉE TOPPING
OR CARAMELIZING WITH
A PROPANE TORCH

Here's how to create a crisp caramelized crème brulée style topping on individual custards and puddings.

Have desserts well chilled. Sprinkle 1½ teaspoons sugar evenly over the top of 1 dessert. Light the torch with a match and adjust the flame to high. Tilt the torch and sweep the surface of the dessert with the flame at a distance of about 12 inches, stopping only long enough to melt and caramelize each area. If sugar starts to burn, blow out the flame. The rim of the cup will be hot: Handle with a potholder. Put in the freezer for about 15 minutes, then put back in the refrigerator. Repeat with each dessert.

Note
Do not try to caramelize the tops of delicate mousses set with gelatin. The heat will melt the mousse. Instead, place an ultra-thin flat Sugar Tuile (page 156) on the surface of each mousse just before serving.

THE NEW CREAMS AND FRUIT SAUCES

A little something, in the way of a sauce or a dollop, is often just the right finishing touch. Whipped cream may be the most sorely missed accompaniment in the low-fat dessert world, so it is nice to have a few alternatives. My suggestions include a truly low-fat cream made from cottage cheese, as well as three much richer creams made from light sour cream and or/real heavy cream, all stretched with Safe Meringue (page 138). These are ultra rich by our standards and you may play around and stretch any of them even farther by using more Safe Meringue. The key is not to stretch them so far that they cease to taste like the real thing and to use them very sparingly.

Fruit sauces and purees are more desirable than ever as fat-free enhancements. It is worth remembering that raspberries are not the only fruit in the world worth pureeing and that most fruit sauces are exquisite because they are fresh, only lightly sweetened, and uncooked—do not destroy their fragility by heating them. Keep them only a day or two in the refrigerator, or freeze for longer storage.

MAIDA'S CREAM

I love Maida Heatter's story of her discovery of the wonderful qualities of cottage cheese that's been processed within an inch of its life in a food processor, then lightly sweetened. She was right. The trick is to process the cottage cheese long enough to eliminate all curds, at least two or three minutes. I do it with low-fat or regular cottage cheese, according to my needs. Regular (4%) cottage cheese, of course, makes a richer cream. It makes a substitute for cream or sour cream that can be used to garnish or sauce any number of desserts. Spoon it over sweetened chestnut puree or fresh fruit. This cream will become a staple in your repertoire—and not just for desserts. I use it, unsweetened, in place of sour cream with Mexican food, to garnish soups, even on toast instead of cream cheese for a very lean breakfast.

INGREDIENTS

1 CUP LOW-FAT (2%) COTTAGE CHEESE
1-1/2 TABLESPOONS SUGAR,
OR MORE TO TASTE
1/8 TEASPOON VANILLA EXTRACT,
OR MORE TO TASTE

NUTRITION INFORMATION

CALORIES PER 3 TABLESPOONS: 52
FAT: .8 G
% CALORIES FROM FAT: 14%
PROTEIN: 5.8 G
CARBOHYDRATES: 5 G
CHOLESTEROL: 3.6 MG

MAKES 1 CUP

Work time: 5 minutes

Put the cottage cheese in a food processor and process it for 2 to 3 minutes, or until silken. Add the sugar and vanilla. Taste and add more if necessary. Chill. *Cream may be refrigerated, covered, for 3 to 4 days.*

ENLIGHTENED CRÈME FRAÎCHE

Use on Pumpkin Nests, Sweet Chestnut Torte, or Chocolate Walnut Torte. For a richer version, use half a cup each cream and light sour cream.

INGREDIENTS

1/16 TEASPOON CREAM OF TARTAR
1 EGG WHITE
2 TABLESPOONS SUGAR
1/3 CUP HEAVY CREAM
1/2 TEASPOON VANILLA EXTRACT
1/3 CUP LIGHT SOUR CREAM

EQUIPMENT

INSTANT-READ THERMOMETER

CALORIES PER TABLESPOON: 16.7

FAT: 1.31 G

% CALORIES FROM FAT: 67%

PROTEIN: .41 G

CARBOHYDRATES: 1.03 G

CHOLESTEROL: 9.99 MG

MAKES 2 CUPS

Work time: 10 minutes

1. Make the safe meringue. Bring 1 inch of water to a simmer in a large skillet. Combine cream of tartar and 1 teaspoon water in a 4- to 6-cup stainless steel bowl. Whisk in the egg white and 2 tablespoons of sugar. Place thermometer near stove in a mug of very hot tap water. Set bowl in skillet. Stir mixture briskly and constantly with a rubber spatula, scraping the sides and bottom often to avoid scrambling the egg white. After 45 seconds, remove bowl from skillet. Quickly insert thermometer, tilting bowl to cover stem by at least 2 inches. If less than 160°F., rinse thermometer in skillet water and return it to mug. Replace bowl in skillet. Stir as before until temperature reaches 160°F. when bowl is removed. Beat on high speed until cool and stiff. Set aside. (For more details on safe meringue, see pages 138–140.)

2. Beat heavy cream with vanilla until it holds soft peaks but is not too stiff. Fold in the sour cream and meringue. Cover and chill until needed. *May be refrigerated for up to 8 hours.*

ENLIGHTENED SOUR CREAM

This is the lightest enlightened cream. It is particularly good with Spicy New Orleans Gingerbread.

NUTRITION INFORMATION

CALORIES PER TABLESPOON: 12.6

FAT: .6 G

% CALORIES FROM FAT: 38%

PROTEIN: .6 G

CARBOHYDRATES: 1.7 G

CHOLESTEROL: 0 MG

MAKES 1-2/3 CUPS

Work time: 10 minutes

Proceed as for Enlightened Crème Fraîche through Step 1. Fold meringue into ½ cup light sour cream. Omit the heavy cream and vanilla. Cover and chill until needed. *May be refrigerated for up to 8 hours.*

ENLIGHTENED WHIPPED CREAM

This is the richest one of all. Use wherever a dollop of whipped cream is wanted!

NUTRITION INFORMATION

CALORIES PER TABLESPOON: 15.6

FAT: 1.38 G

% CALORIES FROM FAT: 78%

PROTEIN: .16 G

CARBOHYDRATES: .7 G

CHOLESTEROL: 5.12 MG

MAKES ABOUT 2-2/3 CUPS

Work time: 10 minutes

Proceed as for Enlightened Crème Fraîche through Step 1. Whip ⅔ cup heavy cream with the vanilla until it holds soft peaks but is not too stiff. Fold meringue into cream. Omit light sour cream. Cover and chill until needed. *May be refrigerated for up to 8 hours.*

RASPBERRY SAUCE

If raspberry puree has become a culinary cliché, it is because some chefs put it on absolutely everything—like ketchup. In truth, it does not enhance every dessert, but when it's good, it's great. I use it with The New Chocolate Decadence and Chocolate Roulade. I sometimes use it with a plain or Chocolate Marble Cheesecake to gild the lily.

INGREDIENTS

2 (10- OR 12-OUNCE) PACKAGES FROZEN RASPBERRIES

SUGAR (OPTIONAL)

NUTRITION INFORMATION

CALORIES PER 2 TABLESPOONS: 30

FAT: .05 G

% CALORIES FROM FAT: 1%

PROTEIN: .2 G

CARBOHYDRATES: 7.74 G

CHOLESTEROL: 0 MG

MAKES 2 TO 2-1/2 CUPS

Work time: 10 minutes

Thaw the raspberries. Drain them and reserve the juice. Puree berries briefly in a food processor. Sieve the puree to remove seeds. Thin it with some of the reserved juice if desired. If the puree seems too tart, sweeten it to taste. Cover and refrigerate until serving. *Sauce may be refrigerated for up to 3 days or frozen for 6 months or longer.*

BLACKBERRY AND OTHER BUSHBERRY SAUCES

Proceed as for Raspberry Sauce, using fresh berries when possible.

STONE FRUIT COULIS

Peaches, nectarines, apricots, plums, and mangoes make delicious purees, usually requiring even less sugar than the tangy bushberries. A few drops of lemon juice keep lighter colored fruit from discoloring and perk up the flavor of the less acidic fruit.

Peel and slice the fruit and puree it in a food processor, adding drops of lemon juice and sugar to taste.

SIMPLE CHOCOLATE DECORATIONS

Use chocolate decorations strategically to get the maximum visual effect with the least chocolate. Here are the simplest techniques I know.

FINE CHOCOLATE SHAVINGS

With feather light, very fine chocolate shavings it takes less than three quarters of an ounce to coat the sides of an eight- or nine-inch cake two to three inches tall and a fraction of that to decorate just the bottom edge of a cake. Shavings may be used on both refrigerated and room-temperature desserts.

1. To make shavings: Scrape a sharp paring knife against the flat side of a bar of chocolate. Shavings are very delicate. Do not try to pick them up with your hands—they will melt almost instantly. Transfer shavings by sliding a metal pancake turner or icing spatula under them.

2. To apply shavings: Hold the dessert, on a cardboard base or the metal bottom of a cake pan, over a plate of chocolate shavings. Using a metal icing spatula, lift shavings and gently touch them to the moist or sticky sides of the dessert, letting the rest fall back onto the plate. Continue until desired effect is achieved.

THICK CHOCOLATE SHAVINGS

Let the bar of chocolate sit in a warm kitchen and rub it with the heel of your hand. Or set it briefly under a desk lamp or sweep it with a hairdryer. Do not melt the chocolate. Hold the knife blade at a 45° angle to the chocolate and scrape toward you while anchoring the bar with your other hand. This yields thick, sturdy shavings and curls. Pick up the curls with a toothpick. Milk chocolate and white chocolate are softer than dark chocolate, so they yield larger shavings and curls with less warming.

CHOCOLATE SHARDS AND SHEETS

Ultra-thin pieces mean a little goes a long way. They melt at room temperature, so use these only on desserts that will be served immediately or kept refrigerated until serving time.

1. To make shards and sheets: Microwave chopped chocolate on Medium (50% power) or melt in a water bath or double boiler, stirring frequently until completely melted and smooth. Spread chocolate on a sheet of wax paper. Cover with a second sheet of wax paper and spread the chocolate very, very thin by rolling with a rolling pin. Refrigerate for at least 1 hour, or until needed.

2. **To apply:** Remove from the refrigerator and peel away the top sheet of wax paper. Slide a thin spatula under the chocolate and break it into irregular pieces. They melt easily—try to handle as little as possible.

CHOCOLATE SPLINTERS

*I invented these splinters when
I wanted some long narrow shapes with
a little curve to them instead
of flat shards. Use on the sides of the
Pavé, for example, or as an
alternative to the chopped or shaved
chocolate for Mini Misùs.*

1. Melt chopped chocolate as for shards and sheets. Tear off several square sheets of plastic wrap. For splinters 2½ inches long, use a small spatula to spread a 2½-inch-wide band of melted chocolate slightly thicker than paper thin down the center of a sheet of plastic wrap. It is not necessary to spread perfectly neatly or in any exact width. Pleat as follows: Use the fingers of both hands to pinch and gather the plastic on both sides of the chocolate into tiny pleats so that the chocolate-coated plastic becomes pleated as well. The chocolate pleats can touch one another. Refrigerate the

pleated sheets for at least 1 hour. Continue to spread, pleat, and refrigerate as many sheets as you wish.

2. Form splinters by pulling the pleated plastic flat. Splinters will pop up and off the plastic. If they stick or melt, refrigerate remaining plastic pieces longer or freeze to speed up the process. Splinters are fragile and melt easily. Handle as for shards and sheets.

CHOCOLATE LACE OR FILIGREE

*Irregular pieces of broken lace or
individual pieces of filigree are fun to
make. No skill required. These
melt at room temperature, so use them
only on refrigerated desserts or add them
at the last minute before serving.*

1. Have ready a piece of wax paper taped to a baking sheet. If you are planning to pipe a specific pattern, slide a copy of it under the wax paper so you can trace it directly.

2. Microwave chopped chocolate on Medium (50% power) or melt in a water bath or double boiler, stirring frequently until completely melted and smooth. Scrape the chocolate into the corner of a plastic food

storage bag or a disposable decorating cone. Twist the bag to secure the chocolate. Snip the tip of the bag and pipe filigree patterns, a random loopy scribble, a not-too-precise crosshatch. Refrigerate for at least 1 hour, or until needed.

3. Slide a thin metal spatula under the chocolate to release it. Lacy scribbles can be broken up. Handle pieces with a metal spatula to avoid melting.

CHOCOLATE CURLS

*One of the biggest challenges for readers
of my first book was the technique
for scraping chocolate cigarettes or curls
from the back of a baking sheet.
However beautiful and worthwhile the
results, it took lots of time, effort,
and chocolate to master the technique.
In contrast, this mixture is
simple to make and remarkably easy
to work with. It is adapted from a not-
so-good tasting concoction used
by food stylists when appearance, not
taste, is most important. My
version tastes quite wonderful.*

6 OUNCES SEMISWEET OR
BITTERSWEET CHOCOLATE, CHOPPED FINE,
NOT CHOCOLATE CHIPS
1-1/2 TEASPOONS CLARIFIED BUTTER
OR 1 TABLESPOON VEGETABLE SHORTENING

1. Line a small loaf pan with plastic wrap. Place the chocolate and clarified butter in a small heatproof bowl. Set the bowl in pan of barely simmering water and stir constantly until the mixture is melted and smooth. Scrape into the loaf pan and chill for at least 2 hours, or until firm.

2. Lift the plastic to remove the chocolate from the pan. Let stand for 10 to 15 minutes to soften chocolate slightly. Cut chocolate lengthwise to form 2 long bars no wider than the cutting blade of a vegetable peeler. Scrape chocolate firmly with the peeler for curls and cigarette shapes. If curls splinter or crack, chocolate is too cold; wait a few more minutes and try again. If chocolate becomes too soft, put it back in the refrigerator to harden. Handle chocolate curls with a toothpick to avoid fingerprints. *Curls and unused chocolate may be stored indefinitely in the refrigerator, in an airtight container or tightly wrapped, or frozen.*

CLARIFIED BUTTER

Clarified Butter is butter without the milk solids and the water. Brush or spray it between phyllo sheets for crisp tart shells or add it to chocolate to make chocolate cigarettes and curls. It is excellent for sautéing because it does not burn as easily as butter does.

It's convenient to melt several sticks at a time to keep on hand in the refrigerator or freezer. The more you make at a time, the better the yield.

◎◎◎

CLARIFIED BUTTER

INGREDIENT

4 OUNCES (1 STICK) UNSALTED BUTTER

NUTRITION INFORMATION

CALORIES PER TABLESPOON: 112
FAT: 12.7 G
% CALORIES FROM FAT: 100%
PROTEIN: .04 G
CARBOHYDRATES: 0 G
CHOLESTEROL: 32.8 MG

MAKES 6 TO 7 TABLESPOONS

Work time: 5 minutes

Melt the butter in the microwave or on the stovetop. Let stand until it separates into 3 distinct components: water with some milk solids on the bottom, foam with milk solids on top, and clear yellow clarified butter oil in the middle. Tilt the container and carefully skim off and discard the foam. Spoon or pour as much of the clear butter oil as possible into another container. Discard the liquid on the bottom.

BLANCHED AND TOASTED NUTS

Almonds and hazelnuts are sometimes blanched to remove the skin, which may be bitter. If you are unable to find unsalted pistachios, blanching will remove the salt as well as the skin from salted pistachios, leaving them bright green and very decorative. Although blanched almonds are available in the supermarket, recent concern about chemicals used in commercial blanching may induce you to blanch your own. Blanched nuts may be toasted for extra flavor or simply recrisped.

BLANCHED ALMONDS AND PISTACHIOS

Drop raw nuts in a saucepan of boiling water for 1 minute. Remove 1 nut and pinch it under cold water. If the skin slips off, nuts are ready. If not, continue to simmer nuts until ready. Drain and rinse nuts under cold water. Pinch or peel off skins. It is sometimes easiest to do this in a bowl of cold water. To recrisp, spread nuts on a baking sheet. Bake almonds at 350°F. for 5 minutes. Bake pistachios at 300°F. for 10 to 15 minutes.

BLANCHED HAZELNUTS

Traditionally, hazelnut skins, which are somewhat bitter, are removed after toasting, by rubbing toasted nuts together in a dishtowel or against a coarse wire strainer and allowing the skins to fall through. I do not find it any more effective to rub the nuts while they are still hot, as opposed to allowing them to cool first. In either case, some stubborn bits of skin always remain. For more complete skin removal, blanch hazelnuts before toasting, using Rose Beranbaum's superb technique, as follows:

Bring 1½ cups water to a boil in a medium saucepan. Add 1 cup raw hazelnuts and 2 tablespoons baking soda. Boil for 3 minutes; the water will blacken from nut skins. Remove 1 nut and pinch it under cold water. If the skin slips off, drain and rinse the nuts under cold water. If not, continue to simmer until ready. Pinch or peel off the skins. Recrisp at 350°F. for 5 minutes.

TOASTED NUTS

Spread nuts in a single layer on an ungreased baking sheet. Bake in a preheated oven for 10 to 20 minutes, depending on whether nuts are whole, sliced, or slivered. Stir once or twice for even toasting. Toast almonds and hazelnuts at 350°F. Toast pecans and walnuts at 325°F. for only 10 to 12 minutes. Taste for doneness. Nuts may also be toasted in the microwave at high power. Spread nuts in a single layer. One cup of nuts takes 3 to 5 minutes, stirring once, depending on type and size. Watch carefully and taste for doneness.

The Theory and Practice of Creating Rich Desserts with Less Fat

Instead of the usual tips and technique instructions, I want to present an approach, a way of thinking about lower-fat desserts that does justice to the complexity of the subject. Simple how-to's cannot adequately address this vastly interesting and still very new topic. What follows is a combination of personal ideology, common sense, and practical advice. I hope that it will provide a rich introduction to new desserts, and, most important, give you the courage to jump in and try your hand.

THE NEW THEORIES

Not every great light dessert will fit the theories that follow; some may even be contradictory. To be sure, the subject is subtle and complex, but the journey of discovery is fascinating.

MODEL RECIPES

Before moving to more specific concepts, let me introduce you to "modeling," the very simplest approach to creating new light recipes. Whenever you find a low-fat recipe you like, use it as a model. Try simple variations. Extrapolate, experiment. I began to learn about light desserts in precisely this manner. Leaps of imagination came much later.

LIGHT PAIRED WITH RICH

A successful low-fat dessert may be comprised of both high-fat and low-fat elements that when put together average out nicely. Meringues are low in fat; cream is high. Meringues with a modest quantity of whipped cream and fruit will average out to a low-fat dessert. You might even be able to add a little chocolate! The dessert works because the contrasting tastes and textures are varied and flavorful and certainly indulgent. Some sponge cakes, as well as ladyfingers, are very low in fat—pair them with a richer mousse.

CONTRASTING TEXTURES

Like chips and dip, smooth with crunchy satisfies. Who doesn't love finding the rich soft custard beneath the sweet caramel crust of a crème brulée? The custard need not be as rich as you think—the contrast of flavors and textures plus the sound of the crunch contribute a great deal of satisfaction. My Black Bottom Banana Napoleons and Panna Cotta are good examples of this kind of pairing.

CONTRASTING FLAVORS

Sweet chestnut cream is incredibly good with rich real crème fraîche, of course, but it is also extremely good with a silken puree of slightly tart low-fat cottage cheese, either eaten from a dish or transformed into Sweet Chestnut Torte. The reason is the same— the contrast of very sweet with smooth and tart. Consider the classic contrast of chocolate and vanilla (it helps that the colors are dramatic too) or chocolate and raspberries.

COMPLEMENTARY FLAVORS

This is the opposite of contrasting flavor. Using one flavor, such as chocolate, several times or in several different ways in the same dessert creates extra richness. A chocolate cake or torte sauced or frosted with chocolate tastes ultra rich, extra chocolatey. Ingredients other than chocolate, such as liqueurs, extracts, or nuts, are kept at low levels to enhance and support the chocolate instead of contrasting with it. A rich layering effect is also produced when a flavor is repeated in different textures. Creamy frozen chocolate truffles coated in crisp bittersweet chocolate and dusted with unsweetened cocoa powder (page 109) make this point nicely.

RICH BY ASSOCIATION

Even if they are not themselves rich, some flavors suggest richness. They send a message to the brain, fooling the palate. For example, caramel is a rich flavor. Sweet crusty browned edges of cookies and cakes are slightly caramelized, and we can't get enough of them. Transfer the flavor of these hard-to-resist foods to another context. Caramelized apples, peaches, or pears? Caramelized molds for puddings or flans.

I have been amazed at how powerful flavor associations can be. My recipe for Flans with Brandied Prunes was adapted from a nonfat recipe by Steven Raichlen. This flan tastes positively rich to me because of the flavor associations. One percent milk is steeped in aromatics (cinnamon stick and whole vanilla bean and lemon peel) so that it is richly infused with flavors. My brain tells me that a custard with this depth of flavor must be rich. Put that together with the caramel sauce from the mold and the sweet plump prune and the palate has been totally bedazzled.

FREEZING

Some desserts that are good cold or at room temperature turn into something entirely different and wonderful when frozen. Freezing stiffens the texture and changes the "mouth feel," often creating a perception of greater richness. Beryl's Walnut Truffle Cookies happened quite by accident when I scooped some chocolate mousse between two chocolate walnut cookies and froze them. I was astonished at how deliciously chewy and extremely chocolatey they were. That discovery led to

two of my favorites, Bittersweet Chocolate Truffles and an extraordinary frozen Bittersweet Chocolate Marquise, which I serve with Praline Crème Anglaise. Other mousses and creams may not work as frozen desserts because of the formation of ice crystals. My mousses adapt well because the meringue inhibits the formation of ice crystals and keeps the frozen mixture soft enough to be appealing.

Layered and assembled desserts that pair frozen yogurt with cake or meringues are also wonderful—Sorbet Basket, Frozen Chocolate Praline Torte, Black Forest or Chestnut Bûche de Noël. The cold creaminess of these desserts always seems luxurious to me.

PRESENTATION

The mystique of dessert starts with how it looks. Is it beautiful, dramatic, appetizing, elegant? All of this continues to be important with lighter desserts. I like to use the same kinds of super dramatic and elegant finishing techniques for light desserts that I do for richer ones because of the association those looks have with splurge desserts, splurge restaurants, splurge contexts in general. I don't want to signal lowered expectations with a modest presentation when I can create anticipation with a little chocolate glaze, spun sugar, or gold leaf.

FAT AND SUGAR

When you only reduce fat you will find that desserts suddenly taste sweeter, often too sweet. Fat balances and mutes sweetness, so it may be necessary to compensate for the loss of fat with less sugar, as well. See, there is some good news!

Beware the irony, however. First, sugar contributes to moistness and moisture retention, which keeps baked goods from becoming stale quickly. This may explain the tendency for commercially produced low-fat baked goods to be overly sweet. Second, keeping sugar high (or adding it) is an insidious way of lowering the percentage of calories from fat. Why? Any ingredient that raises total calories (but not fat) automatically lowers the percentage of calories from fat. I have actually heard knowledgeable people tell me that increasing sugar is a technique for creating lower-fat desserts. Humbug!

FAT AND FLAVOR

The idea that fat carries flavor is the single most annoying and facile argument for why it is impossible to make really spectacular desserts with less fat. It is much more productive to look at fat and flavor in a less simplistic way. Does fat carry flavor or bury flavor? Let's see how this works.

First of all, fat does help to blend flavors. It softens or mutes strong or harsh flavors and sweetness, among other things. In this regard it helps flavors to work together to create a pleasing whole.

This became perfectly clear as I tried to balance and blend flavors in desserts with less fat and found it unexpectedly tricky. For example, my traditional Queen of Sheba Torte with lots of butter, chocolate, and eggs is enhanced by three tablespoons of brandy. My lean Fallen Chocolate Soufflé Torte, inspired by the Sheba, wants only one tablespoon of brandy—any more than that stands out and overwhelms the cake. The same thing happened when I was trying to find the right amount of liqueur to brush on the Chocolate Grand Marnier Cake. Less really did turn out to be more. Liqueurs and extracts must be used with a very light hand.

Fat also stabilizes flavors. Flavors are more volatile when there is less fat present. A lean dessert may taste fine one day but not so good the next. Or it will taste best on the second day but doesn't keep until the fourth. Joking with a friend, I said, "Be sure to eat this dessert between 2 and 4:30 P.M. the day after tomorrow." That was an exaggeration, but clearly it is important to know how far in advance things can be made, remembering also that reducing the fat reduces the keeping qualities of most desserts. In the same vein, some of my lower-fat desserts don't freeze as well as I thought they would—not because the texture deteriorates, but the flavors seem to change and wander off in different directions. Like Alice in Wonderland, I thought things were behaving very strangely. Can flavors wander off? I defrosted a plain Buttermilk Pound Cake after only two and a half months to find the texture great but the vanilla flavor transformed into something vaguely unpleasant.

As a consequence of flavor volatility, I often recommend when to make each dessert and tell how long it will remain delicious. I also recommend very conservative freezing times in the recipe, where appropriate.

With fat at a minimum, great ingredients become even more important. While I have always been a fanatic about good ingredients, I now suspect that very rich recipes are more forgiving of mediocre ingredients because of the softening and blending properties of the fat. My leaner desserts really shine with fine ingredients; off flavors from lesser quality ingredients, if they are there, are easy to detect. I am thrilled when I make a lean chocolate torte with excellent bittersweet chocolate and Pernigotti cocoa. I am less happy with grocery store cocoa.

THE FAT BUDGET

I think of fat as a limited resource. The more I use, the less I have to spend. My favorite traditional chocolate desserts—signature desserts in my first book and for my company—were always rich chocolate tortes with little or no flour in them, lots of bittersweet chocolate, eggs, butter, and nuts. I have found that the rich chocolate flavor I like, and the texture, can be approached with a careful combination of cocoa and excellent bittersweet chocolate. But the more I spend the fat budget on chocolate, the more egg yolks and/or butter I must eliminate. Amazingly, this can and does work. The results are a handful of stunning, and very chocolatey tortes, each with its

own character depending on the use of nuts, quantity of flour, ratio of bittersweet to cocoa, and use of egg whites. You will see that I was able to eliminate the butter entirely and work with only a small amount of egg yolk.

I try to think about which fat will contribute the most to my recipe. Working on chocolate frostings and sauces, I found my cocoa-based concoctions good but a little sharp. Because they were very low in fat, they did not stiffen enough to frost a cake. I needed fat to soften the rough edges of the flavor and thicken the mixture. I was about to add just a little butter when I had an even better idea. Why not use a little milk chocolate instead? The reward was threefold: The milk chocolate stiffened the mixture; it added the creamy mellow flavor I needed; and it enriched the chocolate taste. In a milder, sweeter frosting I used a little light cream cheese similarly, to provide body and the illusion of cream. Get your limited fat allowance to do as many things as possible—and all at the same time.

THE NEW PRACTICES FOR LIGHTENING UP YOUR FAVORITE RECIPES

This is lots of fun. Successes are particularly satisfying because the process is not completely straightforward and results can be unpredictable. You will be rewarded for your culinary acumen and creativity on one day and brought down to earth the next when you re-invent rubber or cardboard. There are no finite rules, but there are many guidelines and lots of room for leaps of imagination. Here are some pointers for lightening up a bit.

FIND THE FAT

This is easy. Look for butter or oil, egg yolks, chocolate, nuts, and cream. If you are serious about analyzing recipes, buy a reference book like *Food Values of Portions Commonly Used* by Jean A. T. Pennington or *Nutrition Almanac* by John D. Kirschmann with Lavon J. Dunne. You will quickly learn exactly where the fat is in any recipe as you look up the calories and fat in each ingredient. Each gram of fat has nine calories. Multiply the number of grams of fat in any dish by nine and divide by the total calories in the recipe or serving and you will have calculated the percentage of calories from fat. If you are more serious, you can purchase a computer program that will calculate all of this for you.

Having found the fat, remember that you will not be trying to eliminate all of it. You will be trying to use less and make what you use count. You will budget and strategize.

LEARN TO SPOT RECIPES THAT ARE GOOD CANDIDATES FOR ALTERATION

Some recipes seem defined by the kind and quantity of their fat. Classic butter cookies and shortbread, true pound cakes, and butter cakes are a few of the desserts that seem to rely on fat for taste and texture. These are not good starting points for modification if you are new at the game.

Start with recipes that are moderate in fat to begin with and have ingredients other than fat that contribute to flavor, moisture, and structure. A carrot cake or apple cake (or any other fruit- or vegetable-based cake) will tolerate the reduction of butter, oil, and some egg yolks and all or some of the nuts. A devil's food cake made with cocoa is usually moderate in fat to begin with and can be reduced even further. Buttermilk-based cakes may be made with low-fat buttermilk and can usually survive the removal of twenty to twenty-five percent of their butter and some replacement of egg yolks with whites.

Pies and tarts with fillings that don't break the fat budget are often held together with very rich buttery crusts. A two-crust pie can become a one-crust pie or the pie crust can be traded in for a multilayered flaky phyllo crust (page 154). Tart crusts are heartbreakingly buttery. Instead of compromising the taste and texture of the traditional crust I base my lighter tarts on a very light, crunchy version of Mandelbrot.

REPLACE AT LEAST ONE EGG WITH TWO EGG WHITES

This works if done in moderation. Do not, however, apply this (or any) rule too rigidly. Too many egg whites can create a rubbery texture (from too much baked protein). I sometimes replace a whole egg with only one white. I made unbelievably rubbery brownies by replacing two of the whole eggs with four whites. I made excellent brownies (page 133) by replacing two eggs with only two whites.

USE QUALITY INGREDIENTS

As always, the best chocolate, cocoa, nuts, cream, and butter have more and better flavor. When you use these splurge ingredients, the best quality goes much farther.

USE NUTS STRATEGICALLY

Use fewer nuts than the recipe calls for but try to get the most flavor out of them. Recipes like biscotti usually call for whole nuts—I use chopped nuts so that there are more pieces and no one gets a cookie without nuts. If a recipe calls for ground nuts, I sometimes start with chopped nuts and process them with the flour in the recipe so that the nut oils are dispersed into the flour. I also toast nuts, where appropriate, for more flavor.

FOOL WITH THE FORMAT

I wrote about designer desserts and architectural desserts in *Cocolat*. I talked about constructing desserts so that they decorate themselves, eliminating the need to spread with icing or frost all over with cream. This concept is perfect for lighter desserts. Put the lighter elements (cake, meringue, ladyfingers, phyllo pastry, etc.) around the outside of the dessert to envelop the richer fillings and mousses. Or use a richer cake and roll it around a light filling like a jelly roll. I think of this practice as creating a decorative edible container for the dessert. It offers great presentations, and it changes the ratio of rich to light but still lets you eat some rich. For several desserts in this book I used a springform pan as a mold to assemble layers of cake and mousse. I make sure that the cake layers are slightly smaller than the pan so that the mousse filling flows all around the edges of the cake to provide an even, finished appearance for the top and sides of the dessert; there is no need to add additional frosting. This saves steps and fat.

REPLACE DAIRY PRODUCTS WITH THEIR LOW-FAT COUNTERPARTS

This doesn't get you into much trouble, usually. Light or low-fat (1% or 2%) milk substitutes beautifully for whole milk; nonfat milk seems so much less creamy but works in a pinch. Low-fat buttermilk is excellent and low-fat sour cream, yogurt, cottage cheese, and ricotta cheese are all good bets. Light cream cheese is an acceptable substitute for most packaged brands of full-fat cream cheese, although I wish a lower-fat natural cream cheese were available, without gums and starches.

DON'T TRY TO REMOVE ALL OF THE FAT

Keep a perspective on things. This is dessert! If you are trading pureed sweetened cottage cheese for rich whipped cream, allow yourself the luxury of 4% cottage cheese instead of 2% if it seems creamier to you (although sometimes the 2% is fine). When experimenting with old recipes, don't try to eliminate all of the egg yolks and all of the butter at once. Remove fat a little at a time. If the recipe still tastes good, you may be able to reduce a bit more. Keep notes—your own low-fat diary.

USE SAFE MERINGUE TO LIGHTEN RICH DESSERTS

My Safe Meringue is creamy and nonfat. It can be used to stretch whipped cream, as a topping, or as an ingredient in mousses and fillings. Invent more hot and cold desserts with baked meringue toppings—the contrasting texture and creaminess of meringue adds interest and richness to desserts other than lemon meringue pie and baked Alaska. A layer cake can even be frosted with Safe Meringue and briefly toasted in the oven.

REPLACE SOME BUT NOT NECESSARILY ALL OF THE CHOCOLATE WITH COCOA

This is a trial and error kind of thing. When you substitute cocoa for bittersweet or semisweet chocolate, you must also add sugar (from twenty-five up to one hundred percent of the volume of the added cocoa, depending on what else is going on in the recipe). Reviewing my own recipes, I don't see clear rules of thumb. For example, in one torte that would traditionally have called for six ounces of bittersweet chocolate and three quarters of a cup of sugar, I used only three ounces of bittersweet with half a cup of cocoa and a full cup of sugar. This may work as a guideline for a similarly structured recipe, but certainly not across the board for all recipes. In my original Marble Cheesecake recipe five ounces of bittersweet chocolate was added to one cup of plain cheesecake batter. In the light version (page 44), I used only three tablespoons of cocoa to a cup of plain batter with only one tablespoon of extra sugar. The results in both cases were dark and chocolatey.

There are too many variables in each recipe and too many different types of recipes to make hard-and-fast rules about substitution. A better approach would be to look at different categories of desserts—tortes, loaves and pound cakes, cookies—and study the relationships between major ingredients. What works in one torte will likely work in another but not necessarily in a cookie.

MIND YOUR MIXING TECHNIQUE

Do not skimp or take shortcuts with classic mixing techniques. Cakes made by first creaming fat and sugar together, then adding eggs gradually, and finally alternately adding dry and moist ingredients can be delicate. The final texture is dependent on your technique—especially with minimal fat. Have ingredients, especially dairy ingredients, at room temperature. Move from one step to the next without delay or interruption and carry out each mixing step fully. My Buttermilk Pound Cake can be used as a master recipe for this technique. (For further, in-depth discussions of mixing cakes, consult the excellent technique sections in *The Simple Art of Perfect Baking* by Flo Braker and/or *Great Cakes* by Carole Walter.)

Cookies mixed by the creaming method will also vary considerably in texture depending on whether they are well creamed to incorporate a lot of air or minimally creamed; cookies with minimal fat seem to do best with lots of creaming.

WHAT ABOUT FRUIT PUREES?

Applesauce or strained prunes or other fruit purees can be added to compensate for fat loss and to provide moisture. This is a brilliant technique but one that I use sparingly (unless I am cooking for someone who must eliminate nearly all fat). I am happiest when the added flavor from these purees (in addition to the moistness) enhances the rest of the recipe, as I feel it does in Spicy New Orleans Gingerbread. I am less enthralled when I have to count on the other ingredients to hide the flavor of the puree.

Experiment with fruit purees in quick breads and oil-based cakes that may already include fruits and vegetables. Don't think it's all or nothing—try substituting the puree for a part of the butter or fat.

THE CAKE FLOUR QUESTION

In place of all-purpose flour, cake flour substituted by equal weight (not volume) can tenderize and provide a finer, softer grain in cakes. I use this technique sparingly also, since all-purpose flour provides excellent flavor and character to some cakes. To substitute using a scale, simply substitute cake flour for all-purpose ounce for ounce. If you have no scale, substitute one and a quarter cups unsifted cake flour for every cup of unsifted all-purpose; if the flour called for is a sifted measurement, substitute one and one eighth cups of sifted cake flour for each cup of sifted all-purpose. For a fuller discussion of cake and all-purpose flour, see pages 177–178.

USE ACIDIC DAIRY PRODUCTS

Low-fat or nonfat yogurt or low-fat buttermilk tenderizes doughs and adds a velvet texture to cakes. It stands to reason. Some of the most luscious traditional cakes we know are made with buttermilk or sour cream. I never thought about the nature of their contribution to texture until I was reminded that

sour cream adds tenderness in rich pastries and doughs. If they tenderize the rich ones, I thought while struggling to develop a tender crisp cookie, surely they could help my lean ones. The addition of two tablespoons of nonfat yogurt tenderized them dramatically.

DON'T BORE YOUR AUDIENCE

If you have read this far, you should know by now that different kinds of recipes invite different kinds of lightening techniques. Don't bore your audience by using the same technique on everything! Don't always replace every ounce of chocolate with cocoa. Make some of your lighter desserts exclusively with cocoa, but learn to use combinations of cocoa and chocolate to create more variety and richness in your desserts. Try different chocolates and different cocoas. Don't overdo the egg whites for yolks substitution; don't switch all your cakes from all-purpose to cake flour; and don't put strained prunes or applesauce into everything.

KEEP YOUR STANDARDS HIGH

Never settle for "It's pretty good for what it is." Keep on tasting and evaluating. Let's reeducate ourselves and our techniques to please our palates—not teach our palates to like things that are not delicious. Lighter desserts can be stunningly delicious, but there is still a lot to learn.

MEASURING AND MIXING MATTER

As I tested recipes for this book, I became more aware than ever of the importance of measuring and mixing techniques—not to mention oven accuracy and weight of pans.

All cookbook authors are haunted, at least once in a while, by the reader who says, "It didn't work." Most of the time, after talking through the recipe with the reader, it becomes obvious to me that he or she didn't really think it necessary to follow the instructions exactly; maybe a different size pan was used or the temperature of the oven was way off or the person did not measure correctly. While it is true that many good recipes leave some room for error, desserts and baked goods are less forgiving than other types of foods. Recipes that are low in fat can be even more delicate. If you want to taste the recipe as I created it, it really is important to follow the instructions and measure ingredients precisely.

FLOUR

Properly sifted and measured flour can be up to twenty percent lighter than unsifted flour. Dry ingredients sifted directly into a cup and leveled with the sweep of a knife weigh differently than those sifted onto wax paper and gently spooned into the cup.

These differences may seem too picky for any but a measuring maniac, but they can be crucial with these lighter desserts. I tested endlessly to find the subtle borderline between "less fat but still delicious" and "not so good anymore." I would test a recipe a dozen times varying the quantity of fat or flour by only half an ounce, looking for the formula that was best. If you are cavalier about measuring, you may get a pretty nice cookie, but not as nice as the one I got. You would be surprised at the differences in quality resulting from small changes of fat or flour in cookie or cake recipes. If you do not measure your dry ingredients accurately, you are actually changing the ratio of fat to other ingredients in the recipe by a small but possibly critical amount. Let's review the measuring conventions.

Recipes will designate whether the flour should be measured before or after sifting, as follows:

1 cup sifted flour: This means to sift the flour directly into a measuring cup placed on a piece of wax paper, then sweep a metal spatula or knife across the top of the cup to level the flour without jiggling or rapping the cup.

1 cup flour: This means to scoop the measuring cup directly into the canister to fill it without pressing or packing it in, then sweep a metal spatula or knife across the top to level it. Do not rap the cup to settle the flour or otherwise compress it.

COCOA

I agonized over the measuring of cocoa. First, one cup of one brand of cocoa does not weigh the same as another. Second, sifting cocoa before measuring is messy and I was afraid that people would cheat; or if they did sift first, would they sift into the cup and sweep off; or would they sift onto paper and spoon into the cup. Would they use a strainer, a triple sifter? Finally I decided to list cocoa by unsifted measure. Simply spoon the cocoa lightly into the cup (it is hard to dip the measure into the cocoa container) and sweep the excess off with a metal spatula or knife.

I had planned to include the weight as well as the unsifted measurement, so that those with scales would have the advantage. I decided against this when it became clear that my favorite high-fat cocoas weigh three and three quarter ounces per unsifted cup and a common supermarket brand weighs only three ounces. Other good quality cocoas weigh somewhere in between. I tested recipes with high quality cocoa and common national supermarket brands to find out if the volume measures would work for each. In the end, I decided that the volume measure across the board was the better common denominator because when I used the weight measurement with lesser quality cocoas, I got some harsh flavors.

Here is how to interpret the measuring of other ingredients:

½ cup chopped almonds (2 ounces): This means to measure after chopping or weigh first and then chop.

½ cup almonds, chopped (2½ ounces): This means to measure the almonds while whole. After measuring, chop fine.

If using a scale, you may chop before or after weighing in either example.

Mixing technique can also be a greater variable than even I believed it to be. Working on these recipes I paid more attention than ever to the time and method of mixing; sometimes I felt that I was giving myself a refresher course in basic baking. I read and reread my personal gurus (Flo Braker and Carole Walter) on the technique for mixing butter cakes. I am quite certain that the success or failure of the butter cake recipes in this book (tea loaves and pound cakes) has much to do with mixing procedures. Be attentive to the sequence and timing of mixing, and be sure to have ingredients at room temperature, 68°-70°F.

TIME AND TEMPERATURE COUNT

Great care was taken in testing these recipes to insure that everyone could achieve excellent results. Baking times were checked and rechecked and I had my own ovens calibrated regularly. I was feeling fine until I learned that home ovens are infrequently calibrated and may be off from 25°F. to 100°F. I was shocked at this news, although I know that one can roast a chicken at temperatures ranging from 325°F. all the way up to 500°F., with arguably adequate results. Indeed, many everyday foods are similarly forgiving of precise oven temperatures.

Alas, pastries and desserts are a different story and lower-fat recipes are especially finicky. Baked goods with less fat dry out quickly or become rubbery when overcooked and have a tendency toward sticky moistness when undercooked. If you wish to be rewarded with the best results from the recipes in this book—or any other well-tested low-fat recipes—you'd be wise to have your oven checked, watch carefully for the signs of doneness, and observe the baking times given. The added bonus? You'll probably get better results from all your baking!

About the Nutritional Analysis

Recipes were analyzed with the program Food Processor II, published by ESHA Research (P.O. Box 13028, Salem, OR 97309, 503/585-6242). Where I felt appropriate, data was entered by weight instead of volume for greater accuracy. All recipes which contain cocoa assume medium-fat (18%) Dutch process cocoa, which I added to the ESHA database. Fat grams are rounded up to the nearest tenth. Analysis per serving assumes the larger number of servings (i.e., smaller portion). Thus, a recipe that serves six to eight is analyzed for eight servings.

Optional recipe ingredients are not included in the analysis. Nor does the analysis include any sauces or accompaniments listed as optional. Frostings and glazes integral to the specific recipe are, of course, included in the analysis. I list accompaniments as optional if I feel that the recipe stands on its own merit and the accompaniment is simply a way of varying or dressing it up for an occasion. I also list accompaniments as optional when there are several different ones for you to choose from. For reasons of space, not all recipe variations have nutritional analysis, but they are within the guidelines.

Ingredients

The food industry has responded to Americans' concern about fat with a proliferation of food substitutes, additives, and replacement ingredients. A tidal wave of products made from these ingredients are marketed so aggressively that a Martian roaming the supermarket might believe that "healthy," "fat free" and "low fat" mean a long list of mystery ingredients.

A major motivation for me to write this book was to emphasize that the best and most pleasurable low-fat desserts are still made with the finest ingredients.

Here is a guide to essential ingredients and some selection tips.

CHOCOLATE AND COCOA

In a book that boasts lower fat and fewer calories, chocolate as an ingredient must be a scarce resource. Nevertheless, I wanted as many chocolate desserts as possible in this collection, for myself and everyone else for whom chocolate is virtually the definition of dessert. Knowing that friends jumped to the immediate conclusion, "So that means cocoa, right?", I took it as a challenge. As delicious as some of the available cocoas are, I did not want everything to taste like cocoa. And I could not imagine categorically excluding real chocolate from desserts simply to reduce fat and calories. A challenge, indeed.

CHOCOLATE

Where chocolate is called for in recipes, a quality brand will yield maximum flavor, texture, and aroma. Recipes often call for bittersweet or semisweet chocolate. These two types of chocolate are interchangeable for practical purposes. In these leaner recipes, an assertive bittersweet chocolate is a strategic choice because a little goes a long way. I personally prefer the extra intensity of bittersweet whether the recipe is lean or not. In general, though, select chocolates according to your personal taste. There are so many imported and domestic chocolates to choose from now. Like wine, the aroma and flavor characteristics of chocolate are varied and fascinating. Some people prefer the mildest and smoothest with almost fruity overtones; others like assertive, acidic, highly roasted flavors. Ghirardelli (quite assertive) is one of my favorite domestic bittersweet chocolates for use in dessert recipes. Among the imports, Callebaut and Lindt are excellent (milder, not as acidic or smoky) and Valrhona is positively exotic, with a range of flavors and a luxurious price tag. Do not substitute milk chocolate or white chocolate for semisweet or bittersweet. Do not confuse bittersweet and semisweet chocolate with unsweetened chocolate (also called chocolate liquor).

Strategy is the name of the game if you want to use real chocolate instead of or along with cocoa in lower-fat desserts. Here are some examples of how I got away with it:

• In Black Bottom Banana Napoleons the chocolate is only in the lower layer and the other ingredients are lean enough that I can use real chocolate instead of cocoa to make the custard.

• In several chocolate tortes I want the effect of a flourless chocolate cake—extremely chocolatey and rather dense. Cocoa alone delivers lots of chocolate flavor, but the addition of some bittersweet chocolate adds a surprising richness and depth of flavor. I compensate for the fat in the chocolate by eliminating butter and minimizing egg yolks.

• In chocolate glazes and frostings the addition of a small amount of milk chocolate adds creamy chocolate flavor, rich texture, and body. Otherwise the recipe is made with low-fat milk, no butter, no cream, and plenty of cocoa.

COCOA

Cocoa is an unsweetened powder obtained from the roasted cocoa bean after some of the cocoa fat has been pressed out of it. Cocoa is used extensively in low-fat chocolate desserts because it contains from ten to twenty-four percent fat compared with thirty to thirty-five percent in eating chocolate or fifty percent in unsweetened baking chocolate. The fat difference is even more dramatic than the numbers imply, because only a fraction of the amount of cocoa is used as compared with chocolate in any given recipe.

It is not necessarily an advantage to choose the very lowest-fat cocoas for leaner desserts. Most of the cocoa flavor is not in the fat, but the process of extracting fat can damage the delicate cocoa flavor. The best quality cocoas have higher fat and the deepest, richest flavors. For lighter desserts, the extra fat in the better cocoas pays off by giving us much more and better flavor.

Cocoa brands available to the home cook, unfortunately, do not indicate the fat percentage on the package so consumers don't know if they are buying low-fat, medium-fat, or high-fat cocoa. To confuse things further, manufacturers are now developing new and perhaps better cocoas with little or no fat to meet consumer demand for more low-fat or nonfat chocolate products.

Here is a list of my favorite cocoas, most of which are medium to high fat; they are available at specialty stores or by mail order: DeZaan (D23), Lindt, Pernigotti, Valrhona, and Bensdorp. Each of these cocoas is excellent, but they differ in flavor and aroma. If you like, buy a selection and taste each one.

I found my favorites by conducting a blind tasting of about twelve different brands of cocoa with a few friends. We made a lot of hot cocoa that day!

Dutch process cocoa is specified for the recipes in this book. I like the flavor, aroma, and rich color of it, and the many brand choices available. The brands listed above are Dutch process cocoa; it is also available under more common supermarket brands like Droste and the new Hershey's European Style Cocoa. Since lower-fat chocolate desserts rely more than ever on cocoa for their chocolate flavor, try some of the best brands—at least now and then—for their special richness and aroma.

Dutch process and natural (nonalkalized) cocoas can sometimes be used interchangeably to make hot frostings, sauces, creams, and many confections—but rarely in baked goods. Dutch process cocoa is an alkaline ingredient; natural process cocoa is acidic. Baked goods, especially cakes leavened with baking soda and/or baking powder, rely on a balance of acid and alkaline to rise properly and taste good. Substituting Dutch process for natural cocoa in a cake recipe may cause an imbalance and result in a gummy, rubbery, bad tasting cake.

The recipes in this book all call for Dutch process cocoa, but other cookbooks or recipes may not be specific. In traditional American cookbooks cocoa always refers to natural (nonalkalized) rather than Dutch process cocoa because, historically, only natural cocoa was available to the American home cook. If your cookbook is older and/or the leavening is all or mostly baking soda, you can feel safe in using natural soda, you can feel safe in using natural (not Dutch process) cocoa. Recent cookbooks are a different story. Only some of them specify the type of cocoa and sometimes with a phrase like "preferably Dutch process." If no cocoa type is specified in the recipe, check the front or back of the book to see if the author gives advice in an ingredient section that pertains to all the recipes in the book. If not, look at the recipe. If it is a baked item, look at the leavening. If all or most of it is baking soda, assume you are to use natural cocoa. If there is no baking powder or soda in the recipe, you can probably use either natural or Dutch process cocoa. There are exceptions to every rule, of course, but these are good rules of thumb to follow.

Most Dutch process cocoa is labeled Dutch process or alkalized on the front or side of the package or the ingredient list notes "cocoa processed with alkali." Look sharp. Hershey's uses the phrase "European Style" for its Dutch process cocoa. Natural cocoa, on the other hand, is simply called "cocoa" on the package.

CITRUS PEELS, CANDIED

Candied or glacéed Australian lemon and orange peels are excellent in texture and flavor. They are processed without brining or blanching away the oils that give the peels their flavor, and only the smallest quantity of sulfur dioxide is used to maintain color. Williams-Sonoma stores carry these peels; otherwise, look for the Royal Pacific Label or some designation that the peels are from Australia.

COFFEE

Instant espresso or coffee powder is my preferred coffee flavoring for desserts, and Medaglio d'Oro or Café Salvador instant (but not freeze dried) are my preferred brands. These products are found in specialty stores and fancier supermarkets, somewhat unpredictably. If you must substitute freeze-dried instant coffee for the powder, use about twenty-five percent more than the recipe calls for. Stock up on espresso or coffee powder when and if you see it.

DAIRY PRODUCTS

I'm a label reader. I choose my brand of cream, cottage cheese, sour cream, yogurt, and other cultured and fresh dairy products by the length of the ingredient list as well as the taste. With the exception of milk, the reduction of fat in dairy products often goes hand in hand with the addition of gums, modified food starches, flavorings, and other additives to make up for the lost flavor and texture.

The biggest addition of ingredients usually occurs in the transition from low fat to nonfat. For example, my favorite high quality brand of regular (4%) cottage cheese contains the following: grade A cultured nonfat milk, milk, cream, salt, acetic acid, annatto extract. Low-fat (2%) cottage cheese from the same producer has exactly the same ingredient list. Nonfat cottage cheese from the same producer has the following additional ingredients: dextrin, modified food starch, and natural cream flavor. This happens with other dairy products as well, although, to be honest, many full-fat dairy products have long ingredient lists to start with and the nonfat version may not be all that different.

Where I have called for low-fat instead of nonfat dairy products in my recipes it is because I prefer fewer additives where possible, and also because some of the nonfat products are too tart for my needs.

MILK

Recipes call for 1% milk; you may use 2% if you prefer it. Skim or nonfat milk has no creaminess at all, but you may use it.

CREAM

Recipes call for fresh dairy cream (heavy or half-and-half as indicated). I am adamant about the superiority of fresh natural cream which is pasteurized, but not ultra-pasteurized or sterilized for longer shelf life. The long shelf life of ultra-pasteurized and sterilized cream has made them increasingly the grocer's choice, and it is growing more and more difficult to find natural cream in all parts of the country. Ask for it, and use it if you can find it.

SOUR CREAM

Recipes may call for light sour cream. This is a tricky area. Across the country there are scores of brands of light or low-fat sour cream. They vary tremendously in quality and flavor. I urge you to take the time to taste several brands side by side. Choose a brand without a long list of mystery ingredients. I find that the brands with short ingredient lists do, indeed, generally taste more like natural dairy products. Sour cream with a long ingredient list feels artificially smooth and slippery on the palate. It tastes processed and dull, rather than clean and tangy.

BUTTER

In most of my baking and dessert making I use sweet (unsalted) butter. If the butter is to be melted anyway (in a Genoise, for example) I might brown it lightly for a richer flavor. Stick (not soft) margarine can be substituted for butter to meet religious or dietary requirements. In the light of recent information about transfatty acids, however, margarine may not prove to be the fat of choice for those concerned about cholesterol.

COTTAGE CHEESE

I select low-fat cottage cheese that tastes good, has a short list of ingredients compared with the other brands on the shelf (if there is a choice), and is not too salty. I have been unable to find a widely available unsalted cottage cheese, but this has not mattered. Nonfat cottage cheese is too tangy for dessert making and may have additional stabilizers, gums, and flavorings.

Cottage cheese is very useful for making low-fat desserts. I reduce it to a super puree (processed for a full two to three minutes to make it silken smooth) to eliminate the curds. It can then be used in place of cream cheese or sweetened and flavored in various ways to create creamy accompaniments for richer desserts.

RICOTTA CHEESE

Ricotta can be used similarly to cottage cheese. Whole milk and part skim ricotta are both higher in fat than their cottage cheese counterparts, but they are less tangy and offer a creamier tasting alternative.

LIGHT CREAM CHEESE

I use small amounts of this product although I consider it a slight compromise of my philosophy. When I bake with or eat regular cream cheese, I buy a natural bulk cream cheese from a cheese shop. Unlike the supermarket brands, bulk cream cheese does not contain gums and stabilizers; it tastes cleaner and less processed. I have not found a natural lower-fat cream cheese, so I somewhat reluctantly use a low-fat brand from the supermarket. Used in modest amounts, it thickens (yes, I am sure those gums and stabilizers are working for me here) and adds considerable creaminess; I use it in a delicious chocolate frosting and my Mocha Mousse.

EGGS

Recipes call for fresh eggs, graded large. Since reducing the quantity of egg yolks is one of the fat-reducing techniques that I used in many recipes, you will be using more egg whites than yolks.

EGG SAFETY

The possibility of salmonella poisoning from raw eggs is of concern to many. All of the recipes in this book were created with egg safety in mind. No recipe includes whole eggs, yolks, or whites that have not been heated to at least 160°F. In many of my recipes I have incorporated a new technique, of my own creation, for handling uncooked meringue or whipped egg whites; I call it Safe Meringue (page 138). But even a recipe that incorporates safely heated eggs is no guarantee against contamination due to mishandling or ignorance. Here are a few general rules to observe:

• Keep eggs refrigerated.

• Wash your hands after handling raw eggs.

• Keep raw eggs from coming in contact with cuts or broken skin.

• Wash utensils and containers that come in contact with raw eggs, or mixtures containing raw eggs, before using them again while preparing the same dish. For example, when cooking an egg-based custard, the spatula used to scrape raw eggs into the saucepan should not be used again to scrape the cooked mixture out of the saucepan. Nor should the cooked mixture be scraped back into the bowl that was used to beat the raw eggs.

EGG SUBSTITUTES

Egg substitutes will be of interest to those critically concerned about cholesterol. Most of these products are made with egg whites, and a host of additives and preservatives including MSG, artificial flavor, coloring, and modified food starches. They are cholesterol free, and some are even fat free. Although I understand the demand for these products, I am too much of a purist to like them or use them.

Simply Eggs, reduced cholesterol whole eggs, may be the best alternative to shell eggs possible. Quite different from the others, Simply Eggs is a pasteurized liquid whole egg product that comes in a carton. It contains small amounts of salt, citric acid, calcium, vitamin A palmitin, and thiamine. The eggs have the same nutrients, calories, and fat as fresh whole eggs but eighty percent of the cholesterol has been removed. They are pasteurized and thus safe from salmonella. To substitute in baking, use about a quarter of a cup for each whole egg. Reduce the oven temperature in baked goods about ten to fifteen degrees. Read any additional information on the package.

FLOUR

In this book, all-purpose (bleached) flour should be used where the recipe simply calls for flour. Use cake flour (not self-rising) when it is called for. Pastry flour may be substituted for cake flour.

I had lunch one day with a group of bakers and pastry chefs (admittedly not just any old group, as it included Lindsey Shere, Marion Cunningham, and Flo Braker). It turned out that we didn't entirely agree on when it was better to use cake flour rather than all-purpose flour. For fun, we decided to conduct a tasting for the membership of our professional group, the Baker's Dozen.

From that tasting I learned that the answer wasn't so simple! As expected, all-purpose flour was best for cookies and biscuits. But we had disagreed about Genoise and some other cakes. The tasting revealed that Genoise baked with cake flour is indeed lighter and more delicate. I thought it a perfect vehicle to be brushed with liqueur and filled with buttercream or a rich mousse. However, Genoise made with all-purpose flour, although coarser and heavier, was more flavorful. To me it seemed perfect to accompany fresh fruit and cream or any other dessert where the Genoise itself plays an important role. This accounts for the fact that cake flour is specified for the Genoise for Chocolate Grand Marnier Cake while all-purpose is called for in the Raspberry Genoise.

Substituting cake flour for all-purpose flour is often cited as a tenderizing technique for reducing the fat in baked goods. To properly compare the results of such a substitution, the flours must be measured by weight—a cup-for-cup substitution automatically results in a more tender and richer cake simply because one cup of cake flour weighs less than one cup of all-purpose flour. When I compared cake to all-purpose flour (by weight) in my Buttermilk Pound Cake, the superior flavor of the all-purpose version was more compelling than the slightly finer grain and more tender texture of the one made from cake flour.

WONDRA FLOUR

This quick-mixing flour made of wheat and malted barley is used mostly for sauce and gravy making. I have found that it also gives good results in my New Tart Crust and Double Chocolate "Mandelbrot." Wondra is made by Gold Medal.

GELATIN

In classic no-holds-barred desserts where calories and fat are never counted, I use gelatin sparingly, if at all. I don't like to taste or perceive gelatin in a fine dessert. I look for creamy textures not quivery ones. Because gelatin stiffens and sets soft mixtures without fat, it is seductive to low-fat dessert chefs. I remain careful, however. I do not want to create desserts with the taste and texture of commercial low-fat desserts. So I still use gelatin sparingly. To avoid rubbery desserts, measure gelatin accurately by sweeping across the measuring spoon with a knife rather than shaking the spoon. Where gelatin is called for, I use a widely available brand. If you prefer sheet gelatin, by all means use it.

GINGER

CRYSTALIZED GINGER

Crystalized ginger adds great flavor and texture to cookies, cakes, sauces, and candies. The most tender and mildest ginger comes from Australia. Since it is grown specifically for eating and confectionery, it is harvested young, mild, and virtually fiberless. It is processed in pure cane sugar without sulfur dioxide. Ginger packed in its own syrup is called stem ginger in syrup. When it is drained and sugared, it is called crystallized ginger. To substitute ginger in syrup for crystallized ginger, simply drain the ginger and pat it dry to eliminate excess moisture. Crystallized ginger can be found in gourmet and specialty stores and in some supermarkets. Look for the words "Australian ginger" on the package. The Buderim and Royal Pacific labels also guarantee Australian gin-

ger as does the Williams-Sonoma label. See page 185 for mail order sources.

GINGERROOT

Fresh gingerroot is more widely available than ever across the country. Certainly you will find it in Asian markets. Choose smooth, thin-skinned pieces (they are the youngest) that are relatively heavy for their size. Store in the refrigerator. Use a ginger grater to grate ginger. Grating ginger on a box grater is iffy. If the ginger is young, if you grate it on the next-to-largest holes, if you grate it across the grain, and if the grater is sharp, you will have nicely grated ginger. Otherwise, you'll have ginger juice or long fibrous shreds or cut fingers. If your ginger grating conditions are less than perfect, mince the ginger ultra fine as follows: Peel the skin with a sharp paring knife or vegetable peeler. Slice across the grain into very thin rounds. Mince the rounds of ginger with a sharp chef's knife as fine as you can. Do not use the food processor.

LIQUEURS

It is not necessary to use the most expensive liqueurs, but do use those that are good enough to drink. I use a middle-price California brandy, but I prefer Grand Marnier to other orange liqueurs, and I am partial to Meyer's dark rum.

NUTS

Freshness counts. Lean recipes use nuts sparingly, so buy the best and use them while they are fresh or freeze them. New crop nuts available in the fall are worth buying and freezing. Toasting and caramelizing brings out flavor and allows a small quantity of nuts to go a long way. Where ground nuts are called for, I grind them with the flour in the recipe because some flavor from the nut oils will be dispersed into the flour.

CHESTNUTS

Chestnuts have the least fat (less than 20 percent) of all nuts, yet chestnuts, particularly candied ones, are a very luxurious ingredient often associated with rich foods and desserts.

Chestnut products are imported from France and Italy. The easiest brands to find in the supermarket are Faugier (imported from France) and Reese. I always preferred Faugier but was recently introduced to the Italian Agrimontana's products, which are superb. They are available by mail order from Chestnut Hill Orchards (page 185).

Among the many chestnut products are chestnut spread (also called chestnut cream or *crème de marrons*), a sweetened puree of cooked chestnuts; and chestnut puree (*purée de marrons*), an unsweetened puree of cooked chestnuts. Chestnut spread can be served as is for dessert with a dollop of light sour cream or pureed sweetened cottage cheese. Both the spread and puree can be used as ingredients. Whole chestnuts (*marrons entiers*), cooked chestnuts in water, can be pureed to make an unsweetened puree. Whole or broken chestnuts in syrup (*marrons pièces*), candied chestnuts in heavy vanilla syrup, can be drained and used in other desserts. Chestnut flour is made from dried and ground chestnuts. Though not yet widely used in this country, it has many possibilities in creating new low-fat baked goods.

SUGAR

Where sugar is called for, regular granulated sugar is usually fine for my recipes. In the northeastern United States, however, I have had cake failures because the granulated sugar was too coarse to dissolve properly. Some granulated sugar in the New York area also contains fructose; the labels on those bags counsel against its use for making butter cakes or pound cakes. Knowledgeable home bakers on the East Coast suggest using extra fine, superfine, bar sugar, or something Canadians call "fruit sugar" (because it dissolves easily on fruit, not because it contains fructose) in place of regular granulated. These alternatives are expensive and the crystals are finer than necessary. It is more economical to process regular granulated sugar briefly in a food processor. Even on the West Coast where ordinary granulated works adequately, I buy a ten-pound sack of a particular supermarket brand labeled "fine granulated" whenever I can find it. It is the closest thing to Baker's Special Sugar, which is what professional bakers use.

Baker's Special is the best sugar for baking. It is available in hundred-pound sacks from bakery supply houses. The crystals are finer than ordinary granulated sugar (but not as fine as superfine, extra fine, or bar sugar). It dissolves rapidly and traps air perfectly for pound cake, foam cakes, cookies, and meringue. If you bake a lot, consider it; sugar keeps well, and the price is reasonable. You can always split it with baker friends.

BROWN SUGAR

Here on the West Coast, I have always used C & H brand light and dark brown sugar interchangeably, with a slight preference for dark. However, some brands of dark brown sugar are very inconsistent and can be much too dark and strong in flavor for my recipes. Light brown sugar is the safest choice for baking across the board, unless you have a brand-specific experience to the contrary.

POWDERED SUGAR

Also called 10X sugar or confectioner's sugar in the United States, this is granulated sugar with cornstarch added (to prevent lumping) before it is milled to a consistency like flour. Powdered sugar is used mostly for frosting and icings. It is not normally used for batters, with the exception of some cookies. I use it for decorative techniques and stenciling.

VANILLA

I use pure not artificial extracts. Nielsen-Massey is the finest vanilla available to the home cook. You may choose among Bourbon vanilla (from Madagascar), Tahitian vanilla, and Mexican vanilla. The latter two are fragrant—almost floral—in flavor and certainly have their following. For a change, I might use them in a delicate custard or cream to show off their special qualities, but for all practical purposes the Bourbon vanilla is my favorite.

Equipment

My equipment list is influenced by my professional as well as my home baking experience. I developed most of the recipes for my business in my home kitchen and I have taught classes to home dessert makers for the last fifteen years. I hope my perspective will bring the best of both worlds into your kitchen.

MIXERS

I still love my heavy-duty KitchenAid (model K 5A or K45) mixer. But most of the recipes in this book were tested with an excellent handheld portable electric mixer (also made by KitchenAid) because I believe that it more nearly approaches what most home cooks have in the kitchen. I also have extra pairs of beaters so that I do not have to wash beaters between batters and egg whites, for example.

MIXING BOWLS

As most of these recipes were tested with a handheld mixer, I have come to appreciate the weight and stability of glass and crockery mixing bowls. Bowls that are nearly as deep as they are wide keep ingredients from flying out. They are perfectly shaped for beating egg whites most efficiently without having to move the mixer wildly around the bowl. Glass is also convenient for microwaving. Pyrex makes large glass measuring cups and bowls; I keep two or three of each size. But stainless steel bowls are still my preference for melting chocolate in a hot water bath or warming egg whites for Safe Meringue. Stainless steel heats up quickly in hot water and cools down quickly once removed.

FOOD PROCESSOR

The food processor is invaluable for preparing ingredients, if not always for actually mixing batters and doughs. With lighter desserts in particular, the processor is essential for rendering ordinary cottage cheese or ricotta into a silken cream. You can use the processor to transform hard caramel into caramel powder, to pulverize nuts, to grind granulated sugar extra fine for meringues, to make purees, to mix cookie doughs, to mix a cheesecake, and much more.

MICROWAVE OVEN

The microwave is an essential tool in my kitchen, although I rarely prepare food in it. Rather, I use it to melt and/or to rewarm ingredients from butter to chocolate, to make and remelt caramelized sugar for last-minute Spun Sugar or Caramel Powder. I also use the microwave to bring refrigerated ingredients like eggs, butter, and milk to room temperature (68˚-70˚F.) for cake recipes that require this uniformity of temperature.

LIGHT- OR MEDIUM-WEIGHT 4-CUP SAUCEPAN

Small quantities of caramel burn easily in heavy pans because the retained heat continues to cook the caramel even after it is done and removed from the stove. A lightweight pan offers more control. So even if your cupboards are filled with the finest and heaviest pots and pans, keep just one inexpensive lightweight pot with a 3- to 4-cup capacity especially for caramelizing and spinning small quantities of sugar. This may be contrary to advice you get elsewhere, but I swear by it.

MEDIUM AND FINE STRAINERS

I use a medium mesh strainer for sifting flour and dry ingredients. It can be operated with one hand and it shakes out and cleans easily. Fine mesh strainers are best for dusting or stenciling desserts with powdered sugar or cocoa. With the exception of one or two fine mesh stainless steel strainers, I buy inexpensive strainers with plastic rims so that I can keep many different sizes on hand.

WIRE WHISKS

Who can live without at least two sizes of these very aesthetic hand tools? Use to whisk ingredients together, or even beat egg whites or whipped cream if you are a purist or have no electric mixer. A wire whisk is the very best tool for mixing small quantities of salt and leavenings thoroughly into the flour when making cakes and cookies. The newest whisks are all stainless steel and should last a lifetime. Available from hardware and kitchenware stores.

WOODEN SPOONS

I still use my wooden spoons and stirring paddles for soups and stews but have ceased to use them for custards or anything else that is egg based and may be susceptible to bacterial growth. I use Exoglass spatulas instead.

EXOGLASS SPATULAS

Not really spatulas, these are heat-resistant plastic replacements for the ordinary wooden spoon. They come in the same size, shape, and weight as your favorite wooden spoons. Available from specialty kitchenware shops.

RUBBER SPATULAS

Three sizes cover every contingency. Large professional spatulas are the very best for folding delicate batters and scraping large bowls. A mini spatula is very handy for scraping tiny quantities from small containers and cups. The standard home size handles everything in between. These melt, so get out of the habit of using them on the stove, except when heating something gently in a hot water bath.

OFFSET SPATULA

This is a spatula with a bend or elbow in it, preferably made of stainless steel. I like a blade length of 8 inches or longer. This is the best tool for spreading batter evenly in a jelly-roll pan or any other time you need a thin even layer.

GLASS MEASURING CUPS

Increased use of the microwave makes these cups invaluable, and not only for measuring liquids. I keep 1-cup, 2-cup, 4-cup, and 8-cup measures, with at least two each of the smaller ones.

JELLY JARS

These 8-ounce glass jars are very inexpensive. I buy them by the dozen and use them for melting small quantities of any-

thing—chocolate, butter, caramel, etc. They can go into the microwave or water bath. I also use them to store small quantities in the refrigerator or freezer. The jars keep my 1-cup measuring cups and my small china bowls from getting lost in the fridge and freezer.

SCALE

A scale is the most accurate and simplest way to measure flour, other dry ingredients, and nuts, since you weigh before sifting or grinding.

RULER

I use a ruler for drawing templates, cutting parchment paper, dividing a sheet of sponge cake, measuring pans, cutting brownies into perfect squares, and measuring the thickness of rolled-out cookie dough. It is essential for the otherwise fussy job of marking and cutting of phyllo sheets. My favorite ruler is clear plastic, 18 x 2 inches, with a $\frac{1}{8}$-inch grid pattern.

CALCULATOR

Use it for increasing recipes and figuring out the relative contents of different size pans. Use it to divide phyllo sheets by the number of pieces you need. End guesswork.

BAKING SHEETS AND JELLY-ROLL PANS

Choose the heaviest steel or aluminum baking sheets and jelly-roll pans that you can find. They do not warp or bend, and they cook evenly without hot spots. I like to have at least 1 large cookie sheet that measures 14 x 16 inches. Otherwise I like professional "half sheet" pans; these measure 12 x 16 x 1 inch and fit most home ovens. They can be used as jelly-roll pans in place of the lighter weight standard home size (11 x 17 inches) or as cookie sheets. Buy them in restaurant supply stores—most of which are happy to sell to the public—or send for them from a mail order house (page 185). I do not use specially coated baking sheets or the cushioned variety.

CAKE PANS

I use heavy-duty professional cake layer pans with straight sides. I use 8- and 9-inch round pans that are 2 inches deep. I also use springform pans that measure 6, 8, and 9 inches in diameter. I prefer the kind available in hardware stores. The stainless steel springforms imported from Europe are metric, and thus the 8-inch size actually measures 7½ inches. If you use the imported pans, make some allowances in recipes where layers are cut to fit inside the pan. Even better than springforms, I like aluminum cheesecake pans with removable bottoms. I mostly use the one that measures 8 x 3 inches, but many sizes are available from Parrish (page 185).

FLUTED TART AND TARTLET PANS

I use a 9½-inch fluted tart pan with a removable bottom for classic butter crust tarts as well as the lighter tarts in this book, including those made with phyllo pastry. I use a smaller version, 3½ inches, without a removable bottom, for tartlets. Both are available at any specialty kitchenware shop.

GLASS CAKE, PIE, AND BAKING PANS

Professionals do not generally use glass pans to bake in, so I had to be reminded that even the best home cooks do use glass for some things. I did not test all recipes in glass, only those where I thought the home baker might be used to baking in glass— for instance, a brownie recipe in an 8-inch square pan. Where no glass pan is mentioned, I advise you to use one at your own risk. Remember that most authorities suggest a 25°F. decrease in temperature when baking in glass. In a couple of recipes I specifically advise against using glass because I obtained less than optimal results when doing so. In at least one recipe I specifically advise glass.

PARCHMENT PAPER

This comes in rolls for home use. Use parchment to line baking sheets and cake pans, eliminating the need for grease or butter. Everything, from meringues to macaroons, detaches easily from parchment paper. Sometimes I mention aluminum foil or wax paper as an option; they do not work in every recipe, however.

SOUFFLÉ CUPS, CUSTARD CUPS, AND RAMEKINS

I use 4- to 5-ounce straight-sided glass or porcelain ramekins or soufflé cups for individual soufflés, mousses, and flans. Old-fashioned 5- to 6-ounce Pyrex custard cups will do when the dessert is to be unmolded before serving (Flans with Brandied Prunes, Baby Caramel Cheesecakes, etc.), but do not expect a dramatic rise from a soufflé baked in a cup with flared sides. Pyrex is available at hardware stores. Porcelain and sometimes glass soufflé cups and ramekins are available from kitchenware shops.

OVEN THERMOMETER

Get a good mercury oven thermometer today! Even the best recipes suffer from being baked at the wrong temperatures. Check your oven every now and again to see that it is accurate, and either have it adjusted immediately or compensate for the error yourself until you can have it adjusted.

INSTANT-READ OR BI-THERM MEAT THERMOMETER OR MICROWAVE THERMOMETER

These inexpensive dial thermometers made by Taylor are available in cookware and hardware stores. They have a range of 0° to 220°F.—unlike a candy thermometer, which records temperatures well above 300°F. I use mine to determine the temperature of ingredients, for cooking delicate custards, for melting chocolate, and for Safe Meringue.

WOODEN BARBECUE SKEWERS

These are my preferred cake testers. They are cleaner than broom straws and longer than toothpicks. Avoid the thin metal skewers that are sold as cake testers—nothing sticks to them and it is hard to tell for sure whether the skewer is wet or dry. Wet batter sticks readily to a wooden skewer so you can see the exact consistency of the interior of the cake. Insert the skewer into the cake at a wide angle to test more than one place in the center of the cake. Wooden skewers may be rinsed off and reused.

PASTRY BRUSHES

Natural boar bristle brushes are the best, and you may even buy them (quite cheaply) in the paint or hardware store. Keep brushes for pastry separate—unless you want your cakes and tarts to taste of barbecue sauce. I like a brush 1 inch wide for glazing the fruit on a tart and one 1½ or 2 inches wide for moistening cake layers with liqueur.

SERRATED BREAD KNIFE

A 12-inch blade is the best, but any serrated knife is the perfect tool for cutting a sponge cake or Genoise into thin horizontal layers.

CITRUS ZESTER

This efficient tool removes fine strips of zest (the colored part of citrus peels) from lemons, oranges, and other citrus fruits, leaving the bitter white pith behind. Available at hardware and kitchenware stores.

SCISSORS

Keep a pair in the kitchen for cutting parchment paper, etc.

UTILITY KNIFE

This is handy for cutting stencils and thick cardboard.

CAKE DECORATING TURNTABLE

A cake decorating turntable is a heavy, well balanced, lazy susan you can use to help you frost and decorate cakes. They are available at restaurant supply and kitchenware stores or by mail order (page 185). If you love to make and decorate cakes, you should have one. Lightweight plastic ones are inexpensive but not very satisfying to work with. The heavy metal ones made by Ateco are a joy, though expensive. For nearly half the price you may purchase a 12-inch banding wheel from a ceramics supply shop (potters use them for decorating). They are nicely balanced and heavy. Decorating turntables and banding wheels must never, ever be submerged in water. The stem will rust or corrode, and your wheel will not spin freely. Lubricate the stem now and then with mineral oil.

ICING SPATULA

This should be made of stainless steal with an 8-inch blade rounded at the end. The best spatulas are made by Wearever, Dexter, and Ateco and are available at restaurant supply stores, cookware shops, and cake decorating specialty stores. Cheaper, usually more flexible spatulas are available in the kitchen section of houseware and hardware stores.

CAKE COMB

This triangular piece of stainless steel, aluminum, or plastic has a different size serrated edge on each side. Use to texture the frosting on the tops or sides of cakes. Available at hardware and kitchenware stores.

PASTRY BAG

French pastry bags made of nylon, plastic-coated nylon, or polypropylene are the best ever. They wash out easily, remain supple, and do not become sour or malodorous like old-fashioned cloth bags. Whipped cream does not weep through these wonderful bags either. The bags are available from Bridge (page 185). A 16- to 18-inch bag is best for piping ladyfingers or soft cookies and meringues. A 10- to 12-inch bag is handy for smaller quantities. Since pastry bags should not be filled much more than half full, a bag that is a little too big is better than one that is too small.

PASTRY TIPS

Ateco is the most widely available brand. A useful assortment of tips would include plain tips varying in diameter from ⅜ to ½ inch as well as open and closed star tips #3, #5, #7, and #8.

PROPANE TORCH

A torch is the best tool for caramelizing the top of custards without heating up the entire dessert and without the tricky timing, ice baths, and delicate positioning required when using the broiler. A torch is also good for warming the sides of a springform before releasing them. Torches are available from hardware stores and stores that sell camping supplies. The type with an automatic trigger is expensive but nice. If you live with an artist, sculptor, plumber, or handy person, look in the basement—you may already have a torch! Coleman makes a short, lightweight one with a wide base which is less intimidating and less apt to tip over than some others. An electric heat gun used for stripping paint can be used in place of a torch, but a hand-held hairdryer is not powerful enough.

KRISPY KAN

Fabulous baker Flo Braker told me about this low-tech device. It is a tight-lidded tin with a detachable knob filled with nontoxic crystals that keep the air in the can quite dry. It is excellent for keeping cookies crisp, but it offers an even greater advantage for storing crisp caramel shapes, caramel powder, praline powder, or pastry layers with crisp caramel on them. The knob can also be detached and used in other tight-lidded containers or cookie jars. Knobs are infinitely reusable; all you have to do is dry them out in the oven whenever the crystals become saturated with moisture. Additional knobs can be purchased separately. Look for the Krispy Kan or its equivalent in the housewares section of hardware and variety stores.

RESOURCES

MAIL ORDER AND RETAIL SPECIALTY SOURCES

BRIDGE KITCHENWARE CORP.
214 EAST 52ND ST.
NEW YORK, NY 10022
212/838-1901

Bridge is legendary. You will find an enormous selection of superb domestic and imported kitchenware for home and professional use. If you don't find Fred Bridge's irascibility part of his charm, ask to speak to one of the other Bridges at the outset. You may have to beg to be sent the $3.00 catalogue. Admittedly worth it.

CHESTNUT HILL ORCHARDS, INC.
3300 BEE CAVE RD., SUITE 650
AUSTIN, TX 78746-6663
800/745-3279

Mail order for frozen unsweetened chestnut puree, whole chestnuts, and chestnut flour from Agrimontana.

DEAN & DELUCA

Equipment and ingredients including chocolates, cocoas, and Agrimontana products: chestnuts, candied sour cherries (*amarene candite*), preserves, Australian citrus peels, and candied ginger.
Retail stores:
560 Broadway
New York, NY 10013
212/431-1691

3276 M Street, NW
Washington DC 20007
202/342-2500

MAID OF SCANDINAVIA
3244 RALEIGH AVE.
MINNEAPOLIS, MN 55416
800/851-1121

Terrific assortment of pans, equipment, supplies, and novelties for the dessert maker and cake decorator. Lindt and Callebaut chocolate. Mail order catalogue available.

PARRISH'S CAKE DECORATING SUPPLY, INC.
225 WEST 146TH ST.
GARDENA, CA 90248
800/736-8443

Paradise for cake makers and decorators. You may visit the retail store. Mail order catalogue available.

S.E. RYCOFF
761 TERMINAL ST.
LOS ANGELES, CA 90021
213/622-4131

Imported and domestic ingredients including Callebaut chocolate. Mail order catalogue available.

TORN RANCH
1122 FOURTH ST.
SAN RAFAEL, CA 94901
415/459-1660

All kinds of nuts and dried fruits, crystallized Australian ginger, and fruit peels. You may visit the retail store. Mail order catalogue available.

WILLIAMS-SONOMA
P.O. BOX 7456
SAN FRANCISCO, CA 94120
800/541-2233

Tableware, kitchen and baking equipment. Callebaut chocolate, Valrhona chocolate, Pernigotti cocoa, superb Australian candied orange and lemon peel, and crystallized ginger. Williams-Sonoma has retail stores in many cities across the country. Mail order catalogue available.

THE YELLOW PAGES

Try the following listings in your area for specialized tools and equipment, ingredients, and ideas.

ART SUPPLY STORES
For 23- or 24-carat gold leaf for decorating

CAKE DECORATING SHOPS
For anything to do with cake decorating

CERAMICS SUPPLY
For banding wheels to use as cake decorating turntables

GOURMET FOOD STORES
For ingredients

INDIAN GROCERIES
For edible (23- to 24-carat) gold leaf called Vark, for decorating

NATURAL FOOD STORES
For organic produce, bulk nuts, dried fruits, etc.

RESTAURANT SUPPLY STORES
For heavy-duty half sheet pans and cake pans, Ateco decorating turntables, etc.

PARIS ADDRESSES NOT TO BE MISSED

These two phenomenal emporia are close to one another and offer the opportunity to explore the Place des Victoires, the Passage Colbert, and/or the Rue Montmartre with its additional restaurant and food service suppliers. The Forum des Halles is close by and the Beaubourg (Centre Pompidou) and its adjacent hubbub are but a stone's throw away. Make a day of it.

DEHILLERIN
18 RUE COQUILLIÈRE
PARIS 1
42.36.53.13

Everything for the chef. I've seen some of the same staff here for over twenty years! Look up and you'll see a very old autographed picture of Julia Child behind the sales counter.

M.O.R.A.
13 RUE MONTMARTRE
PARIS 1
45.08.19.24

Ecstasy for the pastry chef and chocolatier. Nothing is priced, but the computer on the sales floor may be operated by customers to look up prices. Prices are listed H.T. (*hors taxe* or exclusive of tax) so don't be surprised when a seventeen-percent value-added tax is added. If you spend a bundle, you are eligible for a tax refund, but you must ask for *détaxe* papers when you pay and you must show your merchandise and the papers at the airport when you exit the country. Same holds true for Dehillerin, above.

BIBILIOGRAPHY

Bayless, Rick, with Deann Groen Bayless. *Authentic Mexican*. New York: William Morrow and Company, 1987.

Beranbaum, Rose Levy. *Rose's Christmas Cookies*. New York: William Morrow and Company, 1990.

Braker, Flo. *The Simple Art of Perfect Baking*. Shelburne, VT: Chapters Publishing, 1992.

———. *Sweet Miniatures*. New York: William Morrow and Company, 1991.

Claiborne, Craig. *The New York Times Cookbook*. New York: Harper & Row, 1961.

Cook, L. Russell. *Chocolate Production and Use*. New York: Harcourt Brace Jovanovich, 1982.

Cunningham, Marion. *The Fannie Farmer Cookbook*. New York: Alfred A. Knopf, 1990.

Field, Carol. *The Italian Baker*. New York: Harper & Row, 1985.

Heatter, Maida. *American Desserts*. New York: Alfred A. Knopf, 1985.

———. *Best Dessert Book Ever*. New York: Alfred A. Knopf, 1990.

———. *New Book of Great Desserts*. New York: Alfred A. Knopf, 1982.

Lenôtre, Gaston. *Faîtes Votre Pâtisserie comme Lenôtre*. Paris: Flammarion, 1975.

McGee, Harold. *The Curious Cook*. San Francisco: North Point Press, 1990.

Medrich, Alice. *Cocolat: Extraordinary Chocolate Desserts*. New York: Warner Books, 1990.

Peck, Paula. *The Art of Fine Baking*. New York: Simon & Schuster, 1991.

Pennington, Jean A. T. *Food Values of Portions Commonly Used*. New York: Harper & Row, 1989.

Purdy, Susan G. "Another Piece of Pie," *Eating Well*, November/December, 1992.

Rombauer, Irma S. and Marion Rombauer Becker. *Joy of Cooking*. Indianapolis, IN: Bobbs-Merrill Company, 1975.

Silverton, Nancy. *Desserts*. New York: Harper & Row, 1986.

Sousanis, Marti. *The Art of Filo Cookbook*. Berkeley, CA: Aris Books, 1988.

Spear, Ruth. *Low Fat and Loving It*. New York: Warner Books, 1991.

Walter, Carole. *Great Cakes*. New York: Ballantine, 1991.

TABLE OF CONVERSIONS

LIQUID MEASURES

Fluid Ounces	U.S. Measures	Imperial Measures	Milliliters
	1 tsp.	1 tsp.	5
¼	2 tsp.	1 dessert spoon	7
½	1 T.	1 T.	15
1	2 T.	2 T.	28
2	¼ cup	4 T.	56
4	½ cup or ¼ pint		110
5		¼ pint or 1 gill	140
6	¾ cup		170
8	1 cup or ½ pint		225
9			250 (¼ liter)
10	1¼ cups	½ pint	280
12	1½ cups or ¾ pint		340
15		¾ pint	420
16	2 cups or 1 pint		450
18	2¼ cups		500 (½ liter)
20	2½ cups	1 pint	560
24	3 cups or 1½ pints		675
25		1¼ pints	700
27	3½ cups		750
30	3¾ cups	1½ pints	840
32	4 cups or 2 pints or 1 quart		900
35		1¾ pints	980
36	4½ cups		1000 (1 liter)

SOLID MEASURES

U.S. and Imperial Measures		Metric Measures	
Ounces	Pounds	Grams	Kilos
1		28	
2		56	
3½		100	
4	¼	112	
5		140	
6		168	
8	½	225	
9		250	¼
12	¾	340	
16	1	450	
18		500	½
20	1¼	560	
24	1½	675	
27		750	¾
28	1¾	780	
32	2	900	
36	2¼	1000	1
40	2½	1100	
48	3	1350	
54		1500	1½

OVEN TEMPERATURE EQUIVALENTS

Fahrenheit	Gas Mark	Celsius	Heat of Oven
225	¼	107	Very Cool
250	½	121	Very Cool
275	1	135	Cool
300	2	148	Cool
325	3	163	Moderate
350	4	177	Moderate
375	5	190	Fairly Hot
400	6	204	Fairly Hot
425	7	218	Hot
450	8	232	Very Hot
475	9	246	Very Hot

INDEX